Crosscurrents/ *Modern Critiques*
Third Series

Edited by Jerome Klinkowitz

Kathryn Hume

PYNCHON'S MYTHOGRAPHY
An Approach to
Gravity's Rainbow

Southern Illinois University Press
CARBONDALE AND EDWARDSVILLE

Printed in the United States of America
Edited by Curtis L. Clark
Designed by Design for Publishing, Inc.
Production supervised by Natalia Nadraga

Library of Congress Cataloging-in-Publication Data

Hume, Kathryn, 1945–
    Pynchon's mythography.   223492

    (Crosscurrents/modern critiques. Third series)
    Bibliography: p.
    Includes index.
    1. Pynchon, Thomas. Gravity's rainbow.
2. Myth in literature. I. Title. II. Series.
PS3566.Y55G7348 1987 813'.52 86–25970
ISBN 0–8093–1357–X

for
Thomas J. Knight

Contents

Crosscurrents/
Modern Critiques/
Third Series

IN THE EARLY 1960s, when the Crosscurrents/Modern Critiques series was developed by Harry T. Moore, the contemporary period was still a controversial one for scholarship. Even today the elusive sense of the present dares critics to rise above mere impressionism and to approach their subject with the same rigors of discipline expected in more traditional areas of study. As the first two series of Crosscurrents books demonstrated, critiquing contemporary culture often means that the writer must be historian, philosopher, sociologist, and bibliographer as well as literary critic, for in many cases these essential preliminary tasks are yet undone.

To the challenges that faced the initial Crosscurrents project have been added those unique to the past two decades: the disruption of conventional techniques by the great surge in innovative writing in the American 1960s just when social and political conditions were being radically transformed, the new worldwide interest in the Magic

Realism of South American novelists, the startling experiments of textual and aural poetry from Europe, the emergence of Third World authors, the rising cause of feminism in life and literature, and, most dramatically, the introduction of Continental theory into the previously staid world of Anglo-American literary scholarship. These transformations demand that many traditional treatments be rethought, and part of the new responsibility for Crosscurrents will be to provide such studies.

Contributions to Crosscurrents/Modern Critiques/Third Series will be distinguished by their fresh approaches to established topics and by their opening up of new territories for discourse. When a single author is studied, we hope to present the first book on his or her work or to explore a previously untreated aspect based on new research. Writers who have been critiqued well elsewhere will be studied in comparison with lesser-known figures, sometimes from other cultures, in an effort to broaden our base of understanding. Critical and theoretical works by leading novelists, poets, and dramatists will have a home in Crosscurrents/Modern Critiques/Third Series, as will sampler-introductions to the best in new Americanist criticism written abroad.

The excitement of contemporary studies is that all of its critical practitioners and most of their subjects are alive and working at the same time. One work influences another, bringing to the field a spirit of competition and cooperation that reaches an intensity rarely found in other disciplines. Above all, this third series of Crosscurrents/Modern Critiques will be collegial—a mutual interest in the present moment that can be shared by writer, subject, and reader alike.

Jerome Klinkowitz

Preface

Pynchon's pyrotechnics—dazzling, fragmented, explosive, surreal, and violent—have convinced most readers that *Gravity's Rainbow* is a new form of fiction. That novel seems bent on rendering problematic all the discourses we associate with traditional and modernist fiction and presents us with an unknowable reality by means of an almost unknowable text, leaving us to cope as best we can. Even our attempts at interpretation are discredited as a form of paranoia, as an open admission of the terror we feel when confronted by chaos. Critics who expound upon this epistemological and ontological hatchetwork in *Gravity's Rainbow* have indeed taught us much about the text and about the philosophical issues facing contemporary literature, but their collective achievement is not a balanced assessment. Despite uncertainties, much that concerns Pynchon can be deciphered, and he is very far from having abandoned all traditional values and novel-writing techniques. As I shall argue, there is a vein throughout the text of *Gravity's Rainbow* that counters all assertions of unknowability. Pynchon has, in fact, used a mythology to give structure and values to his fictive world, and a reading more fully open to the text must take into account his affirmations as well as his denials.

Pynchon has not just created the city or province of realistic literature. His exhausting plenitude, profuse detail, and varied settings—from the Kirghiz Steppes to the interior of a seminal vesicle—all invite readers to see the text as more than just a reflection of the reality that any one individual can know. He has given us a cosmos, the world humanity shapes out of chaos by means of ritual and myth. It is an ordered realm coextensive with and interrelated to a set of interlocking stories or myths. These stories in turn fit into a narrative sequence, or mythology, that conveys, supports, and challenges our cultural values.

Attributing a mythology to Pynchon may seem preposterous, given that most critics revel in what is deconstructive about this avant-garde novel rather than in its traditional elements; they stress the destabilizing structures and techniques, not those conducive to ordinary values. Indeed, because Pynchon attacks our reliance on myth in so many ways, my imputing mythography to him may seem perverse, an attempt to undermine his accomplishment by insisting that he is guilty of a crime he excoriates in others. Pointsman's devotion to the myths of cause-and-effect and stimulus-response relationships, Weissmann's and Pökler's to the myth of transcendence—these draw a good bit of acid from Pynchon. Devotion to certain myths, as much as any one flaw in our culture, underlies his sense of *lacrimae rerum,* and he gives equally short shrift to mythic archetypes. Rubes gawking at the Tree of Creation provoke him into reminding us that a sucker is born every minute. Yet though he treats myth and mythology as dirty words and ridicules many cultural myths, he relies quite heavily for story and structure on his own mythographic pattern.

Given Pynchon's obvious interest in music throughout *Gravity's Rainbow*, one might describe his dialogic consideration of myth with a musical analogy: several voices in this polyphonic work carry mythic materials; others attack well known mythologies; the basso continuo growls insistently that reality is not knowable and hence appears to deny the meaning-giving function of myth. Granted, myth and values are asserted by only some of the voices in this piece. Those voices, however, must be taken into account if we are to understand the whole; furthermore, such voices are intriguing because they move against the more obvious currents, asserting through counterpoint a countermessage.

To date, Pynchon's mythological cycle has been only dimly sensed; fragments have been noticed and commented upon, but the entire sequence has not been identified as such. This book will attempt first to disentangle the mythological pattern from the distracting detail of the whole fictive universe and then to redress an imbalance in critical perspective. I am not just pressing a recuperative traditionalist reading onto *Gravity's Rainbow*, nor arguing that the presence of myth makes this a classical text after all, as T. S. Eliot argued for *Ulysses*. Rather, I shall present a more difficult position: namely, that the reader must learn to maintain simultaneously perspectives that at first seem contradictory—the postmodernist and the mythological—and must learn to integrate them. Yes, Pynchon is postmodernist and deconstructive, but he also relies heavily on very traditional structures to make some of his points. Given his systematic subversion of so many literary conventions, it is all

the more interesting to see what traditional structures
he has chosen to rescue and use.

Because the terms "myth" and "mythological" can be
applied to so vast an empire of phenomena as to be
practically meaningless, chapter 1 lays down restrictive
boundaries. The relevance of anything called myth to
literature must also be established, for traditional Amer-
indian tales and Thomas Pynchon's narrative are not
commensurable by normal standards. For this study of
Gravity's Rainbow, structuralist approaches to mythology
proved the most useful, but only after substantial modifications, so chapter 1 also describes my assumptions
and tools.

Mythography demands a cosmos, not just a setting or
location, so chapter 2 explores Pynchon's cosmos, establishing not only its physical and spiritual dimensions but
also its differences from a fictive world that is merely
mimetic or symbolic.

The mythological sequence, from origin to apocalypse, occupies chapter 3. Pynchon traces the development of the modern world on four levels: (1) the
historical, mostly in terms of Slothrop's ancestors but
also in terms of vignettes from around the world; (2)
the personal, in terms of Slothrop himself; (3) the technological, in terms of coal-tar dyes, plastics chemistry,
and industrial history; and (4) the individual example
of technology, in terms of the V-2. These mythic histories of humanity and its technology come together in
the symbolic marriage of Gottfried to the rocket. The
implicit futures suggested by these histories are not so
much a single apocalypse as any of several, all briefly
sketched in the dense texture of the narrative.

Chapter 4 examines what may be Pynchon's original contribution—a new hero-myth. This myth becomes
visible when we consider what Pynchon's mythology does
to help us measure the universe in human terms, to help
us find patterns of behavior suitable to that chaotic universe. Western mythologies, and many Eastern ones as
well, have relied on variants of the hero monomyth as
model for the individual. The call to action, and the
exaltation of power and control implicit in that pattern,
are not appropriate to the cosmos as Pynchon has re-
defined it, so he offers his own unheroic "hero" pattern.
To jettison the basis of much of world literature is a
radical move, and in this as in other matters Pynchon
does nothing by halves.

Finally, Pynchon's mythology having been disentan-
gled from the chaotic strands of narrative, we need to
consider what he is doing with such mythological material. One approach to this question is to consider his
mythographic writing in the context of contemporary
literature. Italo Calvino and Günther Grass, to name but
two writers who are also mythographers, seem to be
investigating something like Pynchon's new hero pattern
as well. Since both the virtues and defects of Pynchon's
philosophy are commonly held to be deeply rooted in
the American 1960s, it is worth examining this recur-
rence of techniques and ideas in fiction by writers so
different in cultural background and politics.

More central to this final chapter, however, is a series
of interlocking questions. Where does this traditional
mythological material, devoted to imposing values, fit in
a literary cosmos designed brutally to smash values and
absolutes? Pynchon balances the opposing forces of myth

and chaos contrapuntally—but to what end? And how
are we to assimilate, even integrate, such contradictory-
seeming impulses in the novel? In no way do I deny the
presence of the effectiveness of Pynchon's deconstructive activities, his brilliant demonstration that our rou-
tine systems of order founder on contradiction or
crumble under scrutiny; but these demonstrations constitute only half of what he accomplishes. Chapter 5
attempts to fit the two impulses, toward chaos and toward cosmos, into a larger picture.

Objections can be raised to what I am attempting to
do. Any attempt to extract myths or seek patterns can
be called one form of the paranoia that so fascinates
Pynchon. To be an orthodox Pynchon critic, I should
ritually confess to paranoia and express guilt over it,
admit the trespass (given Pynchon's rumored hostility
to literary criticism), and declare that interpretation is
not what we must do when we engage this text. The
critics who follow this protocol are wont to chorus that
the contradictions and gaps in Pynchon's fictive universe
reduce the usual degree of critical assurance to tentative
probabilities at best.

Sanity demands that we not be so ready to deprecate
the human urge to find pattern. All knowledge and much
wisdom depend upon such an urge. Without that urge,
no child would ever learn its native tongue, and while
the communication allowed by that language may be far
from complete or reliable, we cannot and would not
dream of trying to do without it. Even mystics whose
vision has helped them unbuild previous conceptual patterns must make use of pattern-based human activities
to survive. Hence, I feel less apologetic than some pre-

decessors for my critical explorations of *Gravity's Rainbow*. The loss of false certainty is disquieting—as it was for classical physicists—but that loss is not unique to *Gravity's Rainbow*, and it need not bring speculative investigation to a halt. We simply need to learn to recognize the limitations of our tools and methods, and can, if anything, be thankful for texts that force awareness of such shortcomings.

The objection to pattern-seeking criticism as inappropriate is one faced by many Pynchon critics; objections to the terms "myth" and "mythology" are specific to the present study. So unpopular have these terms become that a recent American grants committee secretly decided to throw out all applications using them in the title. That myth has been misused and overused should not rule out all further endeavors, however, and if Northrop Frye is right about the historical sequence of modes, we might well expect more literature with strong mythic components to appear on the contemporary scene. According to his concept of literary modes, irony completes a cycle and the prevailing mode will swing back toward myth. We have watched the extension and development of irony throughout modernist and postmodernist endeavors. Attempts to get beyond its limitations may well demand the sort of leap—even the primitivism—implied by a reliance on myth and by creation of new myth. Indeed, I shall argue briefly in the final chapter that a few major writers are now exploring such possibilities.

The death of the novel or of realism was the cry of the 1960s. Myth, however, has never been realistic. Meaning in myth does not depend on imitation. On one level, such meaning manifests itself in symbolic actions;

on another level, it emerges through redundancies, oppositions, and mediations. Myth is not even bound by
the need for novelty, that inherent limitation now undermining the realist endeavor.

Myth turns chaos to cosmos. The chaos we now feel
to be threatening our world may legitimately be calling
forth a new burst of mythological thinking and writing.
The new cosmos to be defined will have many quagmires
of uncertainty and forests of unknowability. We need
suggestions for dealing with such imponderables. Myth
concerns itself with such psychic orientation, and what
I shall be calling mythological literature—with *Gravity's
Rainbow* my prime example—is a major forum for such
speculative thinking.

A Note on Text and Documentation

Page references are to the Viking Press edition of *Gravity's Rainbow* (New York, 1973). Ellipses in quotations taken
from this text are Pynchon's own; any material I have
cut to shorten a quote is indicated by ellipses within
square brackets.

These quotations may sometimes seem as thick on the
page as fruit in a fruitcake. However, the text is so fragmented, so complex and polyphonic, and so long, that
one cannot make an assertion and expect the reader to
remember where corroborative evidence is to be found.
Far more than is necessary for traditional fiction, the
critic must quote from the novel and must document
every statement with a page reference. I regret the stylistic clumsiness this need entails but hope that readers
may sometimes thus be reminded of lines they had for-

gotten, Pynchonesque felicities overlooked amidst the plenitude.

Another stylistic problem arises from the number of good studies of Pynchon. Giving them due credit necessitates more notes than is altogether graceful. I have attempted to reduce their bulk by giving full bibliographical information in the first reference only, using thereafter the critic's name and, if necessary, a short title. A list of all such sources cited appears at the back of this book.

Acknowledgments

THOMAS J. KNIGHT persuaded me to go back to *Gravity's Rainbow* again, after I had given up around page 100. For that encouragement, and for many hours of passionate and complicated argument over what it all "means," many thanks. Peter Malekin not only showed me some of the mystic material that I had overlooked, but proved that not everyone needs several readings in order to feel at home in Pynchon's fictive cosmos. John Protevi saved me from many philosophical errors and stylistic infelicities. During conversations at the School of Criticism and Theory (Summer 1983), Brian McHale introduced me to his definition of postmodernism and called my attention to aspects of *Gravity's Rainbow* that I was inclined to overlook. The readers for Southern Illinois University Press, David Cowart and Khachig Tölölyan, gave me invaluable suggestions for improving my arguments. Curtis L. Clark did a splendid job of editing the manuscript, for which I am most grateful. My thanks also to Robert D. Hume, who has had to learn much more about Pynchon than is reasonable to demand of any theater historian, however titanic his scholarly and critical powers.

Pynchon's Mythography
An Approach to *Gravity's Rainbow*

1

Separating Cosmos from Chaos

two orders of being, looking identical

TO JUDGE FROM THE CRITICISM, *Gravity's Rainbow* affects readers in a manner reminiscent of such optical illusions as the facing profiles that outline a chalice, or Gombrich's duck-rabbit. The two interpretations—faces or chalice, duck or rabbit—are always present, but in order to see one, viewers mentally block out the other.[1] Pynchon refers to this kind of reversibility in terms of craters or muffins and melody or silences:

But after a while the listener starts actually hearing the pauses instead of the notes—his ear gets tickled the way your eye does staring at a recco map until bomb craters flip inside out to become muffins risen above the tin, or ridges fold to valleys, sea and land flicker across quicksilver edges—so the silences dance in this quartet.[2]

His critics seem increasingly mesmerized by the bulging muffins and silences and no longer see the craters or hear the melody. Critics mostly register the reduction of structures, assumptions, and discourses to contradictions and absences—and validly so, for the process is present and essential to *Gravity's Rainbow* and needs to be explicated in some detail. In focusing on Pynchon's handling of our fallible metaphysics, however, critics become increasingly insensitive to some of Pynchon's relatively stable structures and values; yet those too are present and just as significant, still part of the same literary work. The text is like the reconnaissance map and the quartet: two orders of being inhabit the same body, and when we concentrate on one such order of being, we lose all sense of the other.

Stabilizing and Destabilizing Structures in *Gravity's Rainbow*

In approaching *Gravity's Rainbow* by way of Pynchon's mythography, I hope to redress an imbalance. Of necessity, I shall be discussing the stabilizing more than the destabilizing structures, but this is not to claim priority for them. A reading which focused solely on the mythological elements would be as one-sided as the readings exclusively concerned with disintegration and fragmentation. My immediate aim is to analyze the mythography; the ultimate goal, however, is to find a critical standpoint that will let us be aware of silence and melody at the same time, a perspective that will let us respond to and understand the interdependence of the traditional and postmodernist structures.

Let me sketch briefly what I mean by the postmodernist elements in *Gravity's Rainbow* and by postmodernist or poststructuralist critical approaches to the text. Such elements within the novel are those that foreground unknowability or uncertainty. These elements may have philosophical, scientific, or linguistic foundations in the works of figures such as Nietzsche, Heisenberg, or Saussure. They lend themselves to deconstructive readings. Cumulatively, they function so as to discredit assumptions about system and order; to shake faith in analysis; to deny the romantic concept of individual as entity; to explode literary assumptions about organic unity and generic convention; and to decondition us of our modernist habit of reading for hidden meanings.[3] The critics who focus on these destabilizing elements, which I sometimes call negative or disintegrative for want of a better term, use a variety of poststructuralist methods and terminologies. For all that they belong to no one theoretical persuasion, their analyses of Pynchon's disintegrative techniques all point in the same general direction.

Of course some critics have focused on traditional themes and ordered discourses, but even when presenting such insights, they struggle against the perceived negativity in the text, and their positive insights are weakened by admissions of the ironic dissolutions. One critic may assert that points of transition are important to Pynchon; another, that love is our only answer in the face of chaos—but so far, these interpretations based on positive structures have not coalesced into a whole that integrates the fragments. Far more coherent are the negative approaches with their messages of unknowability, ambiguity, uncertainty, and the failure of meaning.[4]

A statement of the poststructuralist sort is this by Charles Russell:

Pynchon offers us a massive system of analogies of decay and destruction, of repression and fragmentation, analogies that may only fall apart as does the book in its final section. And out of this dismantling—a promise? The art of fragments— whether they portend death or revitalization—this is the final gift of Pynchon. It is an anarchic vision that promises either freedom or impotence, creation or mindless pleasures.

Any pattern of order that people assert follows the same path of the "creation, intensification, and final failure of essential meaning."[5]

Another such statement, by Molly Hite, acknowledges the implicit desire in the novel for the positive and stable but focuses on the frustration of that desire: "He [Pynchon] constructs his radically decentralized texts around the idea that the Center is unaccountably missing. It should be there, and perhaps it was there at one time; as an added incentive he grants, with Yeats, that it may be recoverable." Her argument goes on:

In the same way, the preterite linguistic structure that is *Gravity's Rainbow* is self-defined by the premise that it is *not* that revelation it points toward. . . . But because the novel itself has defined this unity as what is missing it embodies the absence of unity as something unity can never be: as fecundity, as multiple versions of "Holy-Center-Approaching," as a plenitude of failed revelations.[6]

A postmodernist reading by Brian McHale concentrates on all the ways that Pynchon destroys our ontological certainty:

The reader has been invited to undertake the kinds of pattern-making and pattern-interpreting operations which, in the Modernist texts with which he is familiar, would produce intelligible meaning; here, they produce almost a parody of intelligibility. He has been confronted with representations of mental processes of the kind which, in Modernist texts, he could have relied upon in reconstructing external (fictive) reality. In *Gravity's Rainbow,* such representations are always liable to be retroactively qualified as dream, fantasy, or hallucination, while the reconstructions based upon them are always subject to contradiction or cancellation. The ultimate effect is radically to destabilize novelistic ontology.[7]

McHale reads the book as an attack on modernist literary assumptions and modernist habits of reading, which direct readers to look for encoded meanings.

Supporting such orthodox approaches is the undeniable fact that few authors have gone to Pynchon's extremes in breaking conventions of coherence. All of the disintegrative activities that critics note really do take place. We have only to consider what holds traditional narratives together to remind ourselves of just how thoroughly Pynchon rejects such standard meaning structures.

Whereas the novel once promised us a predictable configuration of characters almost always centering on a hero or heroine, Pynchon avoids focusing on personal action or on character and does not keep the personal relationships stable. Tyrone Slothrop may be the main character, but he is no hero, and when others hold the stage, they do so as absolutely as he. Katje shows up in several subplots, but Pynchon does nothing to justify this ubiquity or to bring those plots together. Slothrop and Pökler, Gottfried and Slothrop, Ilse and Gottfried all share experiences in a transpersonal fashion that denies their individuality in any conventional sense. Characters were once expected to be predictable and lifelike (as if those two were always compatible). Much of the time, Pynchon's characters are neither. Pirate Prentice, with his weird ability to manage the fantasies of other people, is hardly predictable. Slothrop's becoming physically invisible is not something we expect. We do not even know, nor can we project, the unknown endings of other major characters. Enzian may go up in a rocket, but we are not sure. Pynchon does not develop characters according to the canons of realism.

Nor does he rely for coherence on genre, raising and then gratifying generic expectations. For a start, we find no aristotelian beginning, middle, and end. In other hands, the love story between Roger and Jessica might have led to marriage, giving us one islet of happiness between grey sea and grey sky. Or, having established an affinity between Slothrop and the V-2, Pynchon might have launched him in one of the last rockets, but he launches Gottfried instead. We expect Slothrop to reach enlightenment in the course of his quest, and he may do so in his role as Zonal Orpheus, but the insight is expressed through wordless music. We may understand Slothrop's warning in general terms but may be hard put to explain what he feels to be the right way of relating to the universe, when all he gives us is harmonica blues. Much of his activity belongs to the romance form: the initial equilibrium, the crossing of the threshold, the quest, the tests, the search for identity (and identity papers), the storming of the holy center, the rescuing of an imprisoned knight (Der Springer). But instead of playing Parsifal all the way to kingship of the Wasteland, Slothrop becomes something more akin to wandering hermit or holy fool, and then disappears. If denied a romance ending, we tend to expect tragedy, but Slothrop is not destroyed as a tormented victim of Them. His fadeout is not tragic, not comic, only marginally ironic. It really eludes most generic models, leaving us with unfulfilled, inchoate expectations.

Normally, we assume a chronological sequence to be coherent. It may be chopped up and shuffled, with parts given analeptically or proleptically, but story lines can usually be sorted out into linearity or into synchronized parallel lines. Although *Gravity's Rainbow's* overall actions can be rationalized, not all parts submit to such treatment. Imipolex G was developed in 1939 yet also apparently was used as a stimulus to condition the Infant Tyrone around 1920. We assume that effects follow causes, but such does not appear to happen when Slothrop's sexual activities correspond geographically to later rocket falls on London. Nor can we find precise chronological clues to date the scene in the Orpheus Theatre in Los Angeles or to date the various Raketen-Städte, all futuristic compared to 1944, though some more so than others.

We are also used to a reasonably stable narrative perspective, but in *Gravity's Rainbow* one can only talk of narrative voices. The narrative voice is at times omniscient, able to use Herero profanities or the equations for determining Brennschluss via capacitor; however, it proves unable to fill in many important gaps, such as Slothrop's end or the correlation between his sexual activities and bombsites. The voice modulates imperceptibly into those of characters, so we may think that a narrator is talking, only to find by the end of a scene that the point of view is that of a character—or even that of two characters combined. One of the voices is occasionally authorial in tone ("you will want cause and effect" [p. 663]) but usually not so clearly authoritative that we can expect it to tell us what belongs in the gaps. When the voice speaks directly to us as "you," we respond as to an encoded author; but that presence disappears in most of the other sequences, and we also discover that "you" can refer not to us as readers, but to other characters, or to the self of someone indulging in interior monologue. An unreliable narrator is one thing, but these voices fade in and out of existence, take different tones, and emanate from different sources unpredictably.[8]

What else usually gives stability and meaning to a narrative? A mood or emotion can do so. Kafka's "The Burrower" exists to convey a mood. Robbe-Grillet's *Jealousy* works within the framework of an emotion. But Pynchon provokes manic highs and lows, excitement, joy, despair, indifference, disgust, personal involvement, and detachment, and insofar as he portrays people and their moods, we find a very wide spectrum. An idea can also organize a book, but critics do not agree on the idea here at all. Tentative claims have been made for entropy, cause-and-effect relationships, gravity, the rationalization of charisma, the V-2, and fragmented postmodernist reality, but the critics considering these possibilities usually admit their insufficiency. *Gravity's Rainbow* cannot be reduced to so narrow a focus. A book can also impart a sense of unity through an arbitrary structural device: *Ulysses* takes place during a single day and relies on the *Odyssey* for its key events. Robbe-Grillet's *The Erasers* uses the Oedipus story. *Gravity's Rainbow* covers a one year span, but the events mentioned extend nearly three centuries into the past, so the one year is not conspicuously cut off from history.

Of the various devices used both to shatter the old patterns and provide new ones, at least three stand out as managing to escape the deconstruction applied to other unifying features: a principle of multiplicity, a group of psychoanalytic theories, and one kind of mythology—three very different sorts of material thus to enjoy protected status. In a sense, the first does not need to be destroyed because it is a technique often used to instill uncertainty: the presentation of multiple realities or multiple inherent possibilities in a situation. Robert Coover's "The Baby Sitter" is a well-known example of the technique; others include Robbe-Grillet's *The House of Assignation* and Calvino's *The Castle of Crossed Destinies*. *Gravity's Rainbow* can be read as an "encyclopedia of all the 'names and methods' by which modern man seeks to surrender to history, to absolute fictions, to any design that promises to shield us from the vulnerability of living with the moments of choice, the so-called 'nodes' of *V.* and the 'cusps' . . . of GR."[9] Encyclopedic multiplicity destroys unitary order, but the encyclopedic tendency itself can be a principle of organization of another sort: the principle of including everything gives one kind of order to this narrative,[10] and this is mocked only to the degree that no encyclopedia can be all-inclusive.

The second organizing technique not openly subverted is the use of psychoanalytic concepts, especially those concerning anality, paranoia, and oedipal anxieties. As has been well argued, Pynchon is familiar with the theories of Norman O. Brown, and uses them in *Gravity's Rainbow:* the numerous scatalogical passages are not just the symptoms of private obsession but are part of Pynchon's diagnosis of what has gone wrong in Western culture.[11] The excremental vision in Slothrop's journey down the toilet is a trip to the repressed side of Western mentality, and it points to the desperate fear of death that motivates the manufacture of weaponry from V 2s to ICBMs. Pynchon also uses paranoia as a unifying theme.[12] We gradually realize that everyone in the Zone is paranoid. All the Zone's inhabitants believe themselves to be the focus of plots, and all find connections in events that to outsiders look like mere coincidences. This is not to say that Pynchon explores his characters psychoanalytically. We see some of Slothrop's paranoid oedipal fantasies but not in enough detail to construct anything like a full interpretation of his background from them. Their presence, however, reminds us that Pynchon is aware of psychoanalytic concerns and uses them without discrediting them (whereas he undercuts behavioral psychology by means of his harsh portraits of Pointsman and Jamf).

The third organizing structure to survive the acid of Pynchon's vision is the one I wish to study, namely mythology. The encyclopedic and psychoanalytic unities have been well examined. The mythological element has not been fully understood, in part because Pynchon so obviously does attack some kinds of myths: the myths of progress, of American innocence, of linear time, and of commonsense logic. We see him subvert German "myths" of "re-education" as he exposes Camp Dora. We see Gottfried going to his unimaginable death bound by a myth of transcendence. Often enough, Pynchon explodes specific "myths"—particularly "myths" as Roland Barthes uses the term, meaning myths or mythologies as propaganda, as the network of values that makes us believe the historical to be natural and inevitable instead of accidental and specific.[13] But his own mythology, though not rigidly consistent, is dependable enough to serve a stabilizing function in this chaotic book and deserves scrutiny for that reason. Particularly because Pynchon attacks some kinds of myths, it is important to see what kinds he accepts, and to speculate on why some are salvaged while others are savaged.

Since each aspect of Pynchon's mythology is covered in its own chapter, I will not enter into details here, but wish merely to indicate the nature of his more obviously mythological elements. The first, only partly recognized by critics, is his mythological cosmos. Readers of *Gravity's Rainbow* know that compass directions matter as they do not in a realistic novel: South is associated with open, non-European societies living within the cycles of nature. These societies have been invaded and colonized, so the original qualities are faded and dying, but remnants of the qualities affect Pynchon's allusions to the south. Other directions have similarly set symbolism. The physical dimensions of his world are also symbolic. Heights and depths not only play a nonrealistically large role in the stories, they also correlate to spiritual adventures. Deserts and wastelands likewise provide *paysages moralisés*.

Pynchon's elaborate references to the Other Side give his cosmos a dimension that cannot be shrugged off. Critics have preferred to ignore the import of this world, but Pynchon does not portray this other region as mere metaphor for the dead hand of the past or use it as a whimsical and euphemistic way of alluding to the dead. Pynchon and his characters, especially those who pass over, treat this further dimension as entirely real and unethereal. The narrative seems to demand that this further dimension be taken seriously at some level, and if so, then we must accept the novel's universe as a mythological cosmos, not just as a fictive world equivalent to those in realistic novels.

Working out destiny against this cosmological background are several strands of mythological action. They involve the history of a people, namely Western, technological humankind. The strands involve crucial symbolic actions equivalent to paradise, the fall, crucifixion (with echoes of Abraham's sacrifice), and apocalypse. There is a strongly structured movement from beginnings toward endings (albeit the sequence does not correspond to the beginning and end of the narrative). The turning points and key developments of this movement are highlighted by means of story, anecdote, whimsy, humor, accumulated facts, and symbolic action.

In addition to mythological actions, Pynchon also makes use of legendary and literary culture heroes: Parsifal, Tannhäuser, Faust, Orpheus, Hansel and Gretel, Alice, and Dorothy, as well as such figures from popular culture as Plasticman. These heroes offer Slothrop a constellation of culturally recognized models for action. Within Pynchon's mythology, such heroes come to suggest the limitations and inadequacies of each, and, in the aggregate, they illustrate the desirability of finding a new hero-myth. The heroes from diverse traditions let Pynchon explore ways that people can invest action with value and ways that they can relate themselves to the universe, both aims being the concern of any mythology.

Such elements are quite conventional, and Pynchon's handling of them does not exemplify his usual impulse to undermine or disassemble. While the answers and relationships presented in this mythological material are not conventional at all, the myths do seem to function in a fairly traditional fashion, one that yields to the application of techniques designed for studying myths themselves.

Myth and Mythic Fiction

A standard objection to myth criticism is politely voiced by Graham Hough when he says, "In its application to any particular literary case myth criticism turns out to be curiously disappointing. It tells much of interest, but not what we really want to know."[14] *Gravity's Rainbow* certainly offers the reader a wealth of concerns besides those touched on by a study of its mythography, but at least two crucial issues cannot be understood apart from myth: the nature of Pynchon's antiempirical vision of the cosmos (on which depends much of the acceptability of what he says philosophically) and the implied messages or warnings promulgated by the mythology. These are indeed matters we might really want to know.

A historical or theoretical survey of what myth can mean would demand many pages and would serve no purpose here. (An excellent survey forms the first chapter of William Righter's *Myth and Literature*.) For my purposes, primary myth is a traditional narrative, usually concerned with gods and heroes, that embodies and reinforces cultural values through its symbolism. It often deals with such socially important subjects as origins and birth, growing up, marriage, death, and humanity's relations to animals, plants, and the cosmos at large. Prominent in such narratives are questions of identity, crises of violence and sacrifice, and struggles with monsters.

As a rule, the actions range over a nonnaturalistic landscape.

Also characteristic of the form is an open-endedness that defies exact translation into a prosaic interpretation. Eric Gould bases his study on this feature:

Myths apparently derive their universal significance from the way in which they try to reconstitute an original event or explain some fact about human nature and its worldly or cosmic context. But in doing so, they necessarily refer to some essential meaning which is absent until it appears as a function of interpretation. If there is one persistent belief in this study, it is that there can be no myth without an *ontological gap between event and meaning*. A myth intends to be an adequate symbolic representation by closing that gap, by aiming to be a tautology. The absent origin, the arbitrary meaning of our place in the world, determines the mythic, at least in the sense that we cannot come up with any definitive origin for our presence here. So what I continually turn to is the fact that myth is both hypothesis and compromise. Its meaning is perpetually open and universal only because once the absence of a final meaning is recognized, the gap itself demands interpretation which, in turn, must go on and on, for language is nothing if it is not a system of open meaning.[15]

This built-in uncertainty, the sense that not all of a myth can be constrained by words, is expressed also by William Righter: "myth fulfils its rôle precisely because it is non-rational, indeterminate, and uncertain in the nature of its ultimate claims" (Righter, pp. 22–23). Righter goes on to say that its "precision of function in its original context is dependent on this very lack of rational tidiness" and suggests that this quality leads to the lack of tidiness in definitions of myth.

When we call a work of literature mythic, we usually mean that it embodies some characteristics of myth; or that it uses the sort of nonrealistic plot devices and landscapes found in myth; or that it borrows actual stories from primary or early literary renditions of myths and legends. The precise relationship between the work and myth can be difficult to pin down. As Righter points out, "*The Tempest* lends itself to mythical interpretations, although it is informed by no particular myth" (p. 25).

The Tempest does seem to have qualities generally called mythic. The specialness of Prospero and his daughter is suggested by means of social class and meaningful names, and those gimmicks still work, for we would not expect tales about Donald Evans, butcher, or Jake Brown, drug-pusher, and their respective daughters, to make the same kind of impact on us. A writer could undoubtedly persuade us to take plebians or criminals as speakers for modern humankind, but it would require special rhetoric.

The action takes place on a nearly deserted island. Life in a suburb or a slum, unless shorn of individual detail, would exhibit such particularity as to work against general significance. Even a modern duke, living in his country seat, would seem too individual, unless that dwelling were made strange—deprived of all but one ancient servitor and situated at great distance from any settlement. Prospero deals with an "other" world of supernatural powers and agencies. In a sense hard to translate into everyday prose, Prospero's intellectual struggles with the power bestowed by magic and Miranda's adventures with the brave new world of humankind both tell us something about humanity's place in the cosmos and about the flaws which keep us from enjoying happy, well-regulated, peaceful lives. By seeing the unfolding of innocence and the temptations of knowledge, the lust for power and the gratifications of force, we are reminded of our mythic origins (the fall) and of the reasons our cultural state and Shakespeare's is more perilous than paradisal. The plot is overtly symbolic rather than realistic. We have only to look at *Measure for Measure,* also about a duke separated from his ducal power for a time, to see a nonmythic play and recognize the degree to which *The Tempest* has characteristics which make literature seem "mythic."

Among more recent works, those of Kafka are generally felt to have mythic qualities. *The Trial* starts with an exceedingly ordinary protagonist, but because he is so quickly isolated on the interface between two worlds, one of them occupied by unreachable, untouchable powers, he becomes special, and his lack of individuality serves to make his experiences seem significant. He tries to deal with mysterious controlling agents; he struggles with problems of identity, responsibility, and guilt—and he dies violently. The indefinability of the powers ranged against him intensifies his anguish and heightens the affective power of his every thought and gesture. An individual's struggle with a specific historical tribunal would not have this general "mythic" applicability. The impossibility of reaching any very firm closure of interpretation is a notorious effect of Kafka's work, true for *The Trial* as it is for the ambiguous ending of *The Metamorphosis.* The ontological gap is filled with words, but they do not manage to close it.

When we consider *Gravity's Rainbow* we find these mythic qualities mentioned above, albeit embedded in a

highly complex web of details, which is relevant to mythology though not to myth. Tyrone Slothrop does not
appeal to many readers as an alter-ego, but his gradual
emergence as something like Western Technological Man
or The American eventually bestows on him one sort of
mythic stature, less obvious but of the same kind as that
enjoyed by Blake's Albion or Spenser's Red Cross Knight.
A somewhat ineffectual if not stupid man, lacking aim
or ambition, Slothrop seems negligible at first, but as an
indictment of Western humanity, he cannot be casually
dismissed. He is trying to make his way through an unusual landscape, a war-torn wonderland where mysterious forces affect his fate in ways he cannot predict or
control. He becomes increasingly isolated in this strange,
nonnaturalistic realm, until at last he disintegrates in a
sparagmos or scattering that takes the form of total loss,
first of individual identity and then of physical form,
until he is literally invisible. Since the loss appears to be
accompanied by some spiritual gains denied ordinary
people, this is not just a personal tragedy, but part of a
symbolic statement.

Other actions in the novel are also mythic in their
configuration. Gottfried's launching in the rocket involves
a ritual wedding, violence, and sacrifice, and implicates
the culture that has launched him. The open-endedness
of all the plot lines, and the gaps never quite filled, are
among the book's most characteristic features. Also present is the intense concern with origins, the beginnings
of modern Western culture, the beginnings of modern
science and technology. Slothrop's adventures let Pynchon explore humanity's relationship to animals and
plants, to society and fellow wanderers, to technology,
and to death. The gap is there—how did we get where

we are?—and so are the words that attempt but cannot fully succeed in filling it. The question of how we reached our culture of ballistic overkill is both answered and unanswerable, and this myth-like ambiguity is reflected in the novel.

Mythology and Mythological Fiction

Northrop Frye points out that myths have two tendencies lacking in folktales:

First, myths stick together to form a mythology, a large interconnected body of narrative that covers all the religious and historical revelation that its society is concerned with, or concerned about. Second, as part of this sticking-together process, myths take root in a specific culture, and it is one of their functions to tell that culture what it is and how it came to be, in their own mythical terms.

He goes on:

The Bible is the supreme example of the way that myths can, under certain social pressures, stick together to make up a mythology. A second look at this mythology shows us that it actually became, for medieval and later centuries, a vast mythological universe, stretching in time from creation to apocalypse, and in metaphorical space from heaven to hell. A mythological universe is a vision of reality in terms of human concerns and hopes and anxieties: it is not a primitive form of science. . . . All mythological universes are by definition centered on man, therefore the actual universe was also assumed to be centered on man.[16]

What Gould says about myth is even more clearly true about mythology: mythologies concern themselves with origins, with the gap between origins and present, with the human condition, and with humankind's relationship to the cosmos—"Stories about our sacred origins are above all explanations of what takes place in the gaps between events and meaning" (Gould, p. 198). Also carried over to mythology from the component myths is the presence of preternatural power and its disturbing implications:

We cannot answer the question of what makes mythology so attractive to writers and readers of modern literature if we remain with structure and semiotics alone and ignore myth's talent for arguing for the numinous signifier and the validity of the supernatural. But, not surprisingly, that has been a much avoided question in modern literary criticism. (Gould, p. 171)

Or, as Righter puts it:

For the importance of myth in a "demythologized" age, is not simply to provide us with the now missing sense of an ultimate frame of reference, but to provide an area of almost deliberate uncertainty as to what such frames might possibly imply. And the strength and weakness in myth reside in the same thing: the weakness in the fact that we can always ask "what is meant by this?" and the strength in some level of conviction that this is not really a relevant query to whatever it may be that the myth "says." (Righter, pp. 96–97)

Mythology, in addition to sharing various features with myths, enjoys a further feature not properly part of the elemental units: complexity of structure, often complemented by complexity of detail. Single biblical stories are simple, but the aggregate is elaborate, and the styles necessary to convey the range of material are varied. To cover any culture's development from origins to end demands fantasy, history, and biography, but as we see in the Bible, lyric, lament, and prophecy are also useful.

When discussing modes and forms, Frye points to this encyclopedic tendency:

We note that traditional tales and myths and histories have a strong tendency to stick together and form encyclopaedic aggregates, especially when they are in a conventional metre, as they usually are. Some such process as this has been postulated for the Homeric epics, and in the Prose Edda the themes of the fragmentary lays of the Elder Edda are organized into a connected prose sequence. The Biblical histories obviously developed in a similar way.[17]

His further examples include the *Ramayana* and *Mahabharata*, *The Romance of the Rose*, and—with modifications—*The Kalevala*. He identifies sacred scripture as the encyclopedic form characteristic of the mythical mode. Frye further suggests that the germ for encyclopedic forms is the oracle and notes that the "oracle develops a number of subsidiary forms, notably the commandment, the parable, the aphorism, and the prophecy" (*Anatomy*, p. 56). The strong oracular strain in *Gravity's Rainbow* is suggestive in this context, given the novel's mythical mode, encyclopedic form, and its mythological/scriptural structure.

We can see the aggregative tendency at work on European arthurian materials. Once Arthur becomes established as the central hero, Tristan, originally an independent figure, gets drawn into Arthur's orbit. The grail legend attaches itself and undergoes a process of further growth and development, so that the wasteland myth comes into being. The vulgate cycle in France and Malory's *Morte Darthur* in England both show a society from its inception to its disintegration. Cultural values are developed and tested. Humankind's place in the universe, however, is not seriously probed, it being fixed by Christian convention; furthermore, Christianity pegs humans so much below the angels that arthurian heroes rarely achieve any sort of superhuman status. Arthuriana falls short of becoming a new mythology, but it illustrates the aggregative tendency well and shows us what came very close to becoming a mythology in the fullest sense.

Modern works embodying mythographic impulses include—to various degrees and in various ways—*100 Years of Solitude* (Gabriel García Márquez), *The Flounder* (Günther Grass), *The Public Burning* (Robert Coover), *Cosmicomics, t zero* (Italo Calvino), and *Shikasta* (Doris Lessing), not to mention occasional works of science fiction, such as Olaf Stapledon's *The Last and First Men*. Like myth, such mythological literature is often episodic, paratactic, and repetitive and hence is well suited to the techniques of structuralist analysis.

Gravity's Rainbow has at least as strong a claim to be called mythological literature as any of the other works here mentioned. Although Pynchon's novel contains a foregrounded time span of only one year, unlike the works of Lessing, Calvino, Grass, and Stapledon, which cover eons, Pynchon fills in considerable detail about the origins and development of modern Western civilization. Slothrop's ancestors, like the patriarchs of Genesis, mark the unfolding of early cultural history. The developments in the coal-tar dye and plastics industries give us the chronicles of more recent stages. His gravestone epitaphs and song lyrics add a free-floating poetic element, and the overall thrust of the book is prophetic:

rockets will descend on Los Angeles (the West) un-less. . . . We frequently contend with cryptic oracular statements, such as that of Walther Rathenau's spirit or of Lyle Bland's astral self; these passages are charged with intensity but not easily translatable into plain ex-position. Pynchon's minor figures give his world some of the scope and variety of a major mythology. We are regaled with the Kirghiz tribes and their Aqyn, the seek-ers at the White Visitation, the lunatic who thought he was the war, Gerhardt von Göll (the subcreator of new cultures through his movies), Laszlo Jamf (the behav-ioral psychologist and organic chemist), and Tchitch-erine (the Russian agent who ends up in love with a witch)—and these are only a sampling of Pynchon's gallery.

Pynchon's origins-to-apocalypse story and his sense of what a mythology consists of probably both stem from the Bible, that being the mythology most known to his culture.[18] Within the scope it offers as model, he con-trives actions with strong mythic elements, such as Sloth-rop's *sparagmos* and Gottfried's launching in the rocket. Indeed, in positively anthropological terms, Gottfried's relations with the 00000 rocket are described in terms of a wedding, man with machine. This union is treated as taboo, the violation of which will produce a new form of life, one in which humanity will depend on machines for life, will lose its independence and sovereignty. In-sofar as many traditional mythologies expend much ef-fort to codify human kinship and marriage rules, as does Genesis (according to Edmund Leach), Pynchon's sym-bolism keeps him startlingly close to the concerns of primary mythologies. The history of the rocket's assem-bly has all the concreteness of the biblical account of establishing the chosen people in the promised land. Indeed, the Zone, as the focus of intense concern, becomes a promised land of sorts, a land of a kind of freedom, and home too of the seekers after rocket information and parts, the scripture and relics of the new order coming into being.

Myth Criticism and Fiction

Literature can share with myths and with aggregated mythologies their various functions of locating humankind in the cosmos, of measuring the universe in human terms, and of presenting emotional images that symbolically explain problems of origin and current condition. We, therefore, naturally wonder to what extent literature and myth share a hermeneutic. Can techniques applied to interpreting myths work on mythological literature? For all that there are similarities, there are also many differences, as anyone comparing *Gravity's Rainbow* to the Bible or to Lévi-Strauss's accounts of Latin American Indian myths would agree.

Further, there is the problem of the work's origins. A myth, according to majority view at any rate, does not stem from the mind of an individual. Italo Calvino—a mythographic writer himself—has argued against this view, suggesting that myth comes from the tribal storyteller's combinatorial play with the givens in cultural folk materials: "At a certain stage something clicks, and one of the combinations obtained by its own mechanisms, independently of any search for meaning or effect on some other level, takes on an unexpected sense or produces an unforeseen effect that consciousness could not have achieved intentionally."[19] Even if myths do originate, however, in the storytelling of individuals, successive tellings would quickly reduce and remove the idiosyncrasies, the traces of personal psychology. As time progresses, the parts to be saved and developed would be those of most general interest. The inability of individualistic features to survive in oral tradition is nicely documented by Constantin Brailoiu. Brailoiu collected a Balkan ballad about a young man who had been

bewitched by a mountain fairy, and a few days before he was to be married, the fairy, driven by jealousy, had flung him from a cliff. The next day, shepherds found his body and, caught in a tree, his hat. They carried the body back to the village and his fiancée came to meet them; upon seeing her lover dead, she poured out a funeral lament, full of mythological allusions, a liturgical text of rustic beauty.

Brailoiu discovered that the event had taken place only forty years prior to his collecting trip; he learned from the heroine herself that

it was a quite commonplace tragedy: one evening her lover had slipped and fallen over a cliff; he had not died instantly; his cries had been heard by mountaineers: he had been carried to the village, where he had died soon after. At the funeral, his fiancée, with the other women of the village, had repeated the customary ritual lamentations, without the slightest allusion to the mountain fairy.[20]

Upon querying his ballad sources and reminding them of the authentic version, Brailoiu found "they replied that the old woman had forgotten; that her great grief had almost destroyed her mind. It was the myth that

told the truth: the real story was already only a falsifi-
cation." This suggests that whether myths originate with
individuals or not, they will lose much of their personal
component in a way that printed fiction does not.

This makes impossible a direct transfer of Lévi-
Strauss's techniques to literature, and he himself has
denied any such transferability. His search for meaning
in myth is based on a concept of meaning that would
work in one way for myth, but quite another for literature. He likens myth study to marxist sociology and
freudian psychology:

At a different level of reality, Marxism seemed to me to proceed in the same manner as geology and psychoanalysis (taking the latter in the sense given it by its founder). All three
demonstrate that understanding consists in reducing one type
of reality to another; that the true reality is never the most
obvious; and that the nature of truth is already indicated by
the care it takes to remain elusive. For all cases, the same
problem arises, the problem of the relationship between feeling and reason, and the aim is the same: to achieve a kind of
superrationalism, which will integrate the first with the second,
without sacrificing any of its properties.[21]

For myth, this second level so different from the outward story would be a cultural anxiety; for fiction, it
would be primarily an individual anxiety and would correspond to a psychoanalytic reading. Even in a mytho-
graphical and philosophical tale like David Lindsay's *A
Voyage to Arcturus* such a meaning level (or at least one
of them) is a cluster of oral-anxiety images whose embedded fears at times even work counter to the overt content
of the story.[22] Lévi-Strauss's approach to myth, if applied
directly to literature, would come up with cultural anx-

ieties only as they are filtered through the individual author's consciousness. At any rate, some modification of the structuralist approach to mythology would seem more promising than direct application to literature.

Edmund Leach sees himself as carrying out the Lévi-Strauss method in his article "Genesis as Myth," but to an outsider his results seem rather different from those of Lévi-Strauss (in his article on Oedipus, for instance).[23] When Lévi-Strauss digs beneath the surface of the Theban cycle, he finds cultural anxiety over humanity's origins: born of earth or of parents. When Leach analyzes Genesis, he finds anxious justifications of endogamy over exogamy, despite the inhering risk of incest. But whereas nothing in Oedipus speaks directly to the possibility of autochthony—so the meaning, as Lévi-Strauss claims, is truly separate from surface concerns—the problems of setting one's people apart as special and of avoiding racial contamination are very much a surface concern of Genesis as well as a deep concern. Leach's analysis suggests that the latent anxieties affect the world picture to a greater extent than the casual reader would anticipate, but the two levels do not seem independent.

What Leach looks for—binary oppositions, redundancies, and mediations—are technical concerns of students of myth, but in other guises they are also the concerns of students of literature. Oppositions—at least major, explicit oppositions—are the natural medium for dialectical exploration of values in literature. The dark heroine versus the fair heroine, action versus contemplation, Gregor Samsa as bug versus his family, the beckettian protagonists versus the shakespearian world in *Rosencrantz and Guildenstern are Dead*—these are obvious oppositions. Some sort of major opposition is necessary if there is to be any plot, though literary oppositions are not always strictly binary. The author may favor one element, or a synthesis, or reject all three.

Redundancies, too, are important in literature. For Leach, they are part of the excess of information given so that the noise creeping into the message will not wipe out crucial elements of that message. Repetition of the main ideas in several different forms makes their survival more likely. In literature, too, we often find replication or repetition of important scenes, actions, and words. Even if the repetitions are no more than the symptoms of shoddy craftsmanship, they usually call our attention to something that mattered to the author. The repetition may be a deliberate ploy for intensifying our concern or response, or it may be unconscious, a reflection of the author's private obsessions. In any event, we are used to paying attention to repetitions and redundancies in literary study; and within the parameters of Leach's method, these play an important role, for in mythological literature such repetitions have a more or less fully mythic function.

The mediations, however, we are not particularly used to looking for, and here Leach's tools may have something new to offer. He argues that the oppositions established in mythic narratives may always seem to be mutually exclusive but that we try to establish sacred mediating categories that resolve the conflict. If a basic antinomy is alive and not-alive, we create the story of an afterlife in which the dead live forever. Religious myth and theology are full of such mediations: virgin mothers, sons who are neither the same nor different in substance from the father, animals declared unclean because they violate basic categories. (Sacredness—as taboo—can be negative as well as positive.) One cannot assume that such mediations exist in literature, for an author may prefer one side to the other, or reject both, rather than seek a synthesis or alternative, but looking for mediations makes sense in fiction heavily reliant on mythology. In Pynchon's case, such mediations can help us work out some of his apparent meanings and values.

Other ways of approaching myth have less that is new to offer study of literature. Most readings of myth are examples of allegorical interpretation, whether the myths are decoded as onomastic play, as weather and nature symbolism, as history misunderstood, or as projections of psychological tensions; such allegoresis is already well known in literary criticism. Structuralism itself offers other practitioners than Lévi-Strauss and Leach as models. Eric Gould practices a form of structuralism or poststructuralism when he reaches back to the linguistic roots of structuralism; he studies myth not just as a reflection of the ontological gaps between our knowledge of events, but reaches back to that gap between every signifier and the signified, the gap between our verbal artifice and the world it tries to deal with. However interesting Gould's theories of mythicity, his comments seem not to apply to Pynchon, partly because Gould thinks in terms of myth rather than mythology. He recognizes the linguistic and philosophical element in *Gravity's Rainbow* but ignores the mythological stories and symbols and their implications. In Gould's own words, Pynchon "has overemphasized the paradigmatic function of literature—particularly its habit of creating arbitrary and even paranoid relations—to the loss of our sense of universal sharing in language itself, which myth depends on" (Gould, p. 115). But the traditional elements of myth, including a symbolic mythological universe and a syntagmatic mythology, are there in the novel. Gould's framework for analysis causes him to filter such elements out and overlook them.

For thoughts about such a symbolic universe, one should turn to writers like Northrop Frye, Paul Ricoeur, and Mircea Eliade, who think in terms of mythology, not just myth. That we need to have some grasp of symbolic universes to read *Gravity's Rainbow* is obvious if we compare its world to that of Austen or Trollope. In the simple matter of direction, they show no preferences. A manor will be north or south of the nearby village without any significance attaching to the fact. A country gentleman may, if he chooses, breed prize cattle as a hobby, but the beasts will not take on the polysemy that pigs enjoy for Pynchon, who associates them with Puritans, with Dutch colonizers of Mauritius, with the side of life that the Puritans reject, with the preterite, with the fertility of compost, with sensual ease, with rockets (as their opposite), with dodos (whom they destroy), with carnivalesque opposition to oppressive police authorities, with companionship along the road, with sex, with grace in several senses of the term, with expressionist painting, and with the comradeship to be found among those marginalized by society.

The interconnectedness of Pynchon's cosmos is one earmark of a symbolic universe: "A logic of correspondences" characterizes "the sacred universe and indicate[s] the specificity of *homo religiosus*'s vision of the world. Such ties occur at the level of the very elements of the natural world such as the sky, earth, air, and water. And the same uranian symbolism makes the diverse epiphanies communicate among themselves, while at the same time they also refer to the divine immanent in the hierophanies of life." Ricoeur goes on: "Within the sacred universe there are not living creatures here and there, but life is everywhere as a sacrality, which permeates everything and which is seen in the movement of the stars, the return to life of vegetation each year, and the alternation of birth and death."[24] Paranoia is not the common form for this sense of connectedness to take, but paranoia, as Pynchon notes, is "perhaps a route In for those . . . who are held at the edge" (p. 703). A crippled mysticism, it is true, but one nonetheless still able to give insight.[25]

In sum, elaborate justifications are not needed for applying various forms of myth criticism to mythological literature. Clearly, literary stories and myths, mythological literature and mythologies are not interchangeable. They share, nonetheless, certain functions, such as delineating ways humankind may interrelate with the cosmos; and they share certain techniques, such as oppositions and redundancies, for conveying values. The critical methods must be applied with due attention to their limitations, but with recognition of that caveat, I shall eschew further defenses and return to my own endeavor.

Approaching *Gravity's Rainbow* via Pynchon's Mythography

Lévi-Strauss uses a metaphor to describe his method of analyzing myth:

As happens in the case of an optical microscope, which is incapable of revealing the ultimate structure of matter to the observer, we can only choose between various degrees of enlargement: each one reveals a level of organization which has no more than a relative truth and, while it lasts, excludes the perception of other levels.[26]

As stated earlier, I have chosen to examine the mythic and specifically the mythological dimensions of *Gravity's Rainbow* not because I believe them to be Pynchon's primary concern, but because they are important concerns and necessary to the understanding of the whole. Ultimately, one must use this approach not on its own, but as part of a critical perspective that seeks to see both the craters and muffins, both the stabilizing and destabilizing elements in their interactions together. After studying one technique for destroying our standard assumptions—Pynchon's habit of "mapping" characters onto each other—Brian McHale concludes: "For the effect of this troublesome novel is, finally, the salutary one of disrupting the conditioned responses of the Modernist reader (and we are all, still, Modernist readers), of de-conditioning the reader." He goes on: "Pynchon's text sets itself against this Modernist mindset, chiefly by luring the paranoid reader—the Modernist reader—into interpretative dark alleys, cul-de-sacs, impossible situations, and requiring him to find his way out by some other path than the one he came in" ("Modernist Reading," p. 107).

This is indeed one possible conclusion and is valid as far as it goes. This is the picture of the muffins, or of the silences. We will see in chapter 3, however, how the technique of mapping produces some interesting redundancies. Certain kinds of situations get repeated. Patterns emerge. Viewing these repetitions as part of the mythological matrix and using Leach's tools for approaching them, we will be able to see that Pynchon may indeed be putting the convention of characters as individuals in question, but his way of doing this calls attention to and reinforces the significance of certain values. Craters and melody are there as well. The presence of the stable values, of the mythic pattern, ultimately does not contradict the postmodernist elements, as I shall argue in the final chapter. Each has a different but interlocking function in the total effect of *Gravity's Rainbow*. When *Ulysses* first appeared, critics reacted most strongly to its dissonant and disturbing elements and stressed its negative effects.[27] Only gradually did Joyce's positive elements also gain recognition. Any avant-garde work, because it rejects prior traditions, will embody violent negative attitudes both philosophical and formal; however, the work is unlikely to command interest for long if it does not stand for some values as well as against others. *Gravity's Rainbow* would soon lose its fascination were it only antimodernist, were it not constructive as well as explosive.

We sometimes forget how very different interpretations can seem—yet still be valid pictures. One can draw a torso in impressionist, expressionist, mannerist, cubist, or primitive styles. One can also photograph the same torso; or produce an abdominal X-ray, or a thermogram, or an ultrasound scan, or a CAT-scan, or a PET-scan. Shown to someone with no artistic or medical training, most of these would seem entirely unrelated and contradictory. They represent different levels of reality as those levels relate to different discourses. Yet these realities coexist and more or less complement each other; furthermore, no one of them should be taken to represent an exclusive reality. The same may be said of a deconstructive reading, a semiotic analysis, a thematic study, and an exploration of Pynchon's mythography. The more such renditions we can draw on, the richer will be our grasp of the realities they represent. All readings do not necessarily merge in perfect harmony; the amount of active participation demanded of each individual reader is far too great for that to be thinkable for this of all texts. I shall argue, nonetheless, that the apparent gulf between postmodernist and more traditional readings, negative and positive in their emphases, is largely illusory. Any first reading of the text will be postmodernist, but subsequent readings develop a more traditional set of satisfactions as well. I shall ultimately suggest that both modes of perception are demanded by the concerns of the book, by Pynchon's orphic aesthetic, and by the nature of the ideal reader his text encodes.

2

The Mythological Cosmos

where you can sit and listen in to traffic from the Other Side

A S ONE STRATUM in *Gravity's Rainbow*'s plenitude, Pynchon gives us an extremely factual account of people, places, and events between December
1944 and September 1945. Many of the countless details
that recreate London, the Riviera, and the Zone have
been traced to historical sources; other details, though
not factual, are realistic.[1] In addition to this tour-de-
force verisimilitude, however, Pynchon also offers us a
mythological cosmos. Since this cosmos underlies the
mythological actions that occur in the novel, echoing and
reinforcing their values, it makes a logical starting point
for studying Pynchon's mythography. Understanding
what Pynchon establishes with his cosmos is crucial to
an overall evaluation of his argument, for what he creates goes beyond our usual empirical assumptions about
the nature of reality. If this cosmos, the foundation of
his argument, seems weak, then his deductions or con-
clusions will not convince us; if, however, he persuades
us to entertain notions of reality differing from those

34

our culture considers true and sane, then he can lead us toward a new vision.

As I am defining it for this study, a mythological cosmos has four significant characteristics.

(1) A mythological cosmos is an interpretation of the universe put in terms of human scale and values. Northrop Frye describes the first characteristic well when he states that a "mythological universe is a vision of reality in terms of human concerns and hopes and anxieties." He goes on: "All mythological universes are by definition centered on man" (*Secular Scripture,* p. 14). This definition eliminates scientific cosmology, which attempts to study the relations between the elements of the system without reference to a human center. In scientific contexts, a mountain is the result of geological pressures, volcanic or tectonic, and it exists as a phenomenon, whether anyone climbs it or not. In a mythological universe, a high place traditionally enters the story to echo, on the geophysical level, a human spiritual illumination. Elevation above sea level does not *cause* insight. It does not even facilitate such insight. Mountains signify or symbolize such illumination, perhaps because of the physical characteristics of high places (one can see farther) and perhaps because of their religious value (they are closer to the sky gods). The relationship between altitude and illumination is parallel, as Leni Pökler would say, not causal, but that relationship is deeply entrenched in nonrealistic literary tradition. In other words, a mythological landscape frequently embodies human values in a way that reality, materially defined, does not.

(2) Mythological cosmoi transcend the empirical. To people embracing their culture's religious myths, these transcendent elements are true, but even believers would

acknowledge that such nonempirical dimensions are not open for casual inspection or scientific investigation. We cannot send a research team to follow Dante's footsteps through Inferno, and neither he nor his Church would have claimed this possible, no matter how real they considered the afterworld to be. The nonempirical may include supernatural beings, various forms of other world, and supernatural sources of power, miraculous or magical. In a cultural context where religion is the primary mythology, such a cosmos reflects the local religious mythology. We have literary examples of such cosmoi in the *Commedia* and in the fantasies of C. S. Lewis. Nonreligious writers have also produced mythological cosmoi, such as those found in Italo Calvino's *Cosmicomics* or in Günther Grass's *The Flounder*.

(3) Mythological cosmoi are serious. Most science fiction and fantasy go beyond the empirical, but their authors do not expect the stories to be taken seriously as cosmological statements. Because mythology is a symbolic form of communication, it need not be taken entirely literally (although it loses most of its religious power when it is felt to be "merely" symbolic), and it can take sportive as well as solemn guise; but at some level, the myth intrinsically demands acceptance as a truth. David Lindsay's *A Voyage to Arcturus* does not demand that we discard the periodic table in favor of green sparks and white vortices, but the statement he makes about the nature of the universe—the struggle between vitalist fragments and enervating, parasitic forces—is offered as an entirely serious truth.

(4) Finally, mythological cosmoi tend to use the traditional components of their form, the archetypes (as these are popularly called). While it might theoretically

be possible to create a mythological cosmos without using such archetypes as creation, apocalypse, *axis mundi*, underworld, and monsterfight, the resultant realm would lack the familiar resonances that guide readers to the desired seriousness of response and would almost certainly lack the human orientation Frye specifies, for the archetypes are mostly the projections of such human experiences as birth and death upon material reality, where they become, in these examples, creation and the end of the world. Without archetypes, a fictive world would seem merely scientific or just fantastic. Lem's *Solaris* offers us both the scientific and the fantastic, but not the mythological, since his ocean resists observers' endeavors to measure it in human terms, or even in humanly comprehensible terms.

Pynchon's cosmos has all four of these characteristics: it is measured in human terms; it presents us with nonempirical realities; it is ultimately serious; and it relies on traditional archetypes. Some of these we accept with the ease of literary familiarity, but we are likely to fight against other features, such as its nonempirical claims and its seriousness, and to wish to withhold our assent. After seeing how Pynchon sets up his cosmos, therefore, we must consider the principles that seem to organize its elements. We can also then study the consistency or fluidity of this structure, which will have bearing on the degree to which Pynchon seems to be demanding acceptance of the nonempirical material. My analysis will start with (1) the physical world and then proceed to (2) the nonphysical realities Pynchon presents, (3) the beings inhabiting this fictive cosmos, and (4) the distribution of positive and negative values. Then, we can evaluate the assertions of new truth Pynchon seems to be making.

The Physical World

The physical world of *Gravity's Rainbow* can be analyzed horizontally and vertically. Horizontal analysis will iden-tify the geographical center and periphery, the core that is valued and the threats that are rejected, repressed, or banished to outer darkness. Vertical considerations will involve what Pynchon does with heights and depths such as mountains and caves under mountains.

The horizontal configuration of most symbolic cosmoi is simple: at the center is a core of light, order, and fellowship; beyond this are the wastes or forests or marshes or seas or deserts inhabited by monsters and outlaws. The hall in *Beowulf* is surrounded by monster-haunted fens; King Arthur's court tries to expand its sway over hinterlands ruled by strongmen who believe only in their own might; tribal villages pit their cooking culture and abstract pattern-painting against the raw and chaotic manifestations of power in nature. Pyn-chon's world, however, is threefold. In the middle is the Zone, the exploded center foretold by Yeats in "The Second Coming." What, but a short while earlier, had been a tense, pressured community losing a war, has lost its cincture, and the fragments fly outward. In the power vacuum that results, people learn to cope with unac-customed freedom: "'It's an arrangement,'" Geli tells Slothrop. "'It's so unorganized out here. There have to be arrangements. You'll find out.' Indeed he will—he'll find thousands of arrangements, for warmth, love, food, simple movement along roads, tracks and canals." The narrator calls Slothrop "as properly constituted a state as any other in the Zone these days" (pp. 290–91). Much evidence suggests that this open life of the Zone, though disapproved and feared by Western culture, is strongly upheld by Pynchon. His placing it where he does reflects this esteem.

Surrounding this core are the Western powers, made by their victory yet more rigid and more obsessed with control. Instead of putting them within the circle of light, Pynchon places them in the location traditionally reserved for monsters, the dark wastes beyond the lighted core. Superimposed on these nations and uniting them are the multinational corporations and the technologies, to whom the war was simply a move in a game plan. Their creed is the "order of Analysis and Death," which started in Europe, then established itself in all the European colonial empires, and now returns to its origins, as "American Death" occupies Europe (p. 722). The disease is carried by rocket at this late stage, and the dispersal of rocket hardware is a metastasis: the tumor at Peenemünde has been excised, but the cells spread.

Beyond the controlling powers, outside them or within their most barren wastes, is a third kind of territory. Those peoples who have been oppressed, dispossessed, and rejected by the dominant group occupy these margins. The Kirghiz tribes, the gauchos of the Argentine pampas, and the Hereros of Southwest Africa—these are the broken and distorted remnants of an alternative to the Western style of living. Within memory, their lives were ahistorical, cyclical, and, in some senses, free. But these peoples are more reminders of lost options than viable choices now: Tchitcherine's mission of spreading literacy in the steppes has diminished and possibly destroyed freedom there. The Argentine anarchists hope that Gerhardt von Göll's film may help break down the fences erected across the pampas, but the fences are there in 1944. The Hereros may once have wandered freely, but von Trotha annihilated most of them. Even Roger Mexico's fantasy island, Puke-a-hook-a-look-i, is welcoming white men into its paradise (p. 685). Closure and control will follow. We are given the impression that such pockets of openness on the distant margins are at best threatened and may, in fact, have already disappeared, overrun by the colonizing great powers. The ring of closed and rigid systems is hostile to any alternatives.

Insofar as the marginalized groups stand for what the controlling powers most fear and therefore desire to reject and oppress, they and what they represent will be missing in the dominant society. Pynchon's tripartite geography embodies Derrida's argument that the margins are the true center, for in the Zone, Western humanity tries to reclaim and live with a form of the marginal life: freedom, arrangements limited to small-scale agreements, avoidance of control, and willingness to go with the current, experiencing time more in cyclical than linear fashion. From the vantage of when he wrote *Gravity's Rainbow*, Pynchon knew that the Zone soon stiffened and hardened into the modern Germanies, so the Zone is another lost realm of relative freedom, important as a reminder of the absent pattern denied us in our control-ridden societies, as a pattern that our culture rejects, but one that may be necessary to ultimate survival.

Orienting this center/periphery model geographically, we find values associated with the points of the compass. Pynchon's symbolism is not exact, and he allows values from adjacent compass directions to overlap, so one can better talk of tendencies than strict associations, but these tendencies are strong enough to make them significant in his cosmos.

The most obvious values are linked with the South and make it the region where barriers break down and openness is, or rather was, possible. European colonial powers, moving into warmer climes, found escape from the regulations and inhibitions of their own rigid cultures:

Colonies are the outhouses of the European soul, where a fellow can let his pants down and relax, enjoy the smell of his own shit. Where he can fall on his slender prey roaring as loud as he feels like, and guzzle her blood with open joy. Eh? Where he can just wallow and rut and let himself go in a softness, a receptive darkness of limbs, of hair as woolly as the hair of his own forbidden genitals. Where the poppy, the cannabis and coco grow full and green[. . . .] No word ever gets back. The silences down here are vast enough to absorb all behavior, no matter how dirty, how animal it gets. . . . (p. 317)

The Argentine pampas and German Southwest Africa are Pynchon's two "Souths" in this book; Italy enjoys a less flamboyant but parallel function in *V.* This openness, though associated with the South and with warmer climes, is also found in the two adjacent compass points in marginal regions. Tchitcherine's experience in the eastern steppes and Crutchfield's exploits in the American West both share some of the characteristic joys of the colonialism just described. Crutchfield's sexual indulgences and Tchitcherine's drugs would not have been possible in the closed societies from which they came.

In the world of *Gravity's Rainbow*, "for danger and enterprise they send you west, for visions, east" (p. 706).

Farthest east in the book are the Kirghiz Steppes and the Kirghiz Light, illumination of a traditional visionary kind. Since the Light is the most spectacular example of illumination in the story, it upholds the reputation of the East. However, Pynchon does not limit spiritual breakthroughs to any one location: Kurt Mondaugen reaches his in the Kalahari Desert, south with respect to Europe though east and inland from European outposts in the area. Lyle Bland achieves his breakthrough in Boston (the American East).[2]

To the west, we find America and within America, the American West, the stomping ground of Crutchfield, and "the edge of the World" to Blicero. This West spelled adventure to those Easterners who heeded Horace Greeley's exhortation, and also to those generations of children who enjoyed cowboy programs through radio, television, and movies. But west, for Pynchon, can also mean the Western world in general, and in that form, west is associated with analysis and death, whose interconnections were explicated by Nietzsche. Death also characterizes north.

The North, with its polar cold and whiteness, Pynchon links to death, rigidity, and entropy. It is the Herero land of death and the direction in which the 00000 is fired. Arctic cold is the foreshadowing of heat death's absolute predictability and stasis, its rigidity and uniformity. If the South is or was in some sense open and the North closed and rigid, European civilization has occupied an interface between the two possibilities but has not found a satisfactory balance between the forces. The Zone is roughly centered by these directional vectors. It is the eye of the storm.[3]

Vertically or cross-sectionally, Pynchon's mythological cosmos is traditional in its assumptions but individual in their embodiment and execution. As the world has mountains and deep places, this fictive world does so also, and they enjoy roughly the same values as elsewhere in mythological cosmoi. When we follow a major figure to a high place, we are not surprised to find the hint of some sort of illumination. Depths usually betoken some sort of ordeal, often with resonances of descent into the underworld, and they too provide illuminations, though these visions usually have a demonic cast. Pynchon does alter traditional values, however, in (1) paying attention to depths below those accessible to humankind (where oil and coal are formed), insisting on the significance of such hidden pockets of transformation and in (2) limiting the amount of high-altitude insight. Pynchon's realm is weighted toward the nether realms. Slothrop's visit to the Brocken introduces him to the Brockengespenst, and his vision of his and Geli's "titanic" shadows is accompanied by rainbows and haloes (p. 330)—terms related elsewhere to the supranatural Other Realm—but Slothrop does not experience any startling breakthrough. Illumination hovers at the edge of his consciousness but does not manifest itself. Later, up still higher in a balloon, Slothrop realizes that the Riviera was where he "broke through the speed of sound"—a minor insight—but again the use of colors and terms from the Other Side suggest that more insight is possible than Slothrop actually achieves.

More specific visions come to Slothrop in his descents. Going down the toilet reveals to him the excremental future, the world of mud and trenches, the world where

Harvard buddies will be known not for family or money but for the kind of "shit" they produce, the world of racial war and political lies. In a sense, the rest of the book, his future and ours, is a continuation of that hallucinated underworld vision.[4] Similarly, his descent into the Mittelwerke shows him the Ugly American at work, Major Marvy being an elaboration of Slothrop's own sexual alter ego, Crutchfield. While there, Slothrop also hears the rocket limericks. He does not sense their import, but readers may put them together with Slothrop's vision of the Raketen-Stadt, a city set up under the Articles of Immachination (p. 297). Immachination is in fact a crucial concept in *Gravity's Rainbow*. The inanimate haunted *V.*, but in *Gravity's Rainbow* humanity wedded or welded to the machine is what threatens us. The limericks celebrate this unholy marriage and its often destructive result. We are illuminated by what the Americans sing, even if Slothrop is not.

Pynchon does not entirely confine illumination to ascents and descents. Solitudes and wastes are equally traditional locations for spiritual adventures. The Kirghiz Light must be sought in the solitude of the steppes. Kurt Mondaugen reached his mystic vision in the Kalahari Desert. Insight may even come in places marked less by geography than by other symbolism, such as the Himmler Spielsaal, with its wheels of chance. We see, however, from the nonrealistic frequency of adventures in mountains, in caves and tunnels under mountains, and in wastelands, that Pynchon accepts certain conventions, even while altering them to his individual purposes. His world has a strong downward tendency toward the demonic. His underworlds render more explicit visions than his high places. As a result, *Gravity's Rainbow* is better at telling us what is wrong than in advising us how to better the situation.[5]

These, then, are the basic parameters of Pynchon's cosmos. One would not produce this world if one were thinking in purely historical or geophysical terms. The Zone is special according to Pynchon's standards because people there are free from the usual cultural and social bonds, not because Germany is physically or geographically unusual. Moreover, this particular kind of specialness is not something Pynchon found from reading history books, for historians pay little attention to the Zone's personal arrangements, as Geli calls them, and the Hiroshima bomb now overshadows the V-2 as a terror weapon. The mythological nature of Pynchon's creation is supported by the end-determined nature of his story materials. The formations and regroupings of power surrounding the V-2 are less significant in themselves than for what they point to thirty years in the future: the world of ICBMs and multinational corporate technologies.[6] Organization through apocalyptic hindsight is suitable to a mythology. It tries to answer the question, How did we get here from there?

Nonphysical Reality

Pynchon's mythological cosmos quickly becomes more complicated when we consider the variety of supernatural or supranatural powers that collectively form the Other Side. This is no simple scheme like Hell and Heaven; it is an array of alternative realities, some of which seem to have a location, others of which seem superimposed on our physical world, and others yet which seem to be not so much a location as a spiritual state. The nonempirical realm cannot readily be mapped, so we must learn what we can of its boundaries through examining the points of contact between the supranatural and the everyday.

Pynchon offers one very structured crossover: that between the séances taking place at Snoxall's and those twenty years earlier in Berlin. Peter Sachsa, the earlier medium, was killed in a riot and now serves as control on the Other Side for medium Carroll Eventyr in London. The spirit, Roland Feldspath, tells his listeners how control has changed the nature of life. Feldspath also makes his influence felt on Slothrop while Slothrop crams rocket specifications at the Casino Hermann Goering. Slothrop never quite senses Feldspath directly but feels an "alkaline aftertaste of lament, an irreducible *strangeness*," and while Feldspath, on the Other Side, is making discoveries about rocket-like patterns of life and control, and about invisible forces and other orders of being (pp. 239–40), Slothrop makes parallel discoveries on This Side.

Nor is Feldspath the only representative from the spirit world. Walther Rathenau comes through for the Berlin circle to answer questions for IG Farben. He too talks of control:

"All talk of cause and effect is secular history, and secular history is a diversionary tactic. Useful to you, gentlemen, but no longer so to us here. If you want the truth—I know I presume—you must look into the technology of these matters. Even into the hearts of certain molecules—it is they after all which dictate temperatures, pressures, rates of flow, costs, profits, the shapes of towers. . . .

"You must ask two questions. First, what is the real nature of synthesis? And then: what is the real nature of control?" (p. 167)

Many critics seem uneasy with this spiritualistic material. Much of it is presented as if it were as real as V-2s. Even when Pynchon makes jokes at the expense of such séances, such as Lamplighter's postmortem failure to report to his erstwhile colleagues, the teasing does not discredit the basic events. When Blobadjian passes to the Other Side, we smile when we hear that "the first thing he learns is how to vary his index of refraction. He can choose anything between transparent and opaque. After the thrill of experimenting has worn off, he settles on a pale, banded onyx effect. 'It suits you,' murmur his guides. 'Now hurry.'" But Pynchon continues: "He has gone beyond—once a sour bureaucrat with an upper lip as clearly demarcated as a chimpanzee's, now he is an adventurer, well off on a passage of his own, by underground current" (p. 355). This sounds less laughable, maybe even heroic, and relatively serious.

Similarly, Lyle Bland's voyages out of his body are amusing but not entirely discredited on that account:

He comes back raving about the presences he has found out there, members of an astral IG, whose mission—as indeed Rathenau implied through the medium of Peter Sachsa—is past secular good and evil[. . . .] but still he is in love with his sense of wonder, with having found it again, even this late[. . . .] To find that Gravity, taken so for granted, is really something eerie, Messianic, extrasensory in Earth's mindbody. . . .

Lest we deem ourselves superior, the narrator goes on: "The rest of us, not chosen for enlightenment, left on the outside of Earth, at the mercy of a Gravity we have only begun to learn how to detect and measure, must go on blundering inside our front-brain faith in Kute Korrespondences" (pp. 589–90).

What we deduce of this spirit world, as seen through the filter of spiritualism and theosophy, is (1) that it too is bureaucratized, has its guides and voices, obligations and adventures; (2) that from beyond death, both cause-and-effect logic and the patterns of organization we perceive give way to other explanations, to patterns we cannot see; (3) that while Pynchon renders his living spiritualists and theosophists individually amusing, he does not overtly undercut the evidence of the Other Side.

Other crossovers between the Other Side and this are less detailed and less insistent in their apparent reality. Slothrop, for example, sees revenants from his past (p. 255); he dances with a ghostly girl (p. 282); and he meets the wraith of Tantivy Mucker-Maffick (p. 552). Revenants, however, do not disturb empiricist readers, since these spirits can be rationalized as hallucinations, dreams, daydreams, or drug visions, and Slothrop may just be imagining these sequences.

A different sector of the Other Side is involved when we collect references to supernatural powers. The Titans are invoked in connection with the roiling forces that went into the creation of Earth: "In harsh-edged echo, Titans stir far below. They are all the presences we are not supposed to be seeing—wind gods, hilltop gods, sunset gods—that we train ourselves away from to keep from looking further even though enough of us do" (p. 720). Pan, though an Olympian, is also a powerful force of nature rather than culture: "The region is lonely and Pan is very close. Geli has been to enough Sabbaths to handle it—she thinks. But what is a devil's blue bite on the ass to the shrieking-outward, into stone resonance, where there is no good or evil, out in the luminous spaces Pan will carry her to? Is she ready yet for anything so real?" (p. 720). Katje too has known Pan (pp. 656–57). Both Pan and the Titans offer a kind of openness, a freedom from system, a creativity or energy. Pynchon is sometimes said to embrace the dionysian outlook (as opposed to the apollonian),[7] and in his treatment of these ancient powers we see some of the evidence that can be cited in support of that interpretation.

The various angels are the most prominent brigade of otherworlders. Rilkean angels, Moslem angels, metaphoric angels—they crowd the pages of *Gravity's Rainbow*, invoked by everything from the bombing of Lübeck to an impression made in the snow. Critics find these angels easy to dismiss as metaphors, but their repeated appearances hammer home the implication that there are other beings living in another world who can cross over into our reality.

At the other end of the spectrum from the grandeur of rilkean angels are the Qlippoth, "souls whose journey across was so bad that they lost all their kindness back in the blue lightning (the long sea-furrows of it rippling), and turned to imbecile killers and jokers, making unintelligible honks in the emptiness, sinewed and stripped thin as rats" (p. 661). These kabbalistic forces are negative, equated with "Ouijaboard jokesters, poltergeists, all kinds of astral-plane tankers and feebs" (p. 746); they will distract questers from true vision, using all their "love for friends who have passed across" against them (p. 750). Because of their desire and ability to cause seekers to fail, they are a notably hostile element in this patchwork pantheon.

Further evidence on the Other Side can be briefly summarized. The possibility of mystic access to another reality is presented through the story of the Kirghiz Light; Tchitcherine cannot assimilate the experience, but the Aqyn has done so, paying with his eyes for the ineffable. Dreams put some dreamers in touch with what one might call an intuitional reality: Kekulé achieves scientific insights via dream, and a narrative voice speculates on what pointsman directed that dream from the collective unconscious to the dreamer (pp. 410–11). Voices and guides are mentioned in passing (pp. 239, 354–55, 589) and so are bodily auras and such phenomena of light and electricity as corposants (p. 489), St. Elmo's fire (p. 491), albedoes (p. 489), and the Heiligenschein or holylight (p. 625). Geli Tripping's witchcraft offers another crossover, and it works: "This is magic. Sure—but not necessarily fantasy" (p. 735). Drugs too offer exposure to some other realities. Their validity and usefulness is left very much in question—they are called mindless pleasures—but Slothrop's sodium amytal vision of the excremental nature of the future appears metaphorically prophetic, and Tchitcherine's oneirine-paranoia is a pathway in, so drugs too may permit some interaction with the transempirical realm.

Most interesting among the remaining crossovers are those that do not follow such conventions as spiritualism or dreams or drugs. The first, which has parallels in mystic thought, is loss of ego-identity. Once Slothrop starts "plucking the albatross of self," he becomes more sensitive to the Other Side. "Omens grow clearer, more specific" (p. 623). He finds he "can sit and listen in to traffic from the Other Side, hearing about the future (no serial time over there: events are all there in the same eternal moment and so certain messages don't always 'make sense' back here: they lack historical structure, they sound fanciful, or insane)" (p. 624). Just before his rainbow vision, he becomes a crossroads, with the implication that what meets in him are the two sides, This and the Other.

Besides loss of self, Pynchon offers other, quite original, crossovers. Color, for instance, is a stimulus to insight or contact with nonmaterial reality. Rainbows, haloes, auras, and Heiligenschein are all part of this phenomenon: Carroll Eventyr experiences haloes of meaning around words, and his séances are saturated with color terms. For instance, we find "salmon," "fawn," "black," "ocher," "creamy . . . yellow," "heliotrope," "sea-green" (p. 145); "murk," "gilt," "red," "ultraviolet" (p. 148); "gold and scarlet," "earth tone," "hedge-green," "clay-brown," "yellow," "citrus light" (p. 149); "milky-white," "lime," "aqua," "lavender," "opalescent," "gold" (p. 150); "poison-green," "red" (twice), "white" (twice), "fiery," "yellow," "rainbowed," "bright blue" (p. 151); "darkwood," "jade," "pastel," "black-and-white," and "yellow" (p. 152). This list is not complete in that it does not mention many things like "blood" or "an orange" that have strong color associations, nor does it mention atmospheric descriptions like "dark," "light," "shadowy," or "autumnal," all of which have color-undertones in context.

When Slothrop soars aloft in a balloon, we find "yellow" (three times), "scarlet," "olive-drab," "golden," "blue" (twice), "red" (twice), "pink," "white," "rose-gray," "the color of boiled shrimp," "green," "black," and "peach"

223492

(pp. 333–36). On the *Anubis,* Slothrop's sexual encounter with Bianca yields "white" (five times), "red" (three times), "lavender," "black" (three times), "dark," "scarlet," "rouged," "shiny," "night-shadowed," "maroon," "snow," "nacreous," "silver-salt dark," "brown," "gentian," "bittersweet," "rut-brown," "rusting," "purple-gray," and "blinding color" (pp. 468–72). These are only a choice sampling of what Pynchon does with color. Color is very important, riotous and unconfinable, especially when close to some manifestations of the Other Side. Primaries and plain colors are especially associated with control, whereas the more outré colors cluster around insight and the Other Side. Rainbows and rainbow lashings of serpentine coils in the sky (pp. 721, 726) remind us of the other reality. So do auras.

Colors signal a level of existence beyond the quotidian when Slothrop intuits an alternative reality superimposed on his own world in the Himmler Spielsaal. On two pages Slothrop "is alone with the paraphernalia of an order whose presence among the ordinary debris of waking he has only lately begun to suspect," finding that "everything in this room is really being used for something different. Meaning things to Them it has never meant to us. Never. Two orders of being, looking identical . . . but, but . . . ." On those same two pages, we find "mahogany," "green," "maroon," "silver," "ebony," "russet," "brass-colored," "pastel," "golden," "brown," "cream," "gray," "black," "white" (three times), and "pink" (pp. 202–3). Pynchon teases us with the meanings withheld: "Why should the rainbow edges of what is almost on him be rippling most intense here in this amply coded room?" (p. 203). Later, when warning Slothrop of higher levels he cannot yet perceive, Katje wears a rainbow-striped dirndl (p. 208), and she refers to the realities beyond the rainbow, the parabola: "You haven't even learned the data on our side of the flight profile, the visible or trackable. Beyond them there's so much more, so much none of us know . . ." (p. 209).

Pynchon's third and fourth crossovers, beyond loss of self and color, are sound and its opposite, silence, which soften the barriers between the Other Side and this, or accompany points of contact. Music not only allows contact but it becomes the vehicle of prophecy.[8] Slothrop, as harmonica Orpheus of the Zone, wails blues, "modulated frequencies" that, like the sun's modulated frequencies, have information for us (pp. 642–43). Yardbird Parker's thirty-second notes tell, to those who can hear, of the machine guns to come: "down inside his most affirmative solos honks already the idle, amused dum-de-dumming of old Mister fucking Death he self" (p. 63). Music brings the atheistic Roger to feel, if not believe, the Christian Other Side at the Advent service. Kazoo music accompanies preterite celebrations of their own preterition. Pinball sounds and Offenbach's *Orphée aux Enfers* accompany the electroshocked pinball Orpheus as he looks "into the heart of the solenoid, [and sees] the magnetic serpent and energy in its nakedness, long enough to be changed, to bring back from the writhing lines of force down in that pit an intimacy with power, with glazed badlands of soul" (p. 584). One of music's several functions in this novel is the orphic function of carrying the awareness across gaps, bridging the abyss between different worlds or planes of reality.

But silence, also a bridge, can provide a way from our own plane of reality to another. The wandering sound shadow, Brennschluss of the sun, opens the portals for those who can really hear. When in the sound shadow, one hears the Titan's drum of one's heart (p. 697) and is open to insights about The Vacuum and Them. The Haydn op. 76 "Kazoo" Quartet, by incorporating a touch of the wandering sound shadow in its sudden quieting from fff to ppp has such effects that "they don't want you listening to too much of that stuff" (p. 712): "Perhaps tonight it is due to the playing of Gustav and André, but after a while the listener starts actually hearing the pauses instead of the notes—his ear gets tickled the way your eye does staring at a recco map until bomb craters flip inside out to become muffins risen above the tin" (p. 713). This quartet-playing is the background music for the banquet that Mexico and Bodine disrupt with alliteration's artful aid. In addition to the alternative reality intruding through the music, we find another irrupting as color: "Their auras, for the record, are green" (p. 714). Simultaneous hallucination spells another departure from consensus reality, for both men share a vision of their being "roasted"—both basted and lambasted, as it were; their joint hallucination expresses social torment in terms of their being cooked, thus superimposing two levels of reality.

As should be clear, this series of other realities making up the Other Side does not divide along pseudogeographical lines into a hell and heaven or Niflheim, Midgard, and Asgard. It is partly a land of the dead but also a realm of phenomena related to the spirit, and one occupied by hierarchies of powers. On the Other Side, time ceases and all events are simultaneously present. These dislocating characteristics help suggest that the Other Side is always available if we only knew how to approach the interface: being open—as Slothrop is after scattering his Self—is enough to gain access. Séances and visions, color, music, and silence can all bridge the gap. Doubtless there are many other points of contact between the worlds, and what really matters is this very multiplicity. Not even empiricist scientists need lack access, as the dream of Kekulé reminds us.

The Beings of this Cosmos

In addition to the nature of Pynchon's mythological cosmos—the physical world mythologically interpreted plus the Other Side—we must examine the inhabitants of this cosmos and the values attaching to them. Pynchon is not given to handing out black and white hats, so assigned values must be tentative at best, but Pynchon's world is not valueless. We think in terms of levels or hierarchies of being, and with reservations, that metaphor is still useful for Pynchon's cosmos.

Within his system, we find more varieties of beings than we are accustomed to acknowledging. Since those of the Other Kingdom seem to exert some power over mortals, they presumably head the loose hierarchy, but there is no clear ranking among these higher orders. Pan, though powerful, is pictured only in terms of terrifying and elevating human consciousness, whereas the Titans are not concerned with humanity but are simply a mad, clangorous life force, possibly not even aware of humans. As Geli's attitude toward Pan suggests, these numina operate in a mode unrelated to good and evil. Insofar as they oppose human systems of closure and control, however, they are functionally, if not absolutely, positive.

Angels come in several guises. Some are kabbalistic: Melchidael, Yahoel, Anafiel, Metatron, and Malkuth (pp. 680, 734). Others, such as the giant vision looming over Lübeck, with its fiery leagues of face and glowing eyes (pp. 151, 214, 217), are rilkean. Even more rilkean than this awesome figure are those angels visible in the sunset:

But out at the horizon, out near the burnished edge of the world, who are these visitors standing . . . these robed figures—perhaps, at this distance, hundreds of miles tall—their faces, serene, unattached, like the Buddha's, bending over the sea, impassive, indeed, as the Angel that stood over Lübeck during the Palm Sunday raid, come that day neither to destroy nor to protect, but to bear witness to a game of seduction. (pp. 214–15)

Given Pynchon's allusions to Rilke's *Duino Elegies,* and especially to the Tenth Elegy angel (at p. 341, for example), these are often interpreted as rilkean manifestations of pure being.[9] Their associations with our inhumanity toward each other, however, suggest another function, that of recording angel, that of intelligence looking at our actions from a great spiritual distance, weighing us and finding us wanting.

Decisions like that are for some angel stationed very high, watching us at our many perversities, crawling across black satin, gagging on whip-handles, licking the blood from a lover's vein-hit, all of it, every lost giggle or sigh, being carried on under a sentence of death whose deep beauty the angel has never been close to. . . . (p. 746)

The bright angel of death turns up: the Hereros see him in Thanatz (pp. 672–73); Osbie Feel's mushroom dope comes from relatives of the poisonous "Destroying Angel." On the novel's last page, the first star of the evening proves to be a "bright angel of death" (p. 760; see also pp. 164, 177). These angels are mostly ornamental figures of speech rather than beings of the same order of reality as the characters of the book, but the rilkean angels, in particular, compel a certain respect, and death's ubiquity gives the angel of death a strong imaginative presence, at least.

Of the rest of the immaterial host on the Other Side, we find specialized forces like the Eis-Heiligen, and metaphoric incarnations like Death or Dominus Blicero as death; but the last major category of beings consists of various guides and voices, such as Blobadjian's guides, or Feldspath, who is "working as one of the invisible interdictors of the stratosphere now, bureaucratized hopelessly on that side as ever on this" (p. 238). These seem the least powerful. None of these last—aside from the Qlippoth—are overtly good or evil, but their organization into an acknowledged hierarchy is deeply suspect. Being bureaucrats, they are concerned with control—their pronouncements are devoted to that subject—and this obsession makes them guilty at least by association with the negative side of Pynchon's creation.

The lack of a deity contributes to our sense that Pynchon's world does not offer humanity the warmth and support it wants from religion. At times, Pynchon's cosmos seems to exist on a plane beyond the modalities of good and evil; but overall, the power of negative forces, negative at least in respect to man's experiences of them, tilts the balance of this creation toward the demonic.

Turning to the material world, we find further varieties of beings, but humanity is not the order of being that comes but little lower than the angels. Instead, Pynchon seems to envision some kind of corporate being as next in rank. These beings amalgamate, divide, multiply, operate across national boundaries and even battle lines. When antimonopolistic pressures grow, they shuffle patents and agreements, but never lose their real power. Far from being hurt by the war, they thrive on it. However, at one point, Pynchon suggests that these corporations are only superficial manifestations of the real, very powerful entities, the technologies:

It means this War was never political at all, the politics was all theatre, all just to keep the people distracted . . . secretly, it was being dictated instead by the needs of technology . . . by a conspiracy between human beings and techniques, by something that needed the energy-burst of war, crying, "Money be damned, the very life of [insert name of Nation] is at stake," but meaning, most likely, *dawn is nearly here, I need my night's blood, my funding, funding, ahh more, more.* . . . The real crises were crises of allocation and priority, not among firms—it was only staged to look that way—but among the different Technologies, Plastics, Electronics, Aircraft, and their needs which are understood only by the ruling elite. . . . (p. 521—square brackets in the original)

Statements like these help establish the ubiquity and the unthreatened existence of these corporate technologies. Individuals may suffer, but the aggregate They, represented by the companies and by the higher technologies, is impervious to everything but lack of funds. Nothing in Pynchon's handling of this level of being suggests that it has redeeming features. The highest earthly rulers seem, therefore, essentially demonic, no longer even able to enjoy their conquests (see, for example, "the joyless hardons of human sultans" [p. 521]).

Subject to the whims of this corporate technological entity are humans, superficially divided into the elect and the preterite. These terms are relative; the same person may be both exploiter and exploited, oppressor and oppressed. Pudding's financial power over Pointsman makes Pudding elect, until we witness his acceptance of his own preterition at Katje's hands. But given a level of ordinary personal life, the vast majority are more obviously preterite than elect; they are passed over, damned. Only members of a small inner circle can consider themselves elect, and for the elect standpoint as such, Pynchon says nothing positive. He may create sympathy or understanding for an elect-seeming individual when that person experiences the preterite side of life, but election itself, control of others, is apparently never beneficial. The most complex organization Pynchon seems to accept in a reasonably positive way are the small-scale personal arrangements that Geli mentions. Even organizations supposedly based on good will, like the International Red Cross, betray their commercial reality by charging for coffee and doughnuts at the Battle of the Bulge (pp. 600, 610).

The preterite condition, as Pynchon portrays it, is described in essentially behavioristic terms. Slothrop is not held fully responsible for his failures in will, love, commitment. Like Watson's Infant Albert, Infant Tyrone was conditioned—sexually conditioned—and the stimulus seems to have been Imipolex G or a chemical forerunner of it.[10] That he gets involved with rockets at all may stem from this experience (unless the coincidence of his sexual conquests and the rocket-falls is just chance[11]) for he appears to be precognitively sensitive to where rockets will land. Ideologically committed to condemning the Protestant work ethic, Pynchon must explain failure more sympathetically, and he chooses a fashion that might otherwise seem paranoid. One fails not out of one's own slackness, but because They prevent one from succeeding. But that failure is not negative. There is a further distinction between accepting one's preterition and not doing so; since those who do not are essentially striving to become part of Them, Pynchon seems to side with those who accept preterition and failure. We follow Pirate Prentice's initiation into acceptance when he attends a fair for double agents (much of this fair, of course, may be hallucinated or may take place on the Other Side of everyday reality). After he and Katje trade pain and hopelessness, "they dissolve now, into the race and swarm of this dancing Preterition, and their faces, the dear, comical faces they have put on for this ball, fade, as innocence fades, grimly flirtatious, and striving to be kind . . ." (p. 548).

Slothrop's acceptance of his preterition and even his *sparagmos* opens him up to a wider spectrum of experience than most mortals can perceive. Roger, upon recognizing his own preterite status, decides to become part of the counterforce. He cannot expect victory (it would make him elect), but he can enjoy the process of resistance. As Roger throws himself into his gestures, he gains insights and becomes sensitive to phenomena beyond the empirical, as we see in his dealings with Rózsavölgyi and his vision at the banquet. Others who accept their preterition include the Hereros, who cultivate their philosophy of *mba-kayere* ("I am passed over"). The lost ones of the Zone—Ludwig, Leni-Solange, Bianca—make their way by accepting their weakness. Not to accept it is automatically to try to raise oneself to the status of the elect.

What the preterite condition seems to mean to Pynchon is a form of openness that lets one respond to the needs of others and to the transempirical phenomena. Those who accept their preterition put off the armor we all construct to protect ourselves from the blows of fate or malice. The closed systems we make and accept are forms of such armor. We subordinate others in order to protect ourselves. By giving up our claim to protection—and after all, as Enzian notes (p. 728), nothing really can protect us from death—we open ourselves to possibilities of touch and contact, with others and with the Other Side.

Being open does not guarantee that our experiences will be good or comforting: Gottfried, approaching the Other Kingdom, "can only try to keep himself open, to loosen the sphincter of his soul" (p. 722)—and his openness gets him his place in the 00000. Gottfried is perhaps unlucky; Tchitcherine, "a giant supermolecule with so many open bonds available at any given time," is given a happier end. Even as Gottfried's openness is expressed in homosexual terms, the openness of the women Slothrop meets and couples with is put in heterosexual terms. They are open to him. They know how to reach out, to help, to make connection of a relatively nonexploitive kind. Nothing human can be entirely open, but Pynchon seems to value openness in personal relations and associates it with those who accept their preterition.

In addition to the technologies, corporations, and elect and preterite, we find references to diminutive subraces:

Pygmies (p. 523), munchkins (pp. 63, 270), dwarves (p. 664), elves (p. 430), and gnomes (pp. 299, 305). Slothrop, dealing with the Mittelwerke, a great cavern under the mountains, sees the toilers there as gnomes and dwarves, and these same workers are called elves by Ilse Pökler (p. 430). Roger Mexico is embarrassed by a swarm of midgets staring at Jessica, who has removed her blouse on a bet. Pirate Prentice, whose past affair with Scorpia Mossmoon parallels that of Roger with Jessica, was surrounded by midgets when he had to bid Scorpia goodbye (p. 37). Enzian's comrade Pavel is haunted by visions of Pygmies when he inhales gasoline. Katje sees a midget in Osbie Feel's film and interprets its presence as a description of the White Visitation's project. Speed and Perdoo are likened to Munchkins. Miniature dwarves, wearing little plastic masks that look like the infinity symbol, pilot vultures who whisk one from the point of a cusp in life into "another world laid down on the previous one and to all appearances no different. Ha-*ha!*" "It will *look* like the world you left, but it'll be different" (p. 664).

These diminutive species vary considerably in the degree to which they are "real" or just metaphoric, and I see no clear logic to their presence. They do not seem to represent the preterite state, something we might have expected, given the precedent of Wagner's Nibelungs, also a small and exploited race under the mountain. These groups vary from nasty to nice, often with a silly, feckless quality to much of their behavior.

Beyond these subraces, sentience seems distributed randomly, or maybe evenly, throughout creation. Human cells parody World-War-I trench heroics as they talk of going epidermal (p. 148). Trees advise Slothrop to steal the oil filter from loggers' tractors (p. 553). Rats in a lab comment on their existential situation (pp. 229–30). A pinball faces *sparagmos* at the hands of Folies-Bergères maenads (pp. 647–55). A lightbulb discovers himself to be immortal and tries to lead a revolution against the electric cartel, the Them of his world. As a rule, these nonhuman awarenesses are commenting on their own preterition, or living with the realities that such preterition entails. Insofar as they are being exploited and injured by humankind, we feel, perhaps, a momentary sense that this exploitation is wrong. But insofar as almost all the cosmos is preterite, we are perhaps meant to wonder why we struggle so frantically to control the future and evade our preterite mortality. Were the inevitability of preterition accepted, life might be easier to bear.

Archetypes and Their Values

Assigning values to members of the human species is complicated by their being elect in one context but preterite in another. When we come, however, to the animal, vegetable, and mineral or inanimate levels,[12] the associations are somewhat clearer. There is indeed a totemistic system of animals and plants identified with human values.

As has frequently been noted, Pynchon approves of pigs.[13] Tyrone's ancestor William Slothrop mused on their preterite condition and wrote a treatise on preterition that grew out of these musings. Slothrop himself becomes Plechazunga, a village pig-god, and accompanies Frieda the sow to Pökler's cottage. Several black marketeers sport Porky the Pig tattoos, and Pig Bodine, gross and disgusting though he is by bourgeois standards, is prepared to help others, and to care. He is the last person physically able to see the disintegrating Slothrop, and he gives him a gift of grace, an undershirt dipped in John Dillinger's blood. The gadarene swine, condemned to take the evil spirits from people and perish with them, may be one of Pynchon's models. That pigs are the most famous of the Bible's taboo or unclean animals makes them especially suitable as emblems of preterition. That they are associated with dirt and earth is to their advantage in Pynchon's system, for rich earth is one of Pynchon's more obvious positive values. Pigs, indeed, contributed to the compost that grows Pirate's bananas, the vital fruit that tells death to "fuck off" (p. 10). The Herero totem, the Erdschwein (aardvark), though not zoologically a pig, partakes in the positive values of swine from its German name and earns that value through its association with earth. Indeed, one might call pigs the totem animal of the Preterite: intelligent, uncomplaining, doomed to be killed that others may consume them, but friendly and happy, living in close contact with the rich earth.

The other animal to serve a positive function, however fleetingly, is Ursula the lemming, Ludwig's pet. His bizarre quest to locate her, his fear that she will follow the fabled instincts of her tribe and throw herself into the sea, evoke love and tenderness from him. Protecting her, he is able to negotiate the fate worse than death with equanimity (p. 729) and survive the currents and rip tides of the Zone. Lemmings' predilection for mass exodus over the sea cliffs echoes the stampede of the gadarene swine and reminds us of lemmings' preterite helplessness under the pressure of forces they do not understand.

The most obvious animal to oppose the pig in Pynchon's bestiary is the lion. Franz Pökler tells Slothrop about Laszlo Jamf and his leonine attitudes:

"Whatever lip-service we may pay to Reason," he told Pökler's class back at the T.H., "to moderation and compromise, nevertheless there remains the lion. A lion in each one of you. He is either tamed—by too much mathematics, by details of design, by corporate procedures—or he stays wild, an eternal predator.

"The lion does not know subtleties and half-solutions. He does not accept *sharing* as a basis for anything! He takes, he holds! He is not a Bolshevik or a Jew. You will never hear relativity from the lion. He wants the absolute. Life and death. Win and lose. Not truces or arrangements, but the joy of the leap, the roar, the blood." (p. 577)

In Pökler's mind, this attitude became embodied in actor Rudolf Klein-Rogge, "whom Pökler idolized, and wanted to be like." In *Metropolis*, Klein-Rogge played "the mad inventor that Pökler and his codisciples under Jamf longed to be—indispensable to those who ran the Metropolis, yet, at the end, the untamable lion who could let it all crash, girl, State, masses, himself, asserting his reality against them all in one last roaring plunge from rooftop to street" (p. 578). In *Dr. Mabuse*, "Klein-Rogge *jumped in,* with all claws out, drove her effeminate husband to suicide, seized her, threw her on his bed, the languid bitch—*took her!*" (p. 579). Real-life lions are lazy and not especially forceful, but Pynchon's lions are shaped by mythological ends. They are appropriate totem animals for the elect and would-be elect.

Other animals with mostly negative emblematic associations include the serpent and the albatross. The serpent has a complex metaphoric ancestry. Eden links it to Satan and to knowledge of good and evil. Kekulé's dream (p. 412) of an ouroboros led him to the idea of a ring-structure for benzene. The Norse Midgard serpent circles the globe, ouroboros fashion, but will let go his tail come the end of the world. Pynchon balances the negative theological and apocalyptic meanings of the serpent with the positive values of the snake in Kekulé's dream: "But the meanness, the cynicism with which this dream is to be used. The Serpent that announces, 'The World is a closed thing, cyclical, resonant, eternally-returning,' is to be delivered into a system whose only aim is to *violate* the Cycle" (p. 412).

Pökler too dreams of Kekulé's serpent, of Jamf asking his students,

"Who sent this new serpent to our ruinous garden, already too fouled, too crowded to qualify as any locus of innocence—unless innocence be our age's neutral, our silent passing into the machineries of indifference—something that Kekulé's Serpent had come to—not to destroy, but to define to us the loss of . . . we had been given certain molecules, certain combinations and not others . . . we used what we found in Nature, unquestioning, shamefully perhaps—but the Serpent whispered, *They can be changed,* and new molecules assembled from the debris of the given. . . .'" (p. 413)

The Orpheus pinball sees the magnetic serpent associated with energy and then with power and with "glazed badlands of soul" (p. 584).

The new serpent in the garden thus offers us power, but as before, we choose how to respond, choose to invent the synthetics, to turn out wearable plastics, erectile plastics, plastic grails. We chose to break the cycle, to give up its promise of continuance in favor of power to armor ourselves, and we put our hope for the future in a dream of transcending. The mythological serpent need not signify the fall; it also serves as totem for a world not divided into preterite and elect; such a serpent (its coils in rainbow lashings in the sky [p. 721]) is associated with Pan and the Titans and a world unconstrained by human power structures. We are the ones responsible for making the serpent into the death-bringer.

The albatross, too, depends on us—and on Coleridge—for its values. In its most general sense, it seems in *Gravity's Rainbow* to mean past mistakes or hang-ups: we are told that "old Czarist albatrosses still hang around the Soviet neck" (p. 354). Imipolex G is called Psychochemie AG's albatross (p. 261). More specifically, though, the albatross is a past self. Enzian says of Weissmann that "he is an old self, a dear albatross I cannot let go" (p. 661). Slothrop in his disintegration is our chief bearer of the albatross of self (pp. 624, 712–13). The spirit of his mother, holding a martini, presides over the *sparagmos* of her son, as did the intoxicated maenad-mother of Orpheus, and as a result, Slothrop becomes "one plucked albatross. Plucked, hell—*stripped*. Scattered all over the Zone. It's doubtful if he can ever be 'found' again, in the conventional sense of 'positively identified and detained'" (p. 712).

We are also told that "the Man has a branch office in each of our brains, his corporate emblem is a white albatross, each local rep has a cover known as the Ego, and their mission in this world is Bad Shit" (pp. 712–

13). The self and the ego are run together here, and declared to be "Bad Shit" by the narrative voice. "The Man" (also referred to in the description of Yardbird Parker's music [p. 64]) seems in this context to be The Establishment or Them. The albatross is the corporate emblem or totem of Them, of the corporate entities that our egos might wish to join. Clearly Pynchon is not concerned with albatrosses as zoological entities. All his uses are symbolic and say nothing about the real bird. They simply belong to a system of animals that he has brought into existence to correspond to his system of beings. Both systems are mythological.

Turning to the vegetable kingdom, we find fewer fore-grounded species, but one or two attract attention. On the plus side, we find trees given prominence. They characterize virgin America, the new Eden we lost. Slothrop's ancestors put their money into "timberland whose diminishing green reaches were converted acres at a clip into paper—toilet paper, banknote stock, newsprint—a medium or ground for shit, money, and the Word" (p. 28). Later, as Slothrop drifts further from ordinary humanity, he becomes aware of trees:

Slothrop's intensely alert to trees, finally. When he comes in among trees he will spend time touching them, studying them, sitting very quietly near them and understanding that each tree is a creature, carrying on its individual life, aware of what's happening around it, not just some hunk of wood to be cut down. Slothrop's family actually made its money killing trees, amputating them from their roots, chopping them up, grinding them to pulp, bleaching that to paper and getting paid for this with more paper. "That's really insane." He shakes his head. "There's insanity in my family." He looks up. The trees are still. They know he's there. They probably also know what he's thinking. "I'm sorry," he tells them. "I can't do anything about those people, they're all out of my reach. What can I do?" A medium-sized pine nearby nods its top and suggests, "Next time you come across a logging operation out here, find one of their tractors that isn't being guarded, and take its oil filter with you. That's what you can do." (pp. 552–53)

The traditional tree archetypes Pynchon mentions by name are the Tree of Creation (p. 411), the tree as pole or *axis mundi* (pp. 321–22), and the sephirotic tree, invoking its kabbalistic system of values in conjunction with the firing of the 00000.

Another member of the vegetable realm to be focused upon is the banana. Pynchon hymns its powers in his description of Pirate Prentice's extraordinary banana breakfasts, and despite the exuberant excesses, bananas remain positive, not sickening: "It is not often Death is told so clearly to fuck off [. . .] so the same assertion-through-structure allows this war morning's banana fragrance to meander, repossess, prevail. Is there any reason not to open every window, and let the kind scent blanket all Chelsea? As a spell, against falling objects . . ." (p. 10).

This rhapsody on bananas would be difficult to top, and Pynchon does not try—though foods do seem to tempt him to special efforts, as we see in the Disgusting English Candy Drill and the alliterative banquet. But he does invoke bananas in the form of banana cream pies thrown in someone's face (p. 197), and faint echoes arise when he mentions other pies in faces (pp. 175, 375, 708): banana cream is the true "American reflex"—the others would appear to be whatever is available in times of shortage. All the pies—even the grape chiffon pie in

Stalin's face (p. 353)—belong to a tradition of making a gooey mess of a stuffed shirt, of one of Them. Like the banana, the banana cream pie tells Them to "fuck off," clearly and forcefully.

When we look for negative members of the vegetable realm, we do not find evil plants, but rather plants transformed by humanity's work or plants invoked to remind us of the positive while we see our own creations. Opposing the virgin forests of America is the wasteland near the rocket site (p. 488). The picture of the Hiroshima bomb fleetingly reminds Slothrop of a tree; the mushroom cloud is the new tree-shape for the postnuclear world. The paper made from slaughtering trees allows the elect to carry out their business: wipe away all traces of shit, spread the Word, and exchange goods for money. Paper takes over other functions: "the real and only fucking is done on paper" (p. 616). Much is made of inflationary German money and of its counterfeit, which Slothrop cheerfully accepts as payment. Rocket information turns up on shit-stained paper from latrines at Blizna. Forged ID papers are necessary to get around Them, even in the Zone. Papers read by Jamf's grave tell Slothrop how he was sold as an infant. Papers Tchitcherine collects on Enzian get into Tchitcherine's own dossier. A scrap of newspaper tells Slothrop that the new era has begun with the Hiroshima bomb. Paper maps of girls and bombs are what get Slothrop into the clutches of the White Visitation group. One does not need paper when exchanging potatoes for cigarettes, making love, or serving as pig-god at a festival. Most of the actions belonging to the openness of preterition get along quite well without paper. Contracts, orders, technical specifications—these are needed to support control, but are not much used otherwise. Paper is not evil in and of itself, any more than potatoes are. But potatoes can be distilled into rocket fuel, and paper can serve many ends for the elect.

Halfway between the vegetable and mineral world, Pynchon creates space for another level of being, the world of petroleum. He seems to approve the mysterious processes by which vegetable wastes sink, compact, and are eventually compressed into coal and oil. Preterite refuse is thus transformed. That the initial material is waste material is important. Critics point out that Pynchon is our poet of detritus, refuse, trash, junk, the abandoned and discarded.[14] Such waste is the preterite of the nonhuman world, and Pynchon finds value in these discards shoved to the periphery. As Walther Rathenau puts it, when summoned to a séance from the Other Side, "The real movement is not from death to any rebirth. It is from death to death-transfigured" (p. 166). Rathenau is talking about coal and coal tars. At first, these coal tars were just dross, "Earth's excrement, purged out for the ennoblement of shining steel. Passed over" (p. 166). When speaking of the mad clangor of overpeaking life and the world's green corona, Pynchon speaks of these wastes transputrifying to coal and oil (p. 720), which sounds less positive, but overall the transformation is treated as if it were magic. Lyle Bland learns that gravity, an eerie force in earth's mindbody, has "hugged to its holy center the wastes of dead species, gathered, packed, transmuted, realigned, and rewoven molecules" (p. 590). Opposing the valorized wastes on the level of oil are the synthetic molecules that the IG scientists create from them, new matter for plastics and fuels. These synthetics are the life blood of dye and chemical companies like IG Farben and ICI; of drug companies like Sandoz, Ciba, and Geigy; of oil companies like Shell; and of power companies like GE and AEG—all corporate powers making up Them.

A more generally negative and more truly geological representative of the mineral world is found in crystals. Crystals appear at least thirty-five times, as Friedman points out: "In *Gravity's Rainbow,* crystals serve as contrast to the irregularity in human affairs. . . . And a highly crystalline structure is never living. So crystals in *Gravity's Rainbow,* of snow, cocaine, or terror, are images of order at the price of death."[15] On the very first page of the text, Pirate dreams of bombs hitting the railway station, and he imagines the fall of that "crystal palace" (p. 3). One page later, the oldest city dirt is the "last crystallizations of all the city has denied, threatened, lied to its children." When Pirate tries to get information from Katje about Blicero, he finds that "the truth's crystal sheets have diffracted all her audible words—often to tears—and he can't quite make sense of what's spoken, much less infer to the radiant crystal itself" (p. 107). To him, the radiant crystal is apparently the location of Schußstelle 3; to her, Blicero is crystal, and her experiences with him partake of crystal's frozen dedication to death. During the pointless but near-fatal runcible spoon fight, Bodine and the two fighters are "burning crystals of awareness in this poisoned gray gathering" (p. 597). Frau Gnahb, when cursing a rock, derides its crystalline structure. Crystals and crystallization turn up in odd places, almost always with negative connotations.

Also belonging to the negative side in the realm of the inanimate and mineral are the artifacts that we build from such inert matter. These artifacts can generally be classed as machines and buildings. The machine that stands for them all is the V-2, metallic *axis mundi*, challenger of gravity, annihilator. Pynchon notes nonbellicose uses of the rocket in Pökler's dreams of going to the moon and beyond, but he does not develop these very thoroughly, and one of his flashes into the future, showing Rocket-City, describes it as set up to introduce terror. The space helmets seen in this vision offer no comfort: "Once inside *these* yellow caverns, looking out now through neutral-density orbits, the sound of your breath hissing up and around the bone spaces, what you thought was a balanced mind is little help" (p. 297). Overall, the rocket and its accessories remain negative, and the dreams of life on the moon do not rescue it, or even introduce serious ambiguity, because we would not yearn so for the escape to the moon if we could change our pattern here on earth.

In keeping with this negative attitude toward our inanimate creations is Pynchon's portrayals of cities—symbolic parts of the mineral world, as Frye points out. The London of *Gravity's Rainbow* is fairly realistic, just a place where people go about ordinary jobs. True, spring there is noticed not from blossoms and birds but in the more revealing clothing of the secretaries (p. 237), but the narrative voice sounds fairly cheerful about that trade-off. Beyond London, however, is a series of less attractive cities: the City Paranoiac (p. 172), the Raketen-Stadt or Rocket-City (p. 297 and *passim*), the City Dactylic, "that city of the future where every soul is known, and there is noplace to hide" (p. 566), the Hund-Stadt (city of killer dogs [p. 614]), Rilke's Leid-Stadt and its drug-cheered counterpart Happyville (pp. 644–45), Hexes-Stadt (p. 718), and The City—an indefinite future world all shiny and clean on the surface, but repressive if you ask the wrong questions (p. 735). Repression, order, closed system, control—these are what cities are about; people cannot crowd closely together without repression and control.

Within the cityscape, Pynchon concentrates on verticality, on towers and chimneys, stationary architectural rockets. Such heights are vulnerable and may be brought down (p. 444). The tarot card called The Tower is expounded as, among other things, a falling structure (p. 747). We are also reminded of falling towers by William Slothrop's hymn, which sings of "the light that hath brought the Towers low" (p. 760). Tall structures, though, may also be ominous because they do not fall. What the narrator says of the relationship between the double integral sign and rockets has echoes for such towers: "To integrate here is to operate on a rate of change so that time falls away: change is stilled. . . . 'Meters per second' will integrate to 'meters.' The moving vehicle is frozen, in space, to become architecture and timeless. It was never launched. It will never fall" (p. 301). The ghost of Rathenau calls attention to smokestacks as structures favoring death (p. 167). One might sum up Pynchon's use of cities and buildings by saying that he handles them in two fashions: in his novelistic vein, he gives us a recognizable picture of London, and recognizable fragments of Zürich and Berlin; he also, however, uses cities mythologically when he makes them abstract embodiments of some element of control or suffering. In the realistic portrayals, he allows for a balance of good and ill, if only because he focuses on people; in the mythological, the negative predominates.

The foregoing pages have offered a brief description of the mythological nature of Pynchon's cosmos. The geography—both physical and spiritual—is fairly traditional but weighted toward the demonic. He envisions a rich array of beings and forces, some of which seem to transcend good and evil, but none of which fit conventional categories of divinity. Even Apollo, when mentioned in passing, is a nietzschean avatar of control, not the god of poetry, healing, and light. The strata of creation—animal, vegetable, oil-bearing, and mineral—do permit some manifestations of good, but just as vivid are the animal avatars of the negative. Before we decide, though, that Pynchon is simply paranoid or obsessed, we should consider a point made by Northrop Frye:

In pointing out the latent apocalyptic or demonic patterns in a literary work, we should not make the error of assuming that this latent content is the *real* content hypocritically disguised by a lying censor. It is simply one factor which is relevant to a full critical analysis. It is often, however, the factor which lifts a work of literature out of the category of the merely historical. (*Anatomy of Criticism,* p. 158)

The Principles of Order

Given these components of Pynchon's cosmos, we can deduce some of its organizing laws and principles, and determine the reliability with which Pynchon applies them. Then we can explore the degree to which Pynchon seems serious about his creation.

Relativism is generally regarded as one of the important principles governing Pynchon's fictive cosmos. An act, event, or person is almost always Janus-faced; from one perspective it may seem bad, but from another, good or acceptable. This is clear in the handling of preterition, where Pointsman and Pudding are elect, seen from the vantage of their subordinates, but prove pitiably experienced in their own forms of preterition. Slothrop's *sparagmos*, insofar as it is carried out by Them, is evil, but judging from his rainbow vision and from his increasing sensitivity to nonempirical phenomena, the net result is in some sense beneficial to him. But then the state he finally achieves is similarly two-faced: he may have achieved some sort of satori or nirvana, some sort of selflessness, but his form of life depends on his being totally divorced from society, and whatever insight he achieves is therefore not available to others.

Another example of such ambivalence of values is seen in Pynchon's handling of music. Music cheers up the masses enough to help them find life worth living. This might seem good, but then again music does so by anaesthetizing their pain; it is the opium that permits them to carry on slaving for Them rather than revolting. Music brings pleasure, but may thereby prolong pain. Music is system and order; its rhythm galvanizes listeners, but that system is also a form of control.

Similarly the war is bad from most perspectives; yet as the Argentine anarchist notes, it blasts open systems of control: "This War—this incredible War—just for the moment has wiped out the proliferation of little states that's prevailed in Germany for a thousand years. Wiped it clean. *Opened it*" (p. 265). Of course, drug and chemical interests might argue that the war has been a good thing because it consolidated their control, extended their markets, and ensured their funding.

But if everything can be stood on its head, are there any stable values or absolutes? Some values seem to cluster about the contrasts between openness and closure, freedom and control. One form of total closure, in physical terms, would be the heat death of the universe, and a degree less absolute would be the nuclear holocaust destroying life or at least human life on earth. Pynchon is too compassionate toward his preterite masses to suggest that this solution might be an admirable way of wiping out the most odious vermin ever to crawl the face of the earth. A much less absolute level of closure and control also seems to be consistently negative in his treatment. In the physical world, this corresponds to crystals; in the social, to a rigid government. While many critics have assumed that entropy will eventually work against the most controlled of empires, Pynchon raises the possibility in Father Rapier's speech that such petrifaction could be irreversible: "Once the technical means of control have reached a certain size, a certain degree of *being connected* one to another, the chances for freedom are over for good" (p. 539). He goes on: "It is possible that They will not die. That it is now within the state of Their art to go on forever—though we, of course, will keep dying as we always have" (p. 539). If such control can be made absolute—and Pynchon's concept of corporate entities does support Father Rapier's argument—then we may have here another absolute, an irreversible change, an ill which will not be altered by viewing it from a different perspective.

When we look at the other pole—openness, freedom—we find the values far less easy to sort out. Ab-

78
Pynchon's Mythography

solute openness, randomness, freedom from all obligations, antiparanoia, total unpredictability—none of these are states that humanity can live with for long. As I shall argue in chapter 5, the question is to find an optimum between control and freedom, closure and openness. At a guess, Pynchon does not favor others imposing controls on us but accepts the more generous limitations we are willing to place on ourselves, the kinds of limits and responsibilities we accept for love or fellowship.

Another principle, related to openness and closure, is based on transition points:

There is a cosmology: of nodes and cusps and points of osculation, mathematical kisses . . . *singularities!* Consider cathedral spires, holy minarets, the crunch of trainwheels over the points as you watch peeling away the track you didn't take . . . mountain peaks rising sharply to heaven, such as those to be noted at scenic Berchtesgaden . . . the edges of steel razors, always holding potent mystery . . . rose thorns that prick us by surprise . . . even, according to the Russian mathematician Friedmann, the infinitely dense point from which the present Universe expanded. . . . In each case, the change from point to no-point carries a luminosity and enigma at which something in us must leap and sing, or withdraw in fright. Watching the A4 pointed at the sky—just before the last firing-switch closes—watching that singular point at the very top of the Rocket, where the fuze is. . . . Do all these points imply, like the Rocket's, an annihilation? (p. 396)

About such transitions, Ozier comments:

Common to all the mathematical images Pynchon has used— the Δt, the double integral, and now the singular point—is the idea of transformation from one world order to another or from one state of being into another. In the novel's terms, the two worlds or states separated by the Δ t/Brennschluss Point/singular point experience seem to be the world of cause-and-effect populated by the Elect and its bureaucracies and a transcendent, atemporal realm of uncircumscribed potential which nevertheless is grounded in the former world and is therefore not pure chaos.[16]

Pynchon also uses zero as such a transition point; he uses the concepts of interfaces, of crossroads, of break-through, of the top of the parabolic trajectory, the stretched suspender-point of a silk stocking. As Ozier notes, these are odd moments of mystery, of potential, of freedom.

In social and political terms, they are moments at which human action can make a difference:

What makes GR a rich but perplexing book is Pynchon's in-sistence upon making his modern jeremiad an encyclopedia of all the "names and methods" by which modern man seeks to surrender to history, to absolute fictions, to any design that promises to shield us from the vulnerability of living with the moments of choice, the so-called "nodes" of V. and the "cusps" (p. 236) of GR. When Tyrone Slothrop speculates about his Puritan past and "the fork in the road America never took, the singular point she jumped the wrong way from" (p. 556), he links personal history to national history, and the landscape of post-war Germany to that of the jeremiads. As Schaub has written, "in the vernacular of Gravity's Rainbow all lives are a succession of such points, where the curves of history, place and heritage form the terrible intersection from which we must choose a direction." (Smith and Tölölyan, p. 180)

These cusps and points give us the chance to make choices, and by working to implement those choices, we give ourselves the chance to achieve a sense of value or worth.

Another principle, one tied to the mythological nature of the cosmos, is Pynchon's insistence that beyond all our rational analyses and knowledge lies mystery, the unknowable, the ineffable. He shows us this in mythic terms with the Kirghiz Light. He suggests it on the Brocken and at the various times Slothrop senses another order of reality. Pynchon gives body to this ineffability by peopling the Other Side with forces from several traditions—the Kabbalah, spiritualism, theosophy, classical religion, and Christianity. This acknowledgment of mystery seems partly to be a mystic or religious assertion, but it also appears to stem from modern physics, from the implications of the uncertainty principle, the principle of complementarity, and other transrational developments in science. Pynchon suggests that our awareness of the mystery and the Other Side is analogous to receiving wave phenomena; our senses respond to such narrow spectra of sound and light that we simply cannot pick up these mysterious frequencies above and below our range.[17]

A final principle of organization is paranoia. The term is used in *Gravity's Rainbow* in many ways, some of them misleading. When Slothrop first notes paranoid feelings on the Riviera, he is not clinically paranoid: there really does seem to be a conspiracy focused on him. Observers note his every move, even to timing his erections; furthermore, the conspirators stay interested long after wartime exigencies would seem to warrant, as is proved by the bungled attempt to castrate him. Everyone else, however, exhibits elements of paranoia in the sense that they believe plots exist and are centered on them. All, including Slothrop, tend to see events as connected in a sinister fashion, malignly directed toward themselves. Two elements matter: the habit of measuring the universe not just in terms of humanity (a mythological outlook), but specifically in terms of one's self; and the interconnectedness of everything. As Pynchon notes, anent the paranoia induced by Oneirine, "Like other sorts of paranoia, it is nothing less than the onset, the leading edge, of the discovery that *everything is connected, everything in the Creation*" (p. 703).

Paranoia as a self-centered mode of interpreting phenomena marks Pynchon's characters and is appropriate to the demonic twist in his mythology. At best, as "creative paranoia," it consists of the myths we create and project on reality in order to handle it.[18] The We-force Roger joins, set up to oppose Them, is an example of such creative paranoia. It is a reasonable tactic so long as one remembers the artificial nature of the projection. The paranoia of most characters, however, is neither adequate nor desirable, for they have forgotten the artifice and believe in their own projections.

Rather more in keeping with the broader values of the book, though, is the idea inherent in paranoia that everything is connected. Given Pynchon's ecological nostalgia for the lost American paradise, given his political insights into the multinational corporations and their needs (whereby what seemed like war was business as usual), given his sense that the ever present Other Side is a perpetual mystery through whose agency anything may be related to anything else, paranoia in this nonclinical sense is a plausible approach to reality. Ecology is the model. Introduce pigs and Protestants to an island, and dodos soon become extinct. Planting potatoes in the spring may be the key to permitting rockets to fly in the fall. Modulated frequencies—shivers, sunset spectra modified by the Hiroshima bomb, hair, the blues played on a harmonica—all possess interrelated meanings. No action is without endless and unforeseeable repercussions. Nothing should be carelessly discarded or heedlessly destroyed. All such warnings for conservation are contributing elements to this principle of interconnectedness.

The most wide-reaching general principles organizing this mythological cosmos are the Janus-faced values attaching to most actions and events: the negative onus put on control; the existence and importance of cusps; and the interconnectedness of everything. As critics have noted, the ethos guiding these principles, particularly that of quasi-ecological interconnectedness, is a product of the 1960s.[19] So too are the individual rather than social answers that Pynchon suggests to the problem of human existence.

Seriousness

Having explored the nature of this mythological cosmos and the kind of principles that set it apart from the usual empirical cosmos, we can now consider the most difficult question: How much of this should we take seriously? How much belief, or at least how much conditional acceptance, are we expected to grant? Where can one draw a line between myth and symbolism? Most of his readers are used to the confines of the empirical world and deeply distrust all claims for alternatives—including even the scientific. They would probably not bother to read very far if Pynchon overtly offered his spiritualist material as something he fervently believed in. If the narrator preached any recognizable religious version of God, others would turn away. Nor does Pynchon demand reverence for mythology as such: "After you get a little time in—whatever *that* means over here—one of these archetypes gets to look pretty much like any other, oh you hear some of these new hires, the seersucker crowd come in the first day, 'Wow! hey—that's th-th' *Tree o' Creation! Huh? Ain't it! Je-eepers!*' but they calm down fast enough" (p. 411). There's an archetype hunter born every minute, all of them doubtless eager to see Pynchon's "egress."

In other words, nothing in the text tries to compel reverence or the sort of solemnity that Protestant tradition associates with religious belief. But belief need not be cast in that one form. For instance, one can believe that science is the new religion of materialist humanity without erecting a theology to support this assertion and without making some kind of solemn avowal. One can look at a story describing the assembly of a rocket as a piece of mythological history that shows humanity becoming fixated on technology, and the fictive nature of the characters does not undermine the point being made. Even readers who cling to strictly empirical procedures can accept this nexus of story-ideas-images as one form of stating a truth about Western civilization, or that part of humanity which has invested science with feelings once channeled by religion. The uses that Pynchon makes of trees, colors, excrement—elements of our cosmos— are acceptable as means of communicating symbolically. The only areas where readers are likely to be uncomfortable are (1) the claims for the existence of an Other

Side, (2) the claims that it is populated by sentient beings and (3) the insistence that everything is connected. The last is a matter of perspective and can be debated more or less rationally. The first two are not open to strictly rational debate.

I would argue that the population—angels, Titans, Qlippoth, guides, and astral influences—is not offered for literal acceptance as a new pantheon, given its heterogeneous nature and religious ancestry, but is a fairly playful embodiment of the argument that there are more ways of interpreting human experience than humans themselves see at any one time. What Walther Rathenau considers reality differs considerably from what his interlocutors think they experience. That the war is a gigantic bonus to the technologies, that all the fighting and killing is windowdressing to ensure funding, is one interpretation. It would not, however, have occurred to most people engaged in the war effort. When we learn that Feldspath has been hovering over Slothrop's personal space, giving him intimations about control, we can take it literally or feel that Slothrop, doing what he is and knowing what he has learned, would be reaching these insights into control and other orders of being anyway.

The *Odyssey* offers us an analogous example. When Athene displays the aegis and terrifies the suitors Odysseus is slaughtering, we can take it literally or recognize that their panic is natural under the circumstances and that Athene is a mythological figure whose appearance calls attention to the appropriateness of their feelings. She is a way of talking about the truth of the situation but functions in parallel with other explanations more than as necessary cause and effect. Likewise, when Ath-

ene makes Odysseus and Penelope beautiful in each other's eyes, romantic readers will feel that they might have
seemed beautiful without divine aid, that the aid only
calls attention to the experienced reality. Pynchon uses
his mythological figures much as Homer does in the
Odyssey. They put into human terms some of the dimensions of experience that we otherwise have trouble
assimilating, that we repress, or that we might not notice.

Where Pynchon seems most serious and most literal
is in his insistence on an Other Side, on some kind of
irreducible mystery, on there being something beyond
the world acknowledged by empirical method. This feeling may stem from a mystical sense of reality, but some
forms of this assertion are also present within the scientific community. We know more or less how gravity,
magnetism, and electricity work, but not really what they
are. We now know there are some things we cannot
know—the simultaneous momentum and location of an
electron, for instance. We are philosophically aware that
the concepts of force and of cause and effect are human
projections upon the world. We are increasingly aware
that the observer affects the phenomena observed, to
the point of undermining the certainty of observation.
For many physicists, time is not a one way arrow. Pynchon seems at times to be creating a metaphoric extension of subatomic realities into the quotidian level of
existence. He knows that the cosmos looks to us as it
does because we have been taught to see it that way. If
another perspective were to develop—for instance, if we
were to evolve an outlook that valued all life, not just
human and not just one's self—then the cosmos we would
see would differ dramatically from what we see now.
What we now dismiss as peripheral or anomalous or

useless might become central. Ultimately if a reader is unwilling to consider the possibility of there being some kind of unknown (and probably unknowable) reality beyond the empirical world, that reader will reject Pynchon's premises and hence the mythology, symbolism, argument—and all the pleasure *Gravity's Rainbow* offers its readers.

To make headway, one must start by at least provisionally admitting that there may be something beyond what is empirically knowable, that there are other interpretations of data—other connections—not available to empirical scrutiny. If one can grant that, then Pynchon's cosmos, and even more, his mythological stories, can make their points and have their effects.

3

Mythological Actions

They are mated to each other:
Schwarzgerät and next higher assembly. . . .

I N SIMPLEST TERMS, myths are stories that tend
to "stick together to form a mythology, a large interconnected body of narrative that covers all the religious
and historical revelation that its society is concerned with,
or concerned about."[1] Societies may exist whose mythologies do not tell of a beginning or predict an apocalypse, but minds influenced by that great template the
Bible tend to demand something like its linear pattern
in a mythology. When Pynchon creates stories to embody
the values of Western culture, he uses that traditional
structure.

Pynchon tells this basic story with at least four concerns in mind. One is cultural history; the second is the
personal history of Tyrone Slothrop; the third, the history of the V-2; and the fourth, the history of technology
in general. These will be the subject of the first half of
this chapter.

Meanings in myth not only reside in the narrative, but are communicated at levels beneath the surface as well. Edmund Leach's structuralist approach to myth points out the connections between various meanings and three characteristics of myth: its redundancies; its binary oppositions; and its mediations or middle terms, which permit value to be affirmed in the face of the binary contradictions. One need not confine Leach's method to traditional myths of Latin American Indians or to the Old Testament. Repetitions and redundancies are generally useful indices to what a literary author values. Two rudderless boats, two attempted rapes, two alien fiancés, and two insanely jealous mothers-in-law, all in Chaucer's *The Man of Law's Tale*, push us to consider the typical structuralist subject of overvaluing versus undervaluing relationships. Chaucer seems to be considering how a woman can live a saintly Christian life while remaining in the secular world of sensuality and twisted desire. Binary oppositions likewise reveal literary as well as mythological values, and if any mediation can transcend the literary oppositions, it too is of interest. In a novel, such mediations may not be sacred, technically speaking, but as in myth, they necessarily embody powerful values. Hence, Leach's structuralist terminology seems to me applicable to *Gravity's Rainbow* in any case, but doubly so as Pynchon is "expressing" a culture's myths—expressing in both senses of "telling" and "driving out."[2] These three characteristics—redundancies, binary oppositions (some of which surfaced in the cosmology examined in chapter 2), and mediations—will take up the last half of the chapter.

Pynchon's Mythological Histories

Gravity's Rainbow has been described as dramatizing "two related assemblings and disassemblings—of the rocket, and of the character or figure named Slothrop. Slothrop is engaged in trying to find out the secret of how the rocket is assembled, but in the process he himself is disassembled. Similarly the book both assembles and disassembles itself as we try to read it."[3] If we double these terms, we get a more complete picture: the rocket and Slothrop make up one such pairing, but technology and Western humankind constitute the other. The latter two terms are the grand movements, of which the former two are individual examples.

The commonplaces of a mythic cycle are most clearly seen in Pynchon's history of modern Western culture. The constituent parts of this cycle are the initial paradise, the fall, the central symbolic action, and the predicted apocalypse. Paradise was America as virgin continent. Pynchon does not argue that it was an actual, historical paradise, only that it represented an immense potential for new beginnings, an alternative to Europe's culture of "Analysis and Death." The potential, however, was never realized; Europeans brought along their death culture. Slothrop, as he drifts through the Zone, comes to value rural landscapes and their denizens—cows, storks, rabbits, and trees—and starts to sense what has been lost in the development of technological America. Slothrop's ancestor William sensed some of this grace in creatures and land. Driving his pigs to Boston for slaughter, "William came to love their nobility and personal freedom, their gift for finding comfort in the mud on a hot day—pigs out on the road, in company together, were everything Boston wasn't" (p. 555). The dream of this unrealized America—vital, unassuming, nonrighteous and nonjudgmental, colors William's memories of America late in life:

the blue hills, green maizefields, get-togethers over hemp and tobacco with the Indians, young women in upper rooms with their aprons lifted, pretty faces, hair spilling on the wood floors while underneath in the stables horses kicked and drunks hollered, the starts in the very early mornings when the backs of his herd glowed like pearl, the long, stony and surprising road to Boston, the rain on the Connecticut River, the snuffling good-nights of a hundred pigs among the new stars and long grass still warm from the sun, settling down to sleep. . . . (p. 556)

Weissmann too saw this incredible potential for new beginnings implicit in the New World: "America was a gift from the invisible powers, a way of returning. But Europe refused it[. . . .] Europe came and established its order of Analysis and Death. What it could not use, it killed or altered" (p. 722).

Slothrop wonders whether his ancestor William might have represented "the fork in the road America never took, the singular point she jumped the wrong way from" (p. 556). Since Pynchon virtually ignores the presence of Native Americans, this new beginning for Europeans may be "mythical" in more than one sense. However, as Pynchon establishes it in his fictive universe, people like William Slothrop might have produced a culture capable of living more or less within the natural cycles, unlike the culture of energy addiction that has resulted from the Puritan reflexes. Taking the wrong fork in the road is the American fall. People with the Yankee drive and ingenuity portrayed by Mark Twain in *Connecticut Yankee* were all too eager to welcome Kekulé's serpent into what had become the already "ruinous garden" (p. 413).

History between the American fall and the central symbolic action is projected through varied fragments. Stories of Tyrone Slothrop's ancestors suggest American parts of the mosaic; the world picture emerges in vignettes concerning characters like Katje's ancestor in Mauritius, or Brigadier Pudding in World War I, or Weissmann in Southwest Africa, or Tchitcherine in Russia. We learn nothing of China or the countries that escaped the expansion of the Western way of life. In addition to the major historical actions, we get some popular culture. The allusions to Dillinger and Dorothy, to figures from movies, radio, and comics (like the Shadow and Plasticman and the Lone Ranger), fill in the popular cultural tradition in America, while references to Hansel and Gretel and Alice and Rilke remind us of European cultural traditions. Pynchon's mélange of materials high and low keeps us from oversimplifying our concept of Western culture. As in the Old Testament, the variety and contrast in styles and forms creates a complex—even a perplexed—sense of the reality being sketched in.

The next major myth after paradise and fall is immachination. This corresponds in Jewish thought to Abraham's offering of Isaac and in the Christian structure to the crucifixion; it is symbolized in *Gravity's Rainbow* by the wedding between Gottfried and a rocket. Humanity and machine mating in order to become a new form of life is central to *Gravity's Rainbow,* even as we find in *V.* a related concern, namely the process by which the animate turns into the inanimate.[4] Immachination is not identical to inanimation; it represents a more threatening, more novel development, the evolution of a new, symbiotic life.

Pynchon names this development in a vision of Rocket-City. Slothrop fantasizes the space-suit fashion show, whose helmets look like titanic skulls, and the wearing of which is one such form of immachination: "The eyesockets are fitted with quartz lenses. Filters may be slipped in. Nasal bone and upper teeth have been replaced by a metal breathing apparatus, full of slots and grating. Corresponding to the jaw is a built-up section, almost a facial codpiece, of iron and ebonite, perhaps housing a radio unit, thrusting forward in black fatality" (p. 297). Such Darth Vader suits will be worn in the high-tech future, in a city or space station that is governed by The Articles of Immachination (p. 297). Lest that word "immachination" slide by us, we are exposed to various kinds of union between human and machine. In the same paragraph, we learn that "Enzian had his Illumination in the course of a wet dream where he coupled with a slender white rocket." On the next page, human controllers and machines apparently interact telepathically in order to monitor the thoughts of individuals in a crowd. Shortly thereafter (p. 301), Pynchon discusses in purely technical terms the equation for determining Brennschluss via capacitor. Later (pp. 517–18), Närrisch faces what he is sure will be his death and muses on that Brennschluss equation, where time (B_{iw}) moves toward the angle (A_{iw}) such that B for "B-sub-N-for-Närrisch, is nearly here—nearly about to burn the last whispering veil to equal 'A'." Närrisch thus identifies psychologically with a rocket and will burn out according to mechanical determinations. The rocket limericks also couple man and machine, often with gruesome results. Slothrop fantasizes a scene with his father, in which he is an electrofreak who dreams that "maybe there is a Machine to take us away, take us completely, suck us out through the electrodes out of the skull 'n' into the Machine and live there forever[. . . .] *We* can live forever, in a clean, honest, purified Electroworld" (p. 699).

The synthesis of people and machines may be fantasized, psychological, or metaphoric at times, but in the central image of Pynchon's mythology, the wedding is made as literal as possible, with "white lace," "bridal costume," and "white satin slippers with white bows." Gottfried's "nipples are erect"; "he fits well. They are mated to each other"; "one pressure-switch is the right one, the true clitoris"; there is a "zone of love" and so forth (pp. 750–51). Gottfried and the rocket become one flesh. Which is the groom and which the bride? The symbols designating sex roles shift back and forth, making this a marriage in which not even sexual identity survives.

Insofar as Gottfried represents the fate of humankind in such a union with machine, we note that his married life will be ominously brief. Similarly, the protagonists of several rocket limericks meet sticky ends:

—"Wrecked Hector's hydraulic connector" (p. 306);
—"What was left of his cock, / Was all slimy and sloppy and spattery" (p. 311);
—"It shrivelled his cock, / Which fell off in his sock" (p. 334);
—"His balls and his prick / Froze solid real quick" (p. 335).

Flesh is reduced to protoplasmal jelly through the electrified orgasms offered by the machine. Admittedly not everyone is so unlucky, and all the men mentioned in the lyrics obviously entered such relationships with the expectation of fulfillment. The mythic pattern brought into focus by Gottfried, however, suggests that such satisfactions for the race, if not for all individuals, will be tragic.

The futures made possible by immachination correspond to the biblical predictions of apocalypse in both senses—as revelation of the new and as warning of destruction. Pynchon seems to face the future much as does the Dragon in John Gardner's *Grendel:* "Pick an apocalypse, any apocalypse."[5] It won't matter unduly which we pick. In any of them, humanity seems to have lost its freedom to the machine.

One of the possible futures involves simple space travel—with humankind obviously wedded indissolubly to its machines. Another produces the rocket-falls of total war. A third future that Pynchon alludes to is more or less realistic; indeed, we may be entering it already:

Pynchon's international scope implies the existence of a new international culture, created by the technologies of instant communication and the economy of world markets. Pynchon implies that the contemporary era has developed the first common international culture since medieval Latin Europe separated into the national cultures of the Renaissance. The distinguishing character of Pynchon's new internationalism is its substitution of data for goods: "Is it any wonder the world's gone insane," somebody asks in *Gravity's Rainbow,* "with information come to be the only real medium of exchange?"[6]

Tchitcherine senses one version of this coming world: "*A Rocket-cartel.* A structure cutting across every agency human and paper[. . . .] a state that spans oceans and surface politics, sovereign as the International or the

Church of Rome, and the Rocket is its soul" (p. 566). Roger senses the existence of such a state when he tells Jessica that the peace is just "another bit of propaganda" and that "Their enterprise goes on" (p. 628). The many factual references to industrial and technological entities operating without regard for wars or national boundaries testify to the existence of an international force. Father Rapier assumes such a "Them" when he preaches that "once the technological means of control have reached a certain size, a certain degree of *being connected* one to another, the chances for freedom are over for good" (p. 539). This economically united world is much like that of Orwell's *1984,* a world of control and of continuing suffering among the hopeless preterite. Pynchon seems to consider this future very probable.

But then again, a fourth future posited in Pynchon's novel is analogous to Huxley's *Brave New World.* This future is sketchily invoked in a description of The City (pp. 735–36), a living complex based on verticality, with elevators whose interiors, with their flowersellers and fountains, are more like courtyards. There, uniformed, good-looking young women, "well-tutored in all kinds of elevator lore," refuse to answer questions about such taboo subjects as the rocket. This vision of the future is followed by recollections of a Hitler Youth Glee Club, reminding us of the polished orderliness that was one of the hitlerian ideals, and which is a powerful force in *Brave New World.* Pynchon develops this future so fleetingly that I may be overemphasizing a minor divagation, but this image of The City echoes such dystopic visions as those in *We, Player Piano,* and *This Perfect Day,* all of which show worlds in which poverty and material suffering have been reduced to negligible levels, only to leave other, more hopeless suffering: the more complete damnation of the preterite because they are inferior to machines. Such worlds find people acceptable only to the degree that they can imitate machines.

Pynchon suggests these possible futures, none of which is the way back to the potential represented by early America. Indeed, none of them offers humankind any freedom. In one way or another, they each rest on an unholy union between people and their machines. In Christian symbolism, Christ's death paradoxically proclaims, "Death thou shalt die." In *Gravity's Rainbow*, Gottfried's wedding negates life rather than death, and the bonds that bind him betoken the control that will rule all the inhabitants of an immachinate culture. The myth, as Pynchon lays it out for Western civilization, is openended but not optimistic. Such hope as he allows us emerges not at the level of mythological action but can be discerned in his binary oppositions and mediations. Before turning to those, however, let us look more briefly at the three other strands of this mythology: those concerned with Tyrone Slothrop, with the rocket, and with the history of technology.

We might have expected Slothrop to ascend in the 00000. As the most prominent among the major characters, he enjoys a quasi-hero status. His infant conditioning by Jamf would seem the ideal symbolic training for the rocket's lover. Because of his American background, however, Slothrop becomes The American, inheritor of the Western cultural tradition. What happens to him as an individual turns out to be something like a paradigm for the possible fate of Western humanity.

The first two stages of the mythological cycle—those of paradise and fall—are played out by Slothrop's ancestors. Like the biblical patriarchs, they established the patterns *in illo tempore* that guide the lives of their descendants. Aside from William Slothrop, the Slothrops were not people to rise above their culture. Their gravestones are a clutter of clichés: "round-faced angels with the long noses of dogs, toothy and deep-socketed death's heads, Masonic emblems, flowery urns, feathery willows upright and broken, exhausted hourglasses, sunfaces about to rise or set with eyes peeking Kilroy-style over their horizon, and memorial verse" (p. 27). These ancestors started working fairly close to nature, processing raw materials to goods that would mostly have been used within their own communities, but they quickly evolved into purveyors of less basic services and goods: "They began as fur traders, cordwainers, salters and smokers of bacon, went on into glassmaking, became selectmen, builders of tanneries, quarriers of marble" (p. 27). Most of them are "Bible-packing" and "word-smitten."

One characteristic they apparently all share is "a peculiar sensitivity to what is revealed in the sky" (p. 26). In a passage employing a standard Christian icon for God speaking, Pynchon shows Constant Slothrop seeing, "and not only with his heart, that stone hand pointing out of the secular clouds, pointing directly at him, its edges traced in unbearable light" (p. 27). His descendants, including Tyrone Slothrop, inherit this sensitivity to things descending from the sky.

What we gather about his immediate parents is filtered through Tyrone's oedipal paranoia. His father made a deal that would ensure Tyrone a Harvard education, but Tyrone's interpretation is wholly negative: "I've been sold, Jesus Christ, I've been sold to IG Farben like a side of beef" (p. 286). Later, his father, Broderick, figures as the villain in daydreams of the Floundering Four and makes foolish-sounding remarks when trying to talk man-to-man (pp. 698–99). Slothrop would agree with Weissmann that "fathers are carriers of the virus of Death, and sons are the infected" (p. 723). When offered the chance of atonement with his father in a dream, Slothrop cannot make the gesture of forgiveness (p. 444). Broderick is thus the oedipal patriarch, and Tyrone would be only too glad to kill this archetypal monster. Nor does he find respite with his mother. She is the maenad, martini in hand, presiding over the dismemberment of her orphic son (p. 712).

His more distant ancestors bequeath to Tyrone his basic mediocrity, his sensitivity to revelation from the sky, and his awareness of words; they also give him their division of the world into the elect and preterite. His parents ensure his sense of being preterite. One of Pynchon's basic images, in fact, is that of Western parents killing their own and other people's children.[7] Margherita Erdmann tries to kill a Jewish boy and may have murdered her daughter, Bianca. Conservative audiences of Rossini operas plot against children (p. 441). In arranging Gottfried's wedding-death, Weissmann stresses their father-son relationship. The children at Zwolfkinder are "sentenced" children (p. 430), and Otto Gnahb describes the Mother Conspiracy to destroy children (p. 505). Innocence has no chance; it is unacceptable to Them and must be corrupted or killed before a youth is allowed to join the adult world. Tyrone's unhappy relationships with his parents thus tie in to a much broader phenomenon, one bearing on our culture's drive to destroy itself.

In Slothrop's own adventures, we find a development that echoes the immachination of Gottfried with the rocket. Säure Bummer removes the horns from a wagnerian helmet, caps Slothrop with this nosecone, and names him Rocketman (p. 366). Slothrop has been amusing himself with Plasticman comicbooks, "Plas" also being a hybrid of human and plastic. As Rocketman, Slothrop becomes a funnies-style hero like Plasticman and roams the Zone, instantly a legendary figure. When he penetrates Peenemünde, Tchitcherine greets him as Rocketman. When on the run and wearing a pig costume, the name of Rocketman gets him aid. Slothrop is a fairly ineffectual person, so the successes he enjoys in his rocket-persona make that human/machine blend attractive to him.

But having become Rocketman, what happens? Slothrop disintegrates. His past selves become independent (p. 624). The albatross of self is plucked, then stripped. He turns into a different kind of figure, the harmonica Orpheus of the Zone. He enjoys his rainbow vision and listens to the Other Side—both of which are forms of revelation from the sky—but then, gradually, loses his material reality. Bodine is the last to be able to see him, and even Bodine has to let him go. Slothrop ultimately just dissolves into "the hostile light of the sky, the darkness of the sea" (p. 742).

This scattering is partly explained earlier; according to Kurt Mondaugen, personal density is directly proportional to temporal bandwidth, and "'Temporal bandwidth' is the width of your present, your *now*. It is the familiar 'Δ t' considered as a dependent variable. The more you dwell in the past and in the future, the thicker your bandwidth, the more solid your persona. But the narrower your sense of Now, the more tenuous you are" (p. 509). Slothrop's vision is limited to the here and now, so he loses personality, individuality, planning ability. His head empties. Some of these losses may have their good aspects, for Pynchon treats the albatross of self, the ego, as "bad shit" and marks as positive the flexibility resulting from not trying to plan the future and the openness to the Other Side that results from plucking the albatross. But Slothrop's modus vivendi is no longer social, no longer a way that society might try in its search for improving itself while still remaining a society, so even if his fragmentation is not all bad, it is not viable as a model for others. Fragmentation signifies loss of much of what by our definition makes us human. This is what threatens individuals within that society in which humankind mates with machine. As the two mythic actions—that of Western culture and that of Tyrone Slothrop—unfold in parallel, Slothrop's fate echoes that of society. As control tightens and the machine dominates, one of the few possible ways of preserving freedom is to disintegrate. But even those who do not wish thus to fade out may be deprived of their identities anyway, as machines become the standard of measurement and humans are found wanting.

Pynchon's mythology involves both humanity and its inventions, so we find equivalents to Slothrop as individual in the V-2 and to humankind in technology. The mythological histories of the V-2 and of technology in its general sense do not cover as wide a chronological span as do Pynchon's human mythologies, but the complexity of Pynchon's technical allusions makes up for the loss of scope.

Nothing is said about American or Russian rocket experiments. Pynchon confines himself to German rocketry and to the Verein für Raumschiffahrt, particularly as seen by Franz Pökler. By chance, Pökler stumbles onto an early firing and is nearly killed by the explosion of this "tiny silver egg, with a flame, pure and steady, issuing from beneath" (p. 161). Despite the violence of his introduction, he is excited and enthusiastic, overwhelmingly attracted to this new creation. The paradisal, amateur stage of rocket development gives way, however, once the army becomes interested in the VfR records. Franz resists Leni's accusation ("They're using you to kill people") and counters with his own vision: "We'll all use *it*, someday, to leave the earth. To transcend" (p. 400). The choice, however, "was between building what the Army wanted—practical hardware—or pushing on in chronic poverty, dreaming of expeditions to Venus" (pp. 400–401), so he pragmatically serves the army.

Pökler is witness and participant through the early stages of the Aggregat or Vergeltungswaffen, and the problems bedeviling these big rockets have not changed from those confronting the rocket "egg":

Problem was just to get something off the ground without having it blow up. There were minor disasters—aluminum motor casings would burn through, some injector designs would set up resonant combustion, in which the burning motor would try to shriek itself to pieces—and then, in '34, a major one. Dr. Wahmke decided to mix peroxide and alcohol together *before* injection into the thrust chamber, to see what would happen. The ignition flame backed up through the conduit into the tank. The blast demolished the test stand, killing Dr. Wahmke and two others. First blood, first sacrifice. (p. 403)

The rocket takes on a kind of solidity through what individuals give to it: Wahmke's life, Pökler's submission ("Pökler was an extension of the Rocket, long before it was ever built" [p. 402]). As the effort progresses from the A-3 to the A-4, Pökler is detailed to sit in a trench precisely at Ground Zero, the target, to observe the premature fall.[8] The latter history of the rocket comes to us mostly through Slothrop (for technical details) and from various Londoners who witness rocket strikes. While on the Riviera, British Intelligence crams Slothrop with every piece of information gathered on the V-2, hoping that the knowledge will strengthen his uncanny affinity for these rockets and enable him to be drawn to their source. And, indeed, in his own wanderings, he is drawn to the Mittelwerke and to Peenemünde. The egg image of Pökler's first vision of a rocket recurs:

Here he is, scaling the walls of an honest ceremonial plexus [. . . .] But oh, Egg the flying Rocket hatched from, navel of the 50-meter radio sky, all proper ghosts of place—forgive him his numbness, his glozing neutrality. Forgive the fist that doesn't tighten in his chest, the heart that can't stiffen in any greeting. . . . Forgive him as you forgave Tchitcherine at the Kirghiz Light. . . ." (pp. 509-10)

The rocket's history is further added to by Enzian and his rocket troops, who not only assemble their own but also live lives devoted to the rocket, taking it for their

Holy Text. This devotion started with Enzian's initiation into technology by Weissmann:

> It began when Weissmann brought him to Europe: a discovery that love, among these men, once past the simple feel and orgasming of it, had to do with masculine technologies, with contracts, with winning and losing. Demanded, in his own case, that he enter the service of the Rocket. . . . Beyond simple steel erection, the Rocket was an entire system *won*, away from the feminine darkness, held against the entropies of lovable but scatterbrained Mother Nature.   (p. 324)

The Hereros have adapted the ignition insignia to their tribal mandala (p. 563), thus assimilating themselves to their machine. The rocket acquires a range of further resonances at the crucial launching, when the narrative voice invokes the Kabbalah, sephirotic tree symbolism, tarot arcana, and human sacrifice, both Germanic and biblical. Besides being thus linked to these disparate concerns, the rocket is also yoked to movies (*Die Frau im Mond*) and to radio heroes, who gather about the launching. And its own magic is hymned at least briefly when it defies gravity.

If the history of early rockets corresponds to Slothrop's ancestors and to the settling of America, the launch has the same crucial significance in this thread of the mythology that it does in the history of humankind. Humanity and machine coalesce. For the rocket's next mythological phase, after origins and marriage, the apocalyptic possibilities are limited to two: rockets falling with warheads upon cities, or rockets heading for space— the moon, Venus, and beyond. Of the two, the latter better extends the dream of immachination. On the moon and in space, humankind will have no choice but be wedded to machinery, since it cannot survive their hostile atmospheres without it. However, total destruction is another form of immachination, a Liebestod.

The rocket "engorges energy and information in its 'fearful assembly': thus its 'order' is obtained at the cost of an increase in disorder in the world around it, through which so many of the characters stumble." And as Tanner and others have stressed, the rocket, "in its fixity and metallic destructive inhumanity . . . is an order of death—a *negative* parallel to the process of nature, since its disintegration presages no consequent renewal and growth."[9] In this, it is opposed to the dream of living within the cycle of nature half-sensed by William Slothrop and reachieved at disastrous cost to self by Tyrone Slothrop. The rocket works against the natural cycle,[10] and its order disorders and fragments the lives of those drawn into its orbit. Its power is measured by the lives it absorbs. Some are taken completely; some give themselves willingly; some maintain a shred of independence. Pökler best embodies this dilemma of attraction and resistance: "so he hunted, as a servo valve with a noisy input will, across the Zero, between the two desires, personal identity and impersonal salvation" (p. 406). This is another version of immachination, one in which humanity will be consumed by the rocket if it continues to serve the machine.

The fourth strand of mythological history traces the progress of technology in general. Though this strand is not a myth in the sense of being unreal or fabulous, it takes on mythic qualities in Pynchon's hands as he isolates certain sequences and connects them, putting discoveries into an end-determined structure with the rocket serving as that symbolic end. The development Pynchon chooses to stress is that of organic chemistry, especially the benzene chemistry of Kekulé and the coal-tar chemistry of the dye industry. Offshoots of color chemistry were pharmaceuticals (including psychoactive drugs), fertilizers, coal-gas and other fuel industries, the rubber and synthetic rubber industry, and plastics. Pynchon sticks mostly to the coal-tar dyes and to plastics, in part because they created products not found in nature, and indeed products that sometimes transcend the cycles of life and decay in this world.

Although Pynchon describes many byways of technology, he brings this history to life with two key figures: Kekulé and Jamf. Kekulé is the shadowy founder, the patriarch *in illo tempore* who may not quite have walked and talked with God, but who was visited by a higher revelation in his 1865 dream of an ouroboric serpent, which "revolutionized chemistry and made the IG possible" (p. 410). Much is made of this dream and of its "cosmic serpent, in the violet splendor of its scales, shining that is definitely *not* human" (p. 411); the history of technology is then mythologized in terms of this snake (p. 412).

The history of coal-tar dyes is sketched by the spirit of Walther Rathenau at the Berlin séance: dyes, their discoverers, and drugs emerge in his pronouncement as strands leading toward something, as a succession. On the surface, this end product is "the growing, organic Kartell. But it's only another illusion. A very clever robot. The more dynamic it seems to you, the more deep and dead, in reality, it grows." He ends, however, by warning in sybilline obscurity about "Death the impersonator" and about "the real nature of control" (p. 167).

In the succession he is outlining, these are apparently its real final terms.

The development of plastics mostly emerges as Slothrop gathers information about the fictional László Jamf, Pökler's old teacher, a polymath who contributed to behavioral psychology, polymer plastics, film emulsions, psychoactive drugs, oil, and invisible ink (activated by semen).

Pynchon graphically illustrates the ways in which all these technologies—rocket, plastics, and coal-tar derivatives—are used to control the preterite.[11] Plastic serves as stimulus to condition Infant Tyrone. Jamf's film emulsion, which can see beneath the human skin, will be used to manipulate audience response to a film of a quarrel between a black man and a white. In order for messages in the invisible ink to be legible, a pornographic picture, elaborately tailored to fit the psychosexual profile of the recipient, is sent along with the message to elicit the semen needed for bringing up the script. The drug sodium amytal is used to force Slothrop to expose parts of his mind he would probably rather keep to himself. And the rocket affects the lives of nearly everyone in the book. It draws Slothrop, Tchitcherine, Enzian, and Pökler. It even exerts control over the lives of people who have no direct connection to it, when it is given priority over the hungry for the potato harvest or over cocaine traffickers in the matter of potassium permanganate.

Despite the potential danger of this technological world and its obvious curtailments of freedom, Pynchon makes plain that it has virtues and attractions. Pökler, for instance, enjoys its democracy: "It was a corporate intelligence at work, specialization hardly mattered, class lines even less. The social spectrum ran from von Braun, the Prussian aristocrat, down to the likes of Pökler, who would eat an apple in the street—yet they were all equally at the Rocket's mercy" (p. 402). Pökler cannot accept Mondaugen's electro-mysticism, but longs for the sense of certainty such a rocket religion could give him.

The various futures Pynchon sketches for his history of technology all show humanity and machine inseparable, but beyond this likeness are the same variants shown in the other strands of the mythology: space exploration, nuclear holocaust, the world of *1984,* or the superficially attractive dystopia of *Brave New World.* Raketen-Stadt was a wartime nickname for Peenemünde and is applied by Pynchon to various versions of the technological future. In addition, he mentions the possible future in which we would run out of energy. Technology may emerge as in some sense the superior partner in the human marriage, but it too may fragment for lack of energy. Pynchon does not specify the most likely future here any more than in the other strands.

These then are the basic mythic actions: Western culture, an individual, the V-2, and technology. In various ways, they all explore the development of symbiosis between humanity and its technological creations. This story is mythic in one sense because it tries to fill in the gap between absent origins and our present condition. It is mythological in another sense because the technologies become quasi-animate, to the point that critics grouse about Pynchon's paranoia.[12] These strands are also mythic in the accumulation of myth-like stories: paradise, the fall (complete with serpent), the symbolic marriage between Gottfried and the rocket, the glimpses of a future city not so unlike the New Jerusalem with its symmetries, its metals and precious stones as architectural members. Or, alternatively, the holocaust that will end life. Pynchon has chosen to focus on the V-2, but in the background—outside his mythological history—are the atomic bombs whose debris create such vivid sunsets. Pynchon establishes so many "Kute Korrespondences," as we shall soon see, that he hardly needs to emphasize this most important one. When a colonel asks "Is the sun's everyday spectrum being modulated? Not at random, but systematically, by this unknown debris in the prevailing winds? Is there information for us?" (p. 642) we can answer in the affirmative without being prompted by the narrator.

Redundancies

Edmund Leach calls attention to the role of repetitions or redundancies for conveying meaning in myth:

If myth be a mode of communication, then a part of the theory which is embodied in digital computer systems ought to be relevant. The merit of this approach is that it draws special attention to precisely those features of myth which have formerly been regarded as accidental defects. It is common to all mythological systems that all important stories recur in several different versions. Man is created in Genesis (I, 27) and then he is created all over again (II, 7). And, as if two first men were not enough, we also have Noah in Chapter VIII. Likewise in the New Testament, why must there be four gospels each telling "the same" story yet sometimes flatly contradictory on details of fact? (Leach, p. 317)

Pynchon's recasting of story material so that it applies redundantly to two or more people has been noted by

Brian McHale. He calls attention to Carroll Eventyr's speculations as to whether he himself "maps onto" Peter Sachsa, and if so, whether Nora Dodson-Truck maps onto Leni Pökler (p. 218). Slothrop and Margherita Erdmann reconstruct an *Alpdrücken* scene, which at the original showing was also reconstructed with Leni by Franz Pökler: "both Slothrop and Franz Pökler map onto Max Schlepzig [the actor]; Leni maps onto Greta, Ilse onto Greta's daughter Bianca, and Greta onto her own earlier self." Geli and Gottfried intermap; so do Gottfried and Ilse. McHale treats such mappings as a tactic to unsettle our ontological assumptions and analyzes them as a sign of postmodernism ("Modernist Reading," pp. 104–6). On a case-by-case basis, these mappings certainly function in that destabilizing way. Within the larger frame, however, one can argue that they involve messages repeated so that meaning gets through despite background noise.

Slothrop is both the chief character of the novel and the one most involved in such redundancies. He maps onto most of the other characters in one way or another. Tchitcherine, for example, is practically his double. They are both haunted by a fear of blacks, Slothrop's fears being general, Tchitcherine's being centered on his half-brother. Slothrop's ancestors saw the hand from the sky, and Slothrop retains their sensitivity. Tchitcherine too sees such a hand, or rather "a very large white Finger, addressing him. Its Fingernail is beautifully manicured: as it rotates for him, it slowly reveals a Fingerprint that might well be an aerial view of the City Dactylic, that city of the future where every soul is known, and there is noplace to hide" (p. 566). The hugeness and whiteness maps onto the slothropian image of the "giant white cock, dangling in the sky straight downward out of a white pubic bush" (p. 693).

There are other correspondences. Tchitcherine also has an albatross (p. 701). Like most of the major characters, including Slothrop, he experiences an illuminating disillusionment, when he learns that his culture has lied to him, wants him to die to help make history, a history that theoretically should come about inevitably without his personal death (p. 701). He considers the probability that everything he knows has been fed by a lie. Like Slothrop, he suffers from his own brand of paranoia, although in Tchitcherine's case it is the effect of oneirine.

He and Slothrop map onto each other in their reaching the edges of illumination but being unable to break through. Tchitcherine is also open to the Other Side, albeit through the offices of drugs rather than inherited sensitivity. Also like Slothrop, he sleeps with women all over the Zone. Like Slothrop, he is trying to turn up rocket information. Both men sleep with Geli Tripping, and when she takes Slothrop up the Brocken, he urges her—he knows not why—to show Tchitcherine the Brockengespenst. The two men differ most noticeably in their fates. Tchitcherine may be heading for Central Asia with rocket components, to the scuffling mediocrity once promised to Slothrop, but Geli loves him. Her love has blinded him to Enzian's identity and may rescue him from other bogeys as well.

Enzian, as Tchitcherine's double, shares many of his characteristics and so also maps onto Slothrop. Enzian too has an albatross (p. 661). He too is wedded to the rocket, both physically coupling with one (p. 297) and chasing its parts across the Zone so he can construct one. Enzian and Slothrop share insights into the nature of They-reality. Slothrop broke this barrier in the Casino Hermann Goering: "Shortly, unpleasantly so, it will come to him that everything in this room is really being used for something different. Meaning things to Them it has never meant to us. Never. Two orders of being, looking identical . . . but, but . . . " (p. 202). Slothrop feels he has been playing against the invisible House, perhaps for his soul (p. 205). Katje tells him that he may someday understand—"maybe in one of their bombed-out cities" (p. 224).

It is Enzian, though, who achieves the insight from a bombed-out ruin:

There floods on Enzian what seems to him an extraordinary understanding. This serpentine slag-heap he is just about to ride into now, this ex-refinery, Jamf Ölfabriken Werke AG, is *not a ruin at all. It is in perfect working order.* Only waiting for the right connections to be set up, to be switched on . . . modified, precisely, *deliberately* by bombing that was never hostile, but part of a plan both sides—*'sides?'*—had always agreed on. (p. 520)

He and his people had assumed that the rocket was their Holy Text, but he suddenly realizes that the real Text is elsewhere, maybe in the scenery he is passing through. If the factory is as it is supposed to be, "it means this War was never political at all, the politics was all theatre, all just to keep the people distracted . . . secretly, it was being dictated instead by the needs of technology" (p. 521). Finally, like Slothrop discovering that his culture has lied to him (pp. 266, 623, *inter alia*), Enzian makes similar discoveries (p. 728), and these resemble Tchitcherine's discoveries about his government's need for his death.

One of Slothrop's weirder mappings is onto Gottfried. The last fevered harangue Gottfried receives from Weissmann—full of the older generation killing the younger, fathers and sons unable to face their problems with death—seems a fulfillment of Slothrop's oedipal fantasies of Pop trying to kill The Kid, and both echo the experiences of Isaac with Abraham, invoked during the launching of the 00000. Slothrop's giant shadow from the Brocken parallels Gottfried's shadow cast when he and the rocket reach Brennschluss, a "Brocken-specter, someone's, something's shadow projected from out here in the bright sun and darkening sky into the regions of gold" (p. 759). Not only do the two men share this Brockengespenst, but strangest of all, Gottfried echoes Slothrop's infant experience with Imipolex G: "The soft smell of Imipolex, wrapping him absolutely, is a smell he knows. It doesn't frighten him. It was in the room when he fell asleep so long ago, so deep in sweet paralyzed childhood" (p. 754). Gottfried had not experienced the Forbidden Wing; Jamf never conditioned him. Yet here in the rocket—where Slothrop by one train of logic should be—their childhoods become the same. But then too, when Slothrop is making love with Bianca (one of Gottfried's doubles), he experiences being launched in a rocket as he gets the feeling that he is inside his own penis, "his sperm roaring louder and louder, getting ready to erupt, somewhere below his feet[. . . .] He is enclosed. Everything is about to come [. . .] an extraordinary sense of *waiting to rise*[. . . .] Announcing the void, what could it be but the kingly voice of the Aggregat itself?" (p. 470). So Gottfried becomes Slothrop in the rocket, and Slothrop becomes Gottfried at the launching.

Many minor characters intermap with Slothrop in less detail. Both he and Pirate Prentice, his British Intelligence counterpart, experience fantasies of the rocket hitting them directly (pp. 7, 23–24), and Slothrop recognizes that somehow he and Jamf are one (pp. 287, 623). In accompanying a pig, Slothrop maps onto his own ancestor, William. Like Byron the Bulb, he descends down a toilet bowl, through sewer to sea. Like Roger, he discovers the existence of plots centering on him (pp. 188, 285–86). And Slothrop and Pökler both recreate Erdmann's *Alpdrücken* orgy (pp. 394–96, 397), both are extensions of the rocket, and both love little girls, though Pökler's incest fantasy remains fantasy whereas Slothrop does enjoy Bianca, whose double Ilse Pökler is. Pökler also maps onto Slothrop and the other main characters when he discovers the They-reality superimposed on his own. Whereas Slothrop found he had been playing for his own soul, "Pökler understood that he had been negotiating for his child and for Leni" (p. 417).

These doubly and sometimes multiply mapped episodes point to major nexes of values. We find failure to reach higher spiritual illumination but successful breakthrough into the level of insight about Them and Their control of our world. The intermapping also emphasizes insights into our culture's lies to us. Slothrop's symbolic sexual entanglement with rocket and plastic is echoed in the lives of Gottfried and Enzian, his devotion to uncovering the rocket's technical details finding equivalences in the devotions of Tchitcherine, Enzian, and Pökler. His role as victim of the previous generation is given reinforcing shadows and echoes. Even his melting into sky and sea among the preterite souls is doubled by the ends of Pirate and Katje: "so they dissolve now, into the race and swarm of this dancing Preterition, and their faces, the dear, comical faces they have put on for this ball, fade, as innocence fades, grimly flirtatious, and striving to be kind" (p. 548). All these doublings and redoublings call attention to the most important aspects of Slothrop's life, the aspects that are generalizable into symbolic messages about the state of Western humankind and its relationship to this culture and technology. The values turned up by study of the redundancies are the values of Slothrop's story on the mythological level.

When we turn from Slothrop to some of the other characters, we find similar redundancies. Ilse, Gottfried, and Bianca are almost interchangeable. The two girls are children of *Alpdrücken*. Gottfried and Bianca are apparently destroyed by destructive figures who sometimes fulfill parental roles. Gottfried and Ilse dream of living on the moon. The death of Bianca and Gottfried is accompanied by an Imipolex G shroud and is located next to large engines; they both thought of fitting into the rocket. Gottfried and Bianca are also experienced in sexual deviations, and Ilse knows all the tricks necessary to survive in a concentration camp, including (by implication) the sexual. All three are loved by much older men. Their joint stories stress their roles as victims of their parents' generation, as both products and victims of sexual decadence and violence. Yet all three retain awareness of the feelings of others. They ultimately reject defenses and keep themselves open, and they continue to show kindness, even love.

Other intermappings include Katje and Gottfried, Katje and Slothrop (both of whom play out Hansel and Gretel fantasies—Katje with Weissmann and Gottfried, Slothrop with Darlene and Mrs. Quoad), Katje and Geli (as lovers of Pan [pp. 656–57, 720–21]), Katje and Enzian (as lovers of Weissmann), Katje and her victim-lover Brigadier Pudding (both of whom submit themselves masochistically to ordeals, especially elevating their buttocks to receive beatings, in order to feel something real [pp. 234, 662]), Katje and Pirate (in accepting their preterition), and Katje and Slothrop (in their colonizing ancestors who destroyed a natural setting, partly as an exercise of Protestant fanaticism).

Roger, as lover, overlaps both Pökler and Pirate in this role. Like Pökler, he cries an unusual amount when his loved one leaves him (pp. 402, 629). The parallels to Pirate are even more striking. Like Pirate, Roger is past thirty when he falls in love, but both seem innocent and evoke mothering, protective feelings from Jessica and Scorpia. (Both Jeremy and Clive are establishment executive types.) On their last day together, Scorpia fantasizes to Pirate: "You've come and taken me off on your pirate ship. A girl of good family and the usual repressions. You've raped me. And I'm the Red Bitch of the High Seas" (p. 36). Then, as he leaves her at Waterloo, they are surrounded by Fred Roper's company of Wonder Midgets. When Roger and Jessica once drove down a trunk road, Jessica bared herself to the waist, teasing Roger's funk by claiming to be an innocent lamb whom he has forced to perform degrading acts. Then a gigantic lorry overtakes them, filled with midgets "staring down, scuffling like piglets on a sow for position, eyes popping, swarthy, mouths leaking spit, to take in the spectacle of his Jessica Swanlake scandalously bare-breasted" (p. 123). Toward the end of the novel, Pirate and Roger are the two from the White Visitation who manage to care most about Slothrop's fate, who try to find him. When they lose love, what is left is kindness. Pökler too, when the nature of his past life is clear to him, can leave his gold ring with an unknown victim of Camp Dora.

Love's role in *Gravity's Rainbow* is debatable. In some ways, love is ranged against death and therefore welcome; but the repeated patterns just described suggest that a more significant value lies in its inclination to be transmuted into kindness and also in its ability to make one accept openness, accept the probability of being hurt, accept one sort of preterition. Such openness also characterizes Carroll Eventyr, Gottfried, and Bianca.

Only one major figure stands outside the correspondences: Weissmann. Although he has been lover of Enzian, Katje, and Gottfried, his life unfolds in almost original patterns. He goes out as a colonizer but manages to love Enzian. Others who follow the rocket must yield to it or fight the urge, but he seems unmoved, pulled not by the rocket itself but by the promise of transcendence. Whereas Slothrop hunkers down among ants and capercaillies and dreams of the lost America, Weissmann thinks only of transcending the cycles, of going beyond gravity and the grave. His life is a mixture of cruelty and love, extremes of submission or dominance. More obviously than other characters we see, he controls people, especially his lovers, yet they seem to bear him no grudge, even for the pain. The 175s even invent their own Blicero, modeled on Weissmann and his code name. That SS code name is also a medieval name for death and relates to bleaching and whiteness, as does his family name. No other name in the novel is so heavily freighted with such explicit values. Weissmann thus stands outside the patterned network of mappings and meanings.

As the figure who plans, engineers, and hallows the union between Gottfried and the rocket, Weissmann proves to be the one person who really wants humanity and machine joined. We tend to think of people sliding haphazardly into dependence and then addiction to technology, but Weissmann works consciously to bring this about. He is the sort of person the Schwarzkommando mean when they say, "Do you think we'd've had the Rocket if someone, some specific somebody with a name and a penis hadn't *wanted* to chuck a ton of Amatol 300 miles and blow up a block full of civilians? Go ahead, capitalize the T on technology, deify it if it'll make you feel less responsible—but it puts you in with the neutered, brother" (p. 521). Weissmann is bringing the mythological story into being—the marriage of humanity and rocket—he with his energy and dedication, the rest with their neutered passivity.

Some redundancies do not involve characters so much as situations: references to pie in the face; allusions to Orpheus; the diverse institutions credited with the initials CIA (pp. 164, 625, 650, 700). Perhaps the most obvious such repetition—Roger's bomb map and Slothrop's girl map—is the least explicable. Pynchon never does explain the identity of the points. It may be a joke, but eros and thanatos are linked so often that we may find an answer to this correspondence by shifting to

Edmund Leach's other two characteristics of myth—the
binary oppositions and the forces mediating between
them.

Binary Oppositions and Mediations

Binary oppositions are intrinsic to the process of human
thought. Any description of the world must discriminate categories in the form "p is what not-p is not." An object is alive
or not alive and one could not formulate the concept "alive"
except as the converse of its partner "dead". . . .

Religion everywhere is preoccupied with . . . the antinomy
of life and death. Religion seeks to deny the binary link between the two words; it does this by creating the mystical idea
of "another world," a land of the dead where life is
perpetual. . . .

So, despite all variations of theology, this aspect of myth is
a constant. In every myth system we will find a persistent
sequence of binary discriminations as between human/super-
human, mortal/immortal, male/female, legitimate/illegitimate,
good/bad . . . followed by a "mediation" of the paired categories thus distinguished. (Leach, pp. 319–20; the ellipses in
the last quotation are present in the original text.)

Edmund Leach's terms here—as one statement of a
structuralist position—would seem applicable to *Gravity's
Rainbow* even if I were not arguing for its mythological
qualities. One of the most noticeable characteristics of
the work is its use of oppositions: zero and one, white
and black, control and freedom, elect and preterite,
Them and Us, humanity and the machine, European
and primitive civilizations, life-styles that live within the
cycle of nature and those that violate it, history and
timelessness, North and South, openness and closure,

connectedness and unconnectedness, paranoia and antiparanoia, This Side and the Other Side, eros and thanatos, life and death, Dionysus and Apollo, pig and rocket, force and counterforce.[13] Not all of these are true logical opposites, and some are secondary or tertiary embodiments of the more basic oppositions. Many of those mentioned, though, would come to mind as opposed terms in the novel, and insofar as such oppositions express values of the novel, it is worth determining which are the most basic, irreducible oppositions and exploring what kinds of mediations Pynchon offers. He could, of course, create a cosmos without any such mediations, leaving us to deal with a world constructed entirely from contradictions, or he could establish and then reverse all the hierarchies in deconstructionist fashion. I am arguing, however, that Pynchon does suggest various kinds of mediate terms, and that these do point in the direction of solutions to our problems. He does not, however, follow a single formula for all oppositions; in this respect he goes beyond any simple structuralist formula.

Among the various oppositions that seem fundamental, I find three rough groupings, each with its own method of reducing the tension generated by the opposition. Each of the three groups clusters about a major antinomy, those being zero versus one, elect versus preterite, and control versus freedom.

The first group solves the antinomy by means of and/and rather than either/or logic. Zero versus one, the archetypal binary opposition, appears early in the novel and is obviously freighted with significance. Edward Pointsman, the specialist in pavlovian conditioning, expresses his obsession with stimulus-and-response or cause-and-effect relationships in terms of the elegant

0/1 options. His is the world of either/or, of aristotelian logic and classical science. He is just flexible enough to realize that Slothrop's rocket-dowsing abilities may demand modifications in his assumptions of cause and effect, but he makes that concession in order to cling more firmly to stimulus and response, zero and one. His coworker, Roger Mexico, is "the Antipointsman": "To Mexico belongs the domain *between* zero and one—the middle Pointsman has excluded from his persuasion—the probabilities" (p. 55). For Mexico, cause-and-effect relationships are a "sterile set of assumptions" (p. 89). Critics have made much of 0/1 as the basic binary opposition and of the statistical realm between them as a mediation or means of transcending a sterile opposition. The same critics often castigate readers for trying to apply 0/1 logic to a book where that approach is inadequate. Instead of certainty and knowledge, we are told, we must settle for probability and uncertainty.[14]

But such critics are simply forcing us to make another exclusionary decision: either 0/1 or something in between. I would argue that in this and the related group of oppositions, Pynchon does not abolish the extremes in order to exalt an excluded middle. Rather, he implies that we must somehow strive to integrate, or at least accept all the possibilities: and/and rather than either/or. Roger's middle realm is not the answer. He, after all, produces an Angel's-eye view of the bomb-falls but not a humane one; his "sieve" charts a Poisson distribution, it does not cure the sick (p. 56). Instead, we need the binary polarities for what they can tell us—and they are more or less adequate to some realities, such as computer circuits, or even some stimulus/response experiments. To be useful, though, these applications must be put in a broad context, one that includes probability, and humaneness, and many other factors as well. In this group of oppositions, Pynchon stresses inclusiveness as the answer.

The two other oppositions belonging to this group are paranoia versus antiparanoia, and eros versus thanatos. The former is an explicit concern in the novel. Paranoia is the personal credo of just about every character in the Zone. As more than one writer has pointed out, paranoia is the natural disease for people living in the information age, where technology and structures of control dwarf the individual.[15] Paranoia is even comforting, for no matter how threatening the plots one senses, they do testify to one's own importance. With antiparanoia, the rewards are fewer:

If there is something comforting—religious, if you want— about paranoia, there is still also anti-paranoia, where nothing is connected to anything, a condition not many of us can bear for long. Well right now Slothrop feels himself sliding onto the anti-paranoid part of his cycle[. . . .] Either They have put him here for a reason, or he's just here. He isn't sure that he wouldn't, actually, rather have that *reason*.   (p. 434)

No real solution lies between the extremes of paranoia and antiparanoia. Instead, we must step outside of the alternatives because, indeed, they do not cover all possibilities. Creative paranoia is one option, the self-conscious creation of connections and meanings. Moreover, there are also other forms of connectedness besides personal paranoia. One is the Puritans' determination to see the hand of God in all earthly events. Two others emerge as more attractive to modern readers: the kind of connectedness sensed by mystics and the kind discussed by ecologists. Both viewpoints perceive a network of relationships.[16] Pynchon's comments on mysticism are fragmentary and derive from several mystic traditions, so they have received less attention than they deserve. He does address mysticism directly in his references to the Aqyn and Mondaugen, and his sense of reality beyond the material is compatible with the mystic's sense of interrelationships. Ecology is more obviously a concern in the text. After Slothrop has plucked the albatross of self, he achieves a oneness with nature that is another expression of the sense of connectedness of everything. Pynchon also reminds us of other kinds of unforeseen quasi-ecological connectedness when he links the needs of the rocket to potatoes planted in the spring and to despair in the world of cocaine trafficking. As with 0/1, Pynchon seems to say that we must not only preserve these extremes—after all, paranoia is "perhaps a route In for those like Tchitcherine who are held at the edge" (p. 703)—but also consider all the options found between them. With this set of oppositions, Pynchon seems to espouse and/and rather than either/or logic.

The third opposition in this group—eros and thanatos—is implicit rather than explicit. This pairing is often mentioned by critics, partly because sex in its many forms is almost as ubiquitous as death in the narrative, partly because of Freud's linking of the two terms, partly because of the presence of someone named Thanatz.[17] We might distinguish this opposition from that of life versus death (to be discussed later) by narrowing thanatos to the impulse towards destruction; this destruction may take several forms, including obsession with the means of death or even any obsession with something that blinds us and deafens us to the dangerous consequences of our actions, our suicidal addiction to energy, for instance. Balancing this drive toward death is another, the drive for sexual activity. Roger's love for Jessica, though attractive to our romantic culture, is as much an illogical bondage for him as is that which binds Gottfried to Weissmann or that which causes Katje and Pudding to seek masochistic pain. Roger knows that Jessica will not be satisfied with what he has to offer, yet he persists despite his knowledge of the anguish that must ensue. The loves of Carroll Eventyr for Nora Dodson-Truck and of Franz Pökler for Leni are also unequally reciprocated, yet both men persist. Slothrop's multitude of sexual couplings, though not romantic, would also fall under the heading of erotic compulsion.

Neither thanatos nor eros seems ideal, and I get no sense that we are urged to embrace one and reject the other. Avoiding both extremes might be nice, but Pynchon's obsession-ridden world offers no hope for escaping these drives. He does suggest, however, that we can modify them, lessen their destructive effects, through exercise of another impulse—kindness. Not the storm of passions but kindness is upheld as desirable, and most of the characters who exhibit this generous emotion have experienced eros at some earlier point in the story. Pökler leaves his ring with the Dora victim. Pirate and Katje strive to be kind as they join the dance of preterition. Roger and Pirate, in their postproject concern for Slothrop, show such kindness. So does Pig Bodine. So does Commando Connie, who joins Bodine and Roger in their antiestablishment alliteration. (In thinking of her, the narrative voice remarks, "perhaps, Pointsman, there is such a thing as the kindness-reflex" [p. 714]). Many women show Slothrop kindness in bed, and he too shows it insofar as they want the comfort and pleasure he gives. For everyday living, kindness may do more to ameliorate preterition than a more exclusive passion. Bodine helps Slothrop out of concern, not love, just as Slothrop helps Närrisch rescue von Göll. Kindness is no panacea, but if kept in play along with the more forceful drives in an and/and relationship, it ameliorates their effects. As with zero and one or paranoia and antiparanoia, we retain the extremes but also need what lies in between or beyond or outside their polarity.

The second grouping of antinomies strikes a balance according to a different formula. When dealing with control and freedom, and their double, closure and openness, Pynchon definitely emphasizes or upholds the preferability of one of the poles, but backs off to a slightly less extreme position for his "answer."

There is no doubt that closure and control represent strongly negative qualities in Pynchon's cosmos. Controlling others never gets a good word, and a great deal is done to discredit control as it is exercised by Pointsman, by IG Farben, and by the technologies. The story, furthermore, follows the victims of control and presents events from their points of view. Freedom and openness, therefore, at first glance look like natural ideals. They are not really livable, however. In the openness of the Zone, Geli tells Slothrop, one needs arrangements. Since "nowhere in her eyes is there any sign of corrosion" (p. 290), this appears to be the counsel of sane and sensible experience, not the promptings of one seeking power.

The sorts of arrangements she has in mind, however, are not hedged about with rules or written up on paper as contracts. Each person's credit is only as good as his or her reputation, and the stakes are so small and the standard of living so low in the Zone that nobody is ruined by the occasional failure to come through. No one is very uptight about payments. Slothrop takes counterfeit marks as cheerfully as he does authentic ones and bargains for Imipolex G information without any money at all, let alone the five hundred Swiss francs demanded, yet somehow he gets what he wants. Mention of the hashish he brought out of Potsdam as Rocketman is enough to get him help when Muffage and Spontoon are closing in on him. Tchitcherine can hustle some cigarettes and potatoes, so he and Geli need not go hungry one night. Whether we analyze reality in terms of control and freedom or closure and openness, arrangements of this personal sort, freely entered upon, seem to be the modus vivendi treated most positively.

But this is a mediate position between control and true openness. In absolute openness, food would not appear reliably enough to sustain life, and the species would die out, since raising infants is not possible if everyone enjoys total freedom. Someone must forego that freedom for a decade or more, to raise a child to the age of Ilse or Ludwig or Bianca, protecting it until it has a chance of surviving. Leni may be right that "Mother" is a civil service category imposed by Them, but though she rejects the label violently, she does limit her personal freedom in order to look after her daughter. After all, she could have left the baby with Pökler when she walked out on him. Whether we look at eating and living in the Zone, or at family relationships, or at the dealings of the black market, we find limitations voluntarily put on one's absolute freedom. The answer to either/or here is somewhere between the extremes, but the relations Pynchon appears to favor do not show people controlling each other so much as people freely undertaking to control and limit themselves for a specific object—love, family, exchange of goods. The arrangements must be freely made, upheld by no compulsion but inner decision. Keeping such an agreement from becoming a tyranny in personal affairs may not be easy, may not indeed be possible, but must be attempted if any sort of social life is to continue while preserving some element of openness.

As an answer to the demands of choosing either freedom or control, this opting for freely accepted minimal arrangements may seem weak: how can one be urged to maintain a relationship only as long as one freely wants to but also be encouraged to be responsible? How can this be internalized and made the norm for society? As will become clear in the discussion of preterite and elect, there are similar problems to Pynchon's solution there, but when these "weak" answers are all brought together and studied, we find a consistent pattern that makes sense and may not be so weak-seeming in the aggregate.

The third group of antinomies, as one might guess, has affinities with both the others. As is the case with zero and one, we cannot reject one extreme and uphold the other; both must be accepted. But as with control and freedom, special attention is paid to one side of the opposition. The side thus emphasized here, however, is the unattractive option. Only by accepting the unattractive or repressed option can one reach a vantage point not torn by the tensions of the dichotomy. In the opposition between elect and preterite, for instance, improvement is reached by accepting one's preterite state.

Roger, Leni, Slothrop, Pirate, Katje, and Pökler all more or less come to terms with their own preterition, and in doing so, shed most of their fear and anxiety and win a kind of freedom. Slothrop reaches openness with the Other Side, the closest mode of life to pure freedom, and—to judge from his way of living—largely escapes the tensions of fearing for the morrow. His bandwidth narrows to the here and now. Pirate and Katje can live with their decisions and accept what they are. Roger can throw himself into Counterforce gestures, something only possible when he accepts that he is a loser in the power-struggle. This state of living in the here and now was pointed to by William Slothrop's musing on his pigs. They too are preterite, traveling to slaughter, yet they can enjoy a mud wallow and make "happy sounds"; and William can enjoy their "untroubled pink eyelashes and kind eyes, their smiles, their grace in cross-country movement" (p. 555). Ludwig reaches a comparable state of survival without undue worry: "Mostly what he's seen is a lot of chewing gum and a lot of foreign cock. How else does a foot-loose kid get by in the Zone these days? Ursula is preserved. Ludwig has fallen into a fate worse than death and found it's negotiable" (p. 729). He even manages to take care of his pet, no easy accomplishment when living hand-to-mouth.

One of the values Pynchon seems to associate with this state of accepted preterition is "grace": grace of movement in the pigs; grace of action as recommended by Pig Bodine to Slothrop ("What we need isn't right reasons, but just that *grace*. The physical grace to keep it working. Courage, brains, sure O.K., but without that grace? forget it" [p. 741]). It may be an exaggeration to

say that Slothrop "becomes the embodiment of all wisdom by simply riding Fate instead of trying to control
it,"[18] but some wisdom seems to reside in letting go of
fears and tensions, in living in the present.[19] It is not an
attitude by which the elect can live, only the preterite.
It does not guarantee long life—William Slothrop's pigs
were going to slaughter—but it offers a way to make
action and feeling seem meaningful. Leni knows something about abandoning herself to the present: when
discussing street riots with her husband, Franz, "she tried
to explain to him about the level you reach, with both
feet in, when you lose your fear, you lose it all, you've
penetrated the moment, slipping perfectly into its
grooves, metal-gray but soft as latex, and now the figures
are dancing, each pre-choreographed exactly where it
is" (p. 158). Giving up fear, accepting preterition, lets
one find some forms of happiness and significance. Fear
is responsible for Western craving for security, wealth,
control, election—all our inadequate bulwarks against
death.

The antinomy of death versus life is handled similarly.
Death is generally recognized as one of *Gravity's Rainbow*'s main concerns—some voices would say The Concern. One critic points out that from the opening
Wernher von Braun epigraph to the end of the novel,
death is so ubiquitous that its synonyms occur hundreds
of times.[20] As another critic puts it, "Death is the central
terror and mystery in *Gravity's Rainbow;* inability to deal
with it corrupts life."[21] This observation, however, can
be refined: "*Gravity's Rainbow* is obsessed with death.
And yet deaths (singular deaths, terminations, fulfill-
ments) are not narrated. They are sometimes reported
after they happen: the death of Tantivy Mucker-Maffick,

mass deaths in the [concentration] camps and in German Southwest Africa, the extinction of the Dodo."[22] Indeed, there are "both more bizarre weapons, such as the experimental sonic death mirror, and more common forms of killing, such as by bombardment and shooting, as well as constant reference to death in the abstract. There are, however, hardly any actual corpses in the novel, since what is significant is less the 'mere' brutal fact of death, than people's attitudes toward death."[23] Of the relatively major characters, only Bianca and Pudding actually die; Gottfried can be presumed to die, but the narrator leaves him hanging at the zero point of his trajectory's slope. The spectators at the Orpheus Theatre are also only one delta-t away from annihilation, but they have time to reach out, even to sing.

Death lies behind many of the other oppositions. Control would not be so obsessively sought if it were not held to prevent all sorts of death, except that from old age. Since we cannot simply opt for life without death, the mediating term must help us accept death into our lives. This is what religions try to do (as Leach points out), and many mythologies try to make death palatable. Pynchon certainly leaves open the possibility of afterlife: Blobadjian makes the transition, and no spiritualist medium intrudes between him and the reader to allow skeptics to doubt his fictive "reality"; Brigadier Pudding and Peter Sachsa also reappear post-mortem, albeit via medium. Pynchon's often freakish portrayals of the dead, however, make most readers prefer to take them figuratively when possible. Not figurative, though, is his presentation of a solution: the shedding of the fear of death, insofar as that is possible. This seems to be one of the characteristics of those who accept their own preterition. The more one concentrates on the present, the less one worries about the future. Most of the characters do not court death, and they try to avoid it when the threat arises, but they do not live their lives gnawing their nails—or don't do so once they have learned to focus their attention. Leni faces death in the street riots, but relaxes into the groove.

How people are to shed the anxiety about death is not clear, even as it is unclear how man can be persuaded to be free but responsible. Pynchon sets up no machinery for inculcating the masses. Some of his characters shed their fear through reducing the ego-albatross; others, like Roger, through devoting themselves to a cause and accepting their own status as losers; others, like Gottfried and Pudding, through submission (another form of reducing the ego). Fear of death is one key to our craving for ICBMs, for the arsenal of overkill, for our obsession with the means of death. All the energies going into that fear are deflected from the enjoyment of life. Accepting preterition is in part accepting mortality, and with that acceptance comes a form of freedom.

A variation on acceptance as a kind of mediation is to be found in Pynchon's handling of the opposition between life within the cycle of nature and life outside the cycle, of that between humankind and the machine. Examples of people living within the cycles of nature are the inhabitants of the Kirghiz Steppes and of Southwest Africa. Early in his career, Enzian indeed wants to return his people to a life outside of time and history (p. 319).

Life outside the cycle appears in many forms. Weissmann describes one, in the desire for transformation:

"I want to break out—to leave this cycle of infection and death. I want to be taken in love: so taken that you and I, and death, and life, will be gathered, inseparable, into the radiance of what we would become" (p. 724). Pökler too wants to leave the earth, to transcend (p. 400). For both, the rocket becomes the means. To chemists in the dye industry, new synthetic compounds provide a means for departing from cyclical nature. Those who devote their talents to violating the cycle do not see their actions as evil, but they hide from reality, even in little ways: log paper is something that Pökler found useful "for taming the terror of exponential curves into the linear, the safe" (p. 414).

Though Slothrop wonders if we can retrace our steps to the timeless, Pynchon appears to deny that possibility. Western culture, at least, has fallen into time and linearity, and battens on technology. Such, furthermore, has been its drive to colonize that Kirghiz tribes and Hereros alike are all being forced into time. Besides, the attention Pynchon lavishes on technology is not a labor of hatred; he appears to love Brennschluss capacitors as well as trees. Insofar as he offers some kind of middle state between cycles and linearity, it seems to be the necessity for making intelligent choices at various cusps of history.[24] If we have precipitated ourselves into time, we must do the best we can to guide developments and to retract mistakes, repair their damage, and dismantle the systems that perpetuate those mistakes: "And at least the physical things They have taken, from Earth and from us, can be dismantled, demolished—returned to where it all came from" (p. 540). Pynchon offers no formula for acting correctly at cusps but does suggest that there are gaps in "stone determinacy" if we wish to avail ourselves of them. And these cusps must be faced on an individual level rather than be left to the political.

The opposition between humanity and the machine resolves itself similarly. We would not give up technology even if we could. We love what machines and our technologies can do for us, and Herero existence offers Western culture no attractions. We are fallen into time, but we show no inclination to try to trim our coat to fit our cloth. Pynchon does not outline any direct resolution here: indeed, he uses this as the paradigm for the opposition we are not resolving. Theoretically, though, we have the same choice as above: to accept our obsession but exercise intelligent choices so as to improve our chances of survival. Pynchon seems bleakly pessimistic on this point—he shows Liebestod rather than sensible accommodation and reasonable self-limitation—but the cusps are there for technology as well as for any other historical development.

This leaves a final basic opposition: This Side and The Other. In this instance, Pynchon is not so much pushing a middle term as he is trying to get us to recognize the existence of one of the extremes. Our culture identifies This Side as the only reality that matters, which, Pynchon implies, causes us to cherish a badly distorted notion of our circumstances. Phenomena that belong to the Other Side get ignored, repressed, or misinterpreted. The dichotomy is not one of good and bad (few of Pynchon's are), for the Other Side is not morally any better or more enlightened than This, as his quips about bureaucratization and Qlippoth suggest. But he is insisting that the Other exists and that its existence makes nonsense of all one-side-oriented thinking. Hence we must start by accepting the Other Side as a concept (even as we must accept death and preterition), and then we must find a mode of operation that takes both sides into account. The mediating terms for this antinomy seem to be those individuals who are "open" to the phenomena of the Other Side and who form a bridge between the two sides. Such openness, again, is not automatically creditable or admirable by a traditional moral standard. Many of the open characters (Carroll Eventyr and Gavin Trefoil, for instance) seem but poorly able to cope with everyday life. Nor does openness guarantee reward, since both Gottfried and Bianca are open. This Other Side is beyond good or evil, so increasing the contact with it does not make life more pleasant. If there is another side, however, then no philosophy or attitude that fails to take it into account can have any claim to represent reality, and hence any validity. In a cumulative rather than a moralistic fashion, we might hope for improvements as bridges become more common and as humanity bases more of its actions on a more complete model of reality.

Gravity's Rainbow is riddled with such oppositions, and critical response to them varies. Some critics see *Gravity's Rainbow* as working dialectically. Others insist that the reconciliation of opposites is absent from the book, adding variously that Pynchon gives us unlimited freedom or a maze of dead ends. Maybe, as Leach and Lévi-Strauss argue, the tendency to divide our world into oppositions is a fundamental characteristic of the human mind. However, these divisions are inadequate to reality, and myth acknowledges this inadequacy through its construction of mediations. Pynchon too tries to force a space between, in which further alternatives are possible.[25] Riding the interface is one of his metaphors for such a balancing act. So far as I can see, he is not saying that such a course eliminates the extremes. Control is a fact of Western life, probably of all human life. Breaking out of the cycle and into time is probably not reversible, and very few would wish to return to an entirely cyclical, nontechnological life, even if it were possible. Death cannot be eliminated. Paranoia and antiparanoia both remain useful ways of approaching reality. For reasons such as these, I feel that at the center of Pynchon's world there is some positive content, some values, and not just pure void.

Not surprisingly, given his premises, this positive content falls short of being a ringing manifesto. Some of the mediating answers seem weak or idealistic. Telling people to accept preterition and not be afraid of death may be excellent advice, but it is not easy for us to act upon. Kindness seems a very low-keyed answer in a culture that believes in passionate love and crusading fervor. Self-imposed limits have a poor history of being observed. But then if there were easy answers to the problems of death or control, humankind would have found them long ago.

Through several of his characters, Pynchon illustrates an openness, an undemanding flexibility, that seems to increase chances of species survival without making survival a matter of destroying others. In his cosmos, fitness is flexibility, not readiness to use tooth and claw; it does not exult in aggressiveness, nor live barricaded against fears. Pynchon's openness allows great individual variation and any arrangement that avoids too great an element of control. This is not the Western pattern, so it seems spineless and shiftless to many, but for all the lack of rules, Pynchon's attitude toward cusps and his sympathies for children suggest that he does not just advocate passive drift. How much commitment is necessary, though, cannot be dictated, and he makes no effort to do so. Such commitment must come from the individual, or so the mediations he shows seem to indicate.

If we look back at the major redundancies, we find some correspondence between their concerns and those of the oppositions and mediations. Fear of the rocket and sensitivity to revelation from the sky tie in with the death dichotomies and with the This Side/Other Side organization of reality. The repeated albatrosses of self must be plucked to some extent if one is to achieve freedom from fear. The insight into the Them-reality shared by several characters relates to the elect/preterite and control/freedom oppositions. The behavior of companionable pigs gives us one example of acceptance of preterition and helps us create a space between preterition and election. Sexual congress with the rocket defines one form of thanatos, the many other sexual redundancies help outline eros. The displays of kindness from those who have loved make us focus on that quality. I could continue listing redundancies, but the point, I hope, is clear. The repeated episodes that turn up in several lives are essentially all concerned with the major values of the book, as are those defined by the oppositions. This is what one would expect from any complex work, whether mythological or not—but the aptness of the congruences at least suggests the continued usefulness of considering the story as mythology, for techniques evolved in that field may help us further untangle meanings and values in this difficult text.

4

Mythology and the Individual

The Schwarzgerät is no Grail, Ace. . . .
and you are no knightly hero. . . .

MYTHOLOGIES MEASURE THE UNIVERSE in
human terms, telling us what stature and powers
humankind can claim. For patterns upon which to model
individual action, we have the component myths. Many
of the latter follow the hero monomyth pattern, the story
of the hero with a thousand faces, as Joseph Campbell
calls it.[1] Indeed, the monomyth story seems to transcend
the cultures specific to various mythologies. Much the
same pattern can be found in *Gilgamesh,* in the lives of
biblical patriarchs, in Greek heroic legends, in gnostic
fables about Sophia, in stories about Beowulf or King
Arthur, in saints' lives, in Native American legends, and
in subcontinental Indian myths. One of the most original
elements of Pynchon's mythography is his refusal to accept this almost universal hero monomyth. Instead, he
offers us a new pattern for the individual, one compatible with his nonlinear cosmos.

Perhaps few writers hitherto have jettisoned the monomyth because it is the pattern of initiation and bildung, the pattern whereby youth becomes adult and the individual becomes confirmed in selfhood. Though many subtle variations and displacements exist within realistic fiction, one sees the pattern undisguised in various kinds of popular literature, such as folktale, romance, science fiction, and fantasy.

The story begins with initial equilibrium: the hero is at peace with the world or is just a child, cossetted and untried. Then a call to adventure disturbs the equilibrium. The hero may be victimized (as many folktale children are by wicked relatives) or may willingly undertake a dangerous adventure (Beowulf, the Red Cross Knight). In either event, the hero crosses a threshold into a special world where the normal rules of action are no longer adequate. In folktales, romances, and science fiction, the special world is usually the habitat of magic or supernatural forces, whether the marginalized realm of the Danish fens in *Beowulf*, or another planet in science fiction. Within this world, the hero carries out his quest or quests (Parsifal), faces his test or tests (Sir Gawain), and then usually crosses another threshold out, subsequently becoming established back in human society, often as a leader. Sometimes the culminating test proves to be self-sacrifice, and the hero gives his life to save others, but more commonly, the hero reaps such rewards as a spouse, wealth, power, wisdom, and social success. Occasionally, one finds less complacent acceptance of social success as the ultimate good, in which case the reward will be spiritual illumination of some sort, but most monomyth stories basically uphold and justify society. A few villains may need to be evicted to make way for the hero, but once such cleansing has taken place, the society will continue, strengthened by its acquisition of the hero's support.[2]

The same pattern informs many initiation rituals, there the special world of the trial or test is often linked symbolically to the land of the dead, while the two equilibria at beginning and end correspond to childhood and adulthood. The pattern of heroic development corresponds to the formation and centering of the ego that takes place as we reach adulthood. Indeed, the symbolic actions and situations that Campbell discerns in heroic legends correspond very closely to the sequence of psychic archetypes that Erich Neumann hypothesizes for the development of the self.[3]

Such heroes or heroines offer models—either allegorical or literal—for imitation. Bruno Bettelheim discusses the ways in which fairy tales encourage children to believe that they can survive experiences that cause them great anxiety, that the witch-mother can be destroyed and that the good mother will return.[4] Catholic children are enjoined to imitate saints. Adolescents daydream of themselves in the roles of heroes they see on television or at the cinema. By absorbing such material, they learn that one should aspire to rescue damsels, rather than rob and rape them; that one should not bully the elderly and the weak; and that one should be willing to suffer for a worthy cause. The trappings of the hero monomyth change with era, class, and culture, so that the hero may be a peasant, a tailor's son, a knight, or a space engineer, depending on the version, but the events making up the pattern and its basic values have remained remarkably constant over the centuries. For Pynchon to challenge its affirmative, society- and action-oriented assumptions is therefore radical, and that he deconstructs the traditional hero and offers an alternative is noteworthy. To our culture, the developmental pattern of the hero monomyth is not just the norm; it is assumed to be inherent, natural, inescapable. Pynchon, by upholding an alternative, argues that this perdurable pattern is actually historical, accidental, and culturally limited.

Although I propose to analyze parallels between Slothrop and such figures as Goethe's Faust, I am not at all interested in traditional problems of source and influence. Rather, I want to show the many kinds of hero models Pynchon invokes—faustian, wagnerian, juvenile, and orphic—and want to determine which characteristics he deems valuable and which he discredits and discards. Because his recasting of the hero pattern is so original, Pynchon has no terminology or conceptual framework in common with his audience. Qualities he valorizes can only be described in negatives within the existing discourse on the heroic. Hence, he relies heavily on definition by negation: when Slothrop and Faust are paired, we see that the new hero does not have this or that traditional quality. Pynchon brings us to reject the conventional characteristics by mockingly distorting the famous avatars of the heroic. Each one, to be sure, makes some positive contribution to Pynchon's new model, but mostly we are made to see these heroes' inadequacy when measured against Pynchon's explosively fragmented cosmos. After seeing Pynchon's uses and abuses of these traditional culture heroes, we will be more sensitive to the qualities he upholds in his new hero pattern. To our monomyth-shaped minds, openness, kindness, acceptance of preterition, and responsiveness to the Other

Side seem terribly evanescent and fragile, but Pynchon organizes them into a structured model, so we can consider his proposition for its validity as a whole. If it has no survival value, we can justifiably reject both the new model for individual action and Pynchon's philosophy in general. Here, as in the issue of the Other Side, readers will divide on whether they are willing to accept—or feel compelled to reject—fundamental values in the argument of *Gravity's Rainbow*.

Several branches of knowledge have contributed to the decline in our ability to believe in heroes, real or literary. Psychology, by positing an unconscious realm beyond the control of our conscious selves, undercuts the traditional picture of the hero: ostensible motives are no longer the real ones, so the heroism becomes suspect. When selfless sacrifice becomes self-immolation to the uncontrolled internalizations of parental figures, when chastity is interpretable as neurotic anxiety, when a taste for danger and violence are no longer accepted as altogether sane, then the hero stories change their meaning. Sociology too has made the individual negligible. The very notion of an individual is problematic when one tries to evaluate the significance of environmental and hereditary factors. The effects of class and social expectations undermine the credibility of free will and personal responsibility. Whole societies become mere statistics, and the eccentricities of individuals cancel each other out to reinforce the average profile. History also suggests that entire races can be exterminated and become only so many numbers in history books. Belief in the importance of the individual wanes as fewer individuals achieve recognition such that they are remembered even a decade later.

The weaknesses of the hero monomyth as literary structure have not passed unnoticed either. Indeed, the concept of the hero has been under fire on all fronts. A. J. Greimas and Roland Barthes have dismantled standard assumptions about heroes as literary conventions. Greimas focuses on the series of acts performed by various actants that takes us from the initial to the final equilibrium of a narrative; one unified and unifying character thus disintegrates into numerous fragmentary actions, not all performed by a single person. Barthes treats the connective sequence between opening and closing tableaux as a black box transformation, to be analyzed as a sequence, not as quasi-biography. Fredric Jameson, discussing literary romances, discredits the hero category yet further, replacing the hero with "'states' or world configurations: characters would then be understood as so many 'actants' and their deeds as so many properties in the complex mechanism which effectuate a transition from one state to the next; while romance as a whole would be seen as a sequence of what, following Wagnerian opera, we may call 'transformation scenes.' "[5] The hero as integrating focus for a work of literature has fallen on hard times.

Given such corrosion eating away at the concept of the hero, it is no wonder that Pynchon chose to rethink the model for individual action in his mythic cosmos. As I shall try to demonstrate, he goes about constructing his new model from two sets of material: from fragments detached from traditional monomythic heroes, and from the episodes within his own plot where characters map onto each other. Slothrop has very little character at all, and much of what passes for personality is actually constructed through a system of allusions to various kinds of hero from both the American and the European cultural traditions.[6] The concept labeled "Slothrop" in the reader's mind changes when one of these analogues supervenes. This "Slothrop" concept expands and alters in a series of ovidian metamorphoses as Slothrop is refocused by each comparison to such heroes as Faust, Tannhäuser, Dorothy, Rocketman's comicbook confrères, the pig-god Plechazunga, John Dillinger, and Orpheus, to name only the most prominent. Taken all together, the heroes alluded to give us a range of traditional heroic possibilities: young and adult, male and female, ancient and modern, European and American, muscle-bound and spiritual. Repeatedly we are invited to see Slothrop as part of this system of heroic figures, and our first reaction in most instances is likely to be that he falls very short of their standards of heroism. He is no Galahad or Superman. Second and third reactions, however, force us to realize that he does resemble some of these heroes in fragmentary ways, and, more important, that the traditional heroes themselves are inadequate to the reality with which Slothrop has to cope. They are not, in truth, ideals whom Slothrop should be striving to imitate.

In addition to Slothrop, of course, we have an array of other characters, and what tends to stick most in our minds are those traits that are shared by several of them. Much of what we remember about Pirate or Enzian, Gottfried or Ilse, are the points at which they map onto somebody else, and especially onto Slothrop. Insofar as these characters are separable, they suffer different fates and follow somewhat different life patterns, but as their intermapped characteristics and experiences solidify and grow more prominent in the course of the novel, individual differences fade into the background. What we end up with are two sorts of composite heroic pattern. The first is made up of the traditional heroes to whom Slothrop is compared, and out of whose adventures his own take shape. The second consists of the intermappings. The former pattern tells us something about our own culture and about Western heroic dreams and concepts of the individual. It also contributes to our sense of Slothrop's "character" in both positive and negative ways. The latter, Pynchon's new pattern for the individual, constitutes an alternative, one more suited to the uncertain postmodern world projected in this novel.

Because Pynchon's new hero pattern is much the same as that which emerges from analyzing the redundancies and mediations in the mythology (examined in chapter 3), I shall here concentrate on the contrapuntal comparisons Pynchon carries out between Slothrop and traditional heroes. The Faust legend will be discussed first, partly because it is the first unquestionably to superimpose itself onto the events of 1944. I will then analyze wagnerian, juvenile, and orphic hero allusions. The last is particularly important because it is the least discredited and comes closest to the pattern Pynchon advocates for individuals in his cosmos. After seeing what Pynchon does with these patterns of the past, we can look more closely at the alternative he proposes to us in its stead.

Faust as Hero

The spirit of Faust hovers over *Gravity's Rainbow*, becoming an inescapable factor in our responses to Slothrop when Slothrop goes to the Brocken with a witch for a private Walpurgisnacht. Other parallels strengthen our sense that Pynchon is using the Faust story in this text. A Margherita (Greta, Gretel, Gretchen) complicates Slothrop's life. The mysterious Mothers recur, albeit in debased and punning forms, as in Marvy's Mothers, in Otto Gnahb's Mothers' conspiracy, and in the light-bulb sockets (called *Mutter* in German). The ambiguity of Slothrop's salvation or damnation at the end parallels the alternative endings to Faust's story within the European tradition. The obsessive nature of Faust's drive and quest, his selling his soul for he-knows-not-what to assuage an unendurable hunger, is generally relevant to the embedded critique of Western culture. One can indeed argue that Slothrop is an anti-Faust, and the faustian *warum?* becomes the rocket's varoom, the answer that is no answer to questions about the nature of reality.

Goethe's narrative can be said to have roughly four thematic concerns. One consists of Faust's relationship to reality. We see Faust's dissatisfaction with the quotidian surface of this world and Faust's explorations of alternative worlds in Auerbach's Tavern, in the Witch's Kitchen, on the Brocken, and at the classical Walpurgisnacht, to name only a few. The second theme concerns Faust's experiences with manifestations of the feminine: Margarete, the Mothers, and Helen. The third focuses on Faust's interactions with society, his experiments with political power, financial trickery, victory in war, and the reclamation of land from the sea. The fourth includes his death and postmortem vision of a transcendent reality. We learn something about Slothrop by comparing his adventures to these of Faust.

Faust's dissatisfaction stems from the apparent unknowability of reality ("dass wir nichts wissen können" [pt. 1, line 364]).[7] This destroys all delight, causing him to try magic to see if he can reach some understanding of the world. Upon opening Nostradamus's book, he experiences rapture when he sees the interconnectedness of everything in nature ("Wie alles sich zum Ganzen webt, / Eins in dem andern wirkt und lebt!" [pt. 1, lines 447–48]); but once discovered, these harmonies lose their power to excite him, and he is left to wonder how he can get at the eternal nature of reality. After having made common cause with Mephistopheles, he explores the tavern joy of intoxicated states of consciousness, the Witch's Kitchen where he is given the drink of youth, and the Brocken, where the roiling lechery disturbs him by its implicit relevance to his feelings for Margarete. Faust is spiritual kin to the modernist reader; he believes meaning to be "there" and thinks he can apply knowledge of various arcane sorts to discover this meaning. Pynchon's universe is even better calculated to frustrate and defeat him than is the universe Goethe provides.

Slothrop's dissatisfactions are the obverse of Faust's. They are roused not by discontent with everyday reality but by fears that it is not the only reality. He would prefer having to deal with just the one. He is goaded to action by the powerlessness of being controlled rather than by the desire to control. For him, the interconnectedness of everything holds no message of cosmic harmony but rather rouses paranoia. He experiences several irruptions of this superconnected world into his own disjointed reality. In the casino, for instance, he twice finds superimposed orders of existence (pp. 202, 208), and both these visions rouse fleeting repressed memories from infancy, tantalizing wisps of subconscious reality concerning his experience of being conditioned by Jamf.

In sum, Slothrop gradually discovers that other realities exist and that they make nonsense of his previous relationship to everyday existence. The new realities that reinterpret his life are based on money and control, the interests of IG Farben and its subsidiaries. In this reinterpreted reality, sex is not sex and war is not war. Ultimately, he senses dimly that the lust he feels is really aimed at rockets and technology, not at women, and that the war is really about buying and selling, not about ideals and dying. Like Faust, Slothrop is up against new definitions of what is real. Neither finds any rational answer satisfactory.

Corresponding in general ambience and location to the Witch's Kitchen and Walpurgisnacht are Slothrop's adventures in the Mittelwerke and the Brocken. The *Meerkätzchen* of the kitchen are paralleled by the subhuman workers of the Mittelwerke, the gnomes and the girls fantasized as having aluminum-shaving hair. Slothrop welcomes the cold bitter beer given him by the rocket-enamored Americans. It too is a drink of youth, German and American. The presiding witch is Major Marvy, who embodies not only American bondage to weaponry but also the racism (with its arrogance and insecurities) that will make rocket-obsession so dangerous to the rest of the world.

On the Brocken, Slothrop is rather luckier than Faust. Whereas Faust is increasingly angered by his deep dissatisfactions and finds the revelation of his lust's ugly side something he would rather not know, Slothrop reaches a more positive illumination. Like Faust, he is seeing what magic can tell, or rather *show* him—the Brockengespenst. Slothrop's private mythology of comicbook heroes has left him inadequately prepared for this magnificence: the Specter, as he first names his shadow, fades, but not before he and Geli have become Titans, trailing God-shadows, rainbows, and haloed shells. Her magic shows him an unknown dimension of himself, another reality only glimpsable at dawn with the sun at one's back. These special conditions echo those of Faust at the beginning of part 2:

> So bliebe denn die Sonne mir im Rücken!
> ....
>
> Allein wie herrlich, diesem Sturm erspriessend,
> Wölbt sich des bunten Bogens Wechseldauer,
> Bald rein gezeichnet, bald in Luft Zerfliessend,
> Umher verbreitend duftig kühle Schauer.
> D e r spiegelt ab das menschliche Bestreben.
> Ihm sinne nach, und du begreifst genauer:
> Am farbigen Abglanz haben wir das Leben.
> (pt. 2, lines 4715, 4721–27)[8]

Pynchon's rainbows are the ephemeral phenomena that irrupt into everyday reality between gravity and entropy, between zero and one, at Brennschluss, at moments of illumination, and at other instants that defy normal forces and sequences. From *Faust* and from Goethe's *Farbenlehre* we can recognize rainbows as manifestations of the observer's interactions with the cosmos, moments of more comprehensive and hence of truer apprehension of reality (according to Goethe) than Newton could reach by isolating the observer in absolute time and space. To Newton, rainbows were distortions to be removed from his telescope lenses; to Goethe, they were glimpses of the sacred center of things. In Pynchon, the rainbow reality has no necessary meaning beyond its own existence yet has an infinite number of potential meanings that emerge from the interaction between it and its observers, as *Gravity's Rainbow* demonstrates by associating rainbows with covenants, trajectories, moments of illumination, displays of color, optical phenomena, bridges to mythical lands, and conduits to the Other Side. Like the rainbow, reality is an infinite regression and hence unknowable. Both Faust and Slothrop are exposed to versions of this idea, and both assimilate the message only imperfectly.

Faust's concern with the feminine—Margarete, the Mothers, and Helen—again leads him to incomplete experience, to tumultuous feelings that find no fulfilling outlet, to beauty that ultimately cannot be possessed or coerced. In the course of his experiences, he seduces and does grave harm to Margarete, and he is blasted by the Mothers for trying to bend these molds or matrices of cosmic form to his own will. Faust is obsessed with control and Goethe seems to admire this drive, but in this adventure, even Goethe apparently feels that Faust goes too far. Throughout the classical Walpurgisnacht, he seeks beauty as potentially that aspect of universal order most likely to assuage his hunger. He learns, however, that serving Helen may give him experience with beauty but cannot give him endless enjoyment. The limitations of the human mind and body prevent his maintaining ecstasy. Like the homunculus, he must seek to evolve to a form capable of matching his spirit, for his present form cannot give him the joys he has sought any more than it could give continuous orgasm.

Slothrop's equivalent adventures also involve him with two women. Margherita Erdmann corresponds to Helen as a famous beauty (in this case, a pornographic movie star). Faust served his Helen with medieval formality and splendor; Slothrop satisfies his with the dark side of medieval life: dungeons and torture. Slothrop's beauty queen is decadent, murderously antisemitic, and predatory. For Goethe, beauty was a worthy if limited face for reality and a possible route of access to the divine essence behind that reality, but for Pynchon, beauty is no guarantee of worth. Slothrop's Bianca, on the other hand, is more like Faust's Gretchen: young and pathetic, her decadence more outward mannerism and costume than cast of mind. She offers her own form of salvation: "'We can get away. I'm a child, I know how to hide. I can hide you too'" (p. 470). As in *Faust,* an inability to respond to the young woman's needs results in her death.

The *Anubis* episode has something in common with the teutonic Walpurgisnacht (its focus on sexuality), and the early Brocken adventure partly resembles the classical witches' sabbath (in its awareness of the gap between physical limitations and the greater reality). Lest we miss the parallel between ship-orgy and its faustian prototype, the lyric welcoming the newcomers aboard mentions Walpurgisnacht (p. 436). The classical episode in Goethe shows the homunculus attempting to find a form appropriate to the powers of its spirit, and Slothrop's rainbowed vision lets him realize the inadequacy of bodily perceptions to the phenomena of reality. Pynchon's two goethian women and two Walpurgisnacht-like adventures thus mix the separate concerns of their original, but then his quests and concerns are not straight imitations of Goethe's. Treating beauty as an intrinsic good, or offering Slothrop salvation through love, are not on Pynchon's agenda. Neither platonic nor christian assumptions would be adequate to the complexities of life in the Zone.

Faust's mysterious Mothers are mockingly echoed in *Gravity's Rainbow*. Faust finds that the matrices of cosmic forms, that ultimate reality he once sought so passionately, now seem unsatisfying because they offer merely platonic ideals like beauty rather than an embodiment of them that he can grasp and incorporate into his life. The various "Mothers" Slothrop meets are already parts of his life and self, and unwelcome parts at that. Marvy's Mothers are the drunk and ribald soldiers hymning erotic attachment to technology, one of the obvious matrices of Slothrop's life. Otto Gnahb's theory of the Mother Conspiracy ironically caricatures the American momism from which Slothrop has suffered.

Faust's journey to the sacred location of the Mothers also has its equivalent in the raid on Peenemünde, holy center of rocketry. As Kappel puts it, "The ellipse of Test Stand VII is the black hole for Slothrop, his birthplace as the rocket. When Slothrop penetrates the ellipse he is the '1' penetrating the '0,' simultaneous annihilation, consummation, conception. He is the penis entering the vagina, the sperm bombarding the egg, the body returning to earth."[9] He returns to his matrix, to his assembly and his time's assembly and does not recognize the implications for the nature of political and cultural reality. In making the birthplace of the rocket the matrix of the era and of technological humankind, Pynchon challenges the platonic abstractions about reality that contented previous generations.

Faust's political dealings with society are characterized by the financial sleight of hand he performs as court magician, but he develops an interest in more lasting benefits—peace and land. The picture of the new settlement on reclaimed land so enchants him that he proclaims an ultimate vision:

> Das ist der Weisheit letzter Schluss:
> Nur der verdient sich Freiheit wie das Leben,
> Der täglich sie erobern muss.
> ....
>
> Solch ein Gewimmel möcht' ich sehn,
> Auf freiem Grund mit freiem Volke stehn.
> Zum Augenblicke dürft' ich sagen:
> Verweile doch, du bist so schön!
> (pt. 2, lines 11574−76; 11579−82)[10]

Freedom that must be consciously grasped anew each day: this, lived by an entire culture, is Faust's supreme earthly insight, one that produces conditional contentment if not absolute satisfaction.

Slothrop's equivalent adventures consist of sleight of hand in the black market, activities with counterfeit money, and his stint as Plechazunga. Freedom for him, however, is more complex: he preserves it, but not through the assertive stance praised by Goethe. Slothrop experiences freedom rather through openness and relative passivity. With his reacquired harmonica, he gradually lets go of anxieties, quests, and questions: "Slothrop, just suckin' on his harp, is closer to being a spiritual medium than he's been yet, and he doesn't even know it" (p. 622). He wins freedom from the individual will, the albatross of self. He loses the distinction between self and other, and *becomes* a crossroads, a living intersection (p. 625). He becomes pure object, defined by

interactions with his context and observers. He achieves
not heaven, but a wraith-like existence in the Zone. As
many critics have noted, his solution, as a political statement, is purely personal and cannot serve the entire
culture. Some have argued that Pynchon is offering
Slothrop as negative example while insinuating that what
we do need is the faustian freedom affirmed everyday,
at every cusp.[11] Slothrop, however, does make some decisions and take some actions, as do Roger, Katje, Pökler,
and Enzian, but the decisions and actions do not resemble those demanded by the traditional heroic pattern,
so pass virtually unnoticed.

To sum up, Goethe's Faust (if not the traditional
damned Faust) more or less follows the hero monomyth
pattern. Equilibrium turns to discontent; he enters into
a new world and undertakes a series of quest ventures
in which he acts many roles. Ultimately, he is saved.
Goethe's subject is a man with immense cravings for
meaning, purpose, power, knowledge, and achievement,
values upheld by Western civilization. Pynchon deliberately invokes this image and causes it to float along
beside Slothrop, letting the two comment on each other.
Faust's lust for control seems more ugly and more futile
in the context of Pynchon's cosmos; the platonic world
picture implicit in the Mothers seems ludicrous as an
explanation for the Zone. The possibility of salvation
and conventional heaven would seem grotesque if offered to Slothrop in Niederschaumdorf. Indeed, it seems
childishly simple compared to the complex Other Side.
Faust as an appropriate model for Western culture is
rendered even more suspect as we realize that Slothrop
undergoes several experiences similar to Faust's without
all of Faust's strenuous effort. Faust glorying in the new

village and Slothrop enjoying the rainbow conspicuously remain the active versus the passive, but their moments of pure happiness seem similarly fleeting yet complete. As far as earthly experience goes, there is little to distinguish between what the two men accomplish, for many of Faust's accomplishments are spurious, and little differentiates their experiences of happiness. We are used to respecting Faust, with his drive and determination, as a romantic avatar of our culture, but in fact his drive gains him no more satisfaction than Slothrop's flexible drifting gains for him—and this is surely an interesting comment on Pynchon's part. Faust's range of experience is his greatest contribution to Pynchon's melting-pot hero; his other attributes are for the most part roundly rejected.

Wagnerian Heroes

Given Pynchon's immersion in the German cultural tradition, the presence of wagnerian heroes is predictable. There are echoes of *Der Fliegender Hollander*'s homeless ship in the *Anubis* episode, including a proffered innocent love not fully accepted. More generally, the ring made from the Rhinemaidens' gold becomes Kekulé's benzene ring, whose power over the world consists of organic chemistry and the power of synthesis. One must renounce love to gain the power of these respective rings, but all too many men find that a tolerable exchange.[12] Both the *Ring* and the novel, furthermore, are stories constructed about *things*—ring and rocket—and characters exist and are significant only as they interact with that thing. Wagner's characters ultimately fail to achieve redemption on account of their lack of love or compassion or because of their inability to renounce individual will.[13] Similarly, the weakness of Western culture depicted in *Gravity's Rainbow* has been attributed to these same failures.[14] The recurring dwarves, gnomes, midgets, and pygmies who appear in such unlikely droves sometimes resemble the Nibelungs, an elvish race of preterite workers who must slave for those with power. The working out of the ring's curse, up to and including the destruction of the palace of the Gods and its rainbow bridge, are apocalyptic, as is Pynchon's subject matter. While certain details bespeak a general wagnerian influence (the murder of Anton Webern is called, for example, a Götterdämmerung [p. 441]), it is not the heroes from the *Ring* cycle who appear in Pynchon's system of traditional heroes, but Tannhäuser and, via allusions to the grail, Parsifal. These two paradigms of heroic action let Slothrop measure himself, and let us measure him.

Tannhäuser is not very heroic, and for this reason he is frequently invoked in conjunction with Slothrop. The likeness serves Pynchon in two ways: (1) it shows a man enslaved by a love that does him no good, and (2) it shows a man unable to commit himself to serious human love. The two are not contradictory, because the enslavement is to Frau Holda or the V-2, neither one being human. The world under the mountain of the Mittelwerke is a temple to this nonhuman love, and Pynchon introduces us into the sanctum with the comment that "there is that not-so-rare personality disorder known as Tannhäuserism. Some of us love to be taken under mountains, and not always with horny expectations—Venus, Frau Holda, her sexual delights—no, many come, actually, for the gnomes, the critters smaller than you" (p. 299).

In the Mittelwerke, the Nibelung-like gnomes toil to assemble rockets that were as much designed to rule the world as were Alberich's treasures. Under this mountain, rocket lovers sing of their love not in the minnesinger idiom but by declaiming their gross and grisly limericks to a well-known tune. Slothrop sums up his experience here, saying, "But what you've done is put yourself on somebody else's voyage—some Frau Holda, some Venus in some mountain—playing her, its game . . . you know that in some irreducible way it's an evil game. You play because you have nothing better to do, but that doesn't make it right. And where is the Pope whose staff's gonna bloom for you?" (p. 364). Here his whole quest for V-2 information is called in question, but before he has thought this through, Slothrop takes on a new personality and transforms his relationship to his quest by becoming Rocketman. The very name, however, reminds us of his special erotic bondage to rocket technology. He was the infant conditioned in Jamf's experiment to respond sexually to some synthetic stimulus, perhaps Imipolex G, and he apparently retains this inappropriate, nonhuman sexual taste. His nonhuman love is directed toward technology and the V-2 instead of Frau Holda.

Tannhäuser's failure to commit himself firmly to a human love also marks Slothrop's personal relationships. Much is made of the unlikely liaison with Bianca, as if what she offers Slothrop is qualitatively different from the emotions of his other sexual contacts. Intercourse with her produces a visionary ejaculation equated with being launched in a rocket; however, the narrator remarks, "The Pope's staff is always going to remain barren, like Slothrop's own unflowering cock" (p. 470). The Tannhäuser lyric (pp. 532–33) describes a chilling spiritual void; not only can its modernized Tannhäuser not believe in the powers of papal absolution, he cannot find himself any more—"No song, no lust, no memory, no guilt: / No pentacles, no cups, no holy Fool. . . . " Despite Tannhäuser's flaws, however, Wagner deems him worthy of salvation. Since salvation, in Pynchon's Puritan terms, equates with election, we do not find Slothrop rewarded in that fashion. He misses the Pope's messenger (p. 619) and is transformed into an orphic figure, a musician whose subject matter passes beyond Tannhäuser's eroticism into mystic oneness with nature.[15]

Wagner's treatment of the Parsifal story is less specifically relevant to *Gravity's Rainbow* than is the grail legend in general. Wagner exalts the spiritual education of Parsifal, the process that justifies his becoming the Grail King. Slothrop too is a holy fool, but his education does not groom him to become one of Them. Medieval versions of the grail legend pay more attention to the mysterious object of the quest, the grail, and it is the grail to which Pynchon refers frequently. Pynchon's Zone, moreover, bears some relationship to the wasteland myth that was developed in Old French branches of the tale.[16] The wasteland setting, questing fool, and the mystic object make their presence felt in the novel, but the holiness and spiritual transcendence of Wagner only tantalizes us—and Slothrop—as an absence, as a felt ideal, impossible of attainment and ultimately misguided.

Even had Pynchon never mentioned the grail, critics would have associated Slothrop with the grail-seeker because of his obsessive quest. The narrator, however, makes the connection when he mentions "the 'S-Gerät' Slothrop thinks he's chasing like a grail" (p. 275). Later, Slothrop himself ruefully admits, "The Schwarzgerät is no Grail, Ace, that's not what the G in Imipolex G stands for. And you are no knightly hero" (p. 364). Slothrop learns from Greta Erdmann about "a heavy chalice of methyl methacrylate, a replica of the Sangraal" (p. 487) and about the wasteland she found herself in after her Imipolex G orgy at the castle of this grail: "Nothing grew there. Something had been deposited in a great fan that went on for miles. Some tarry kind of waste" (p. 488).

Slothrop's tenuous relationship to Parsifal is extended by references to tarot cards. In the Tannhäuser lyric, the void left by song, lust, memory, and guilt is also noted as an absence of Cups and Fool. We learn (p. 742) that Slothrop may now be contributing an accompaniment to the music of an English rock group named The Fool, and he is last seen in Niederschaumdorf, where a convocation of village idiots is assembling. The associations of Slothrop with holy fool thus grow more frequent as the sequence of Parsifal references develops. What we find lacking is the transformation that Wagner's Parsifal achieves. Slothrop went to a holy center and failed to ask the right questions. Parsifal's initial failure stemmed from his lack of compassion. That same lack arguably kept Slothrop from committing himself to Bianca, and it may limit his responses and awareness when he comes to the birthplace of the rocket, of himself, and of his time. This lack would be symbolically appropriate for technological humankind. Insofar as kingship is a form of control, though, Parsifal's end could not rightly be Slothrop's; Slothrop's education is in riding the inter-

faces and in opening himself to experience and to random changes.

As with Pynchon's references to Faust, we sense a
certain mockery of the wagnerian style of exalted hero.
What Pynchon most seems to value, ironically, is their
lack of slick competence. It makes them akin to the preterite, facing the rigid systems represented by the minnesinger knights of the Wartburg and the company of
the grail. Despite the fact that their prowess and warrior
status considerably exceed Slothrop's, they would have
had no better spiritual tools than Slothrop for dealing
with the complete freedom of the Zone. Their grandiose
self-dramatization is a far cry from Slothrop's easy-come
easy-go attitude, but that I take to be part of Pynchon's
point. Immense striving, emotions torn to tatters by the
winds of passion, and shrieking despair do not gain any
more happiness or ensure any more competence than
do harmonica ditties, insouciance, and a rainbow.

Juvenile Hero Patterns

A number of Slothrop's analogues are heroes and heroines from tales enjoyed by children and adolescents.
The common denominator of these stories is their
freudian content: all embody fantasies that allow young
audiences to deal with aggressive feelings toward their
parents and other authority figures. Three basic configurations are present. The first, the hero as victim, embodies anxieties felt in very early stages of childhood:
Hansel and Gretel, for instance, experience the fear of
being eaten, an oral-stage anxiety. The second configuration—the hero as savior, whether village pig-god or
comic-book superhero—allows audiences of Freud's

phallic stage to assuage worries. Dreams of omnipotence and flying (exemplified by the comicbook heroes) are characteristic fantasies of this level of psychic development.[17] Protagonists may be nominally adult and have no visible parents to struggle with, but they spend their time battling villains who obviously are parental meanies, and these heroes can congratulate themselves on the righteousness of their cause when they save society from such criminals. The last configuration, the hero as rebel, embodies the ideals of discontented older adolescents. In Slothrop's fantasy of the Floundering Four, we see a direct oedipal rebellion against parents who literally try to destroy him. In more displaced rebel stories, the unresolvable conflicts are projected onto other authority figures; thus the electric cartel is Byron the Bulb's oppressor, and the FBI fills that role for the outlaw John Dillinger.

Hansel and Gretel, Lewis Carroll's Alice, and Dorothy, heroine of the Oz books, are all models of victims. Hansel and Gretel are potent figures in Pynchon's cosmos, and they appear associated with characters other than Slothrop as well. Roger and Jessica see a sinister Christmas pantomime about them (pp. 174–75); Gottfried and Katje consciously assume these folktale identities when playing out their rituals of bondage, with Weissmann as witch (pp. 94–96, 102). The Kinderofen—the ultimate threat to the children's survival—emerges repeatedly when Pynchon describes the wartime plight of the young; it becomes a code word for the effect of war and the Third Reich on children. Gottfried's rocket is "the Oven we fattened you for" (p. 751).

Even before Faust's power as hero-model enriches the narrative with its counterpoint to Slothrop's melody, Hansel has made an impression on the Slothropian tabula rasa. Slothrop and Darlene are fed candies by peculiar Mrs. Quoad, who cheerfully admits to being an "outright witch" (p. 115). This culinary tour de force, "the Disgusting English Candy Drill," puts Slothrop in a position of indulging a childish greed for sweets (however unsatisfying he finds them). That overtone of childishness and greed (later shown for women) continues to be part of his character and of our evaluation of him.

Alice and Dorothy are rather minor adjuncts to Slothrop's career, but they have made their presence felt, as critics' comments attest. Slothrop's descent down the Roseland toilet bowl serves as a reminder of Alice's abrupt descent down the rabbit hole, if only because such precipitate, impossible, and claustrophobic descents are unusual. Out of all the beauties at the Perlimpinpin party, Slothrop chooses to associate with one who looked "like Tenniel's Alice, same forehead, nose, hair" (p. 247). He carries a chessman as identity token for dealing with Der Springer, and life in the Zone is likened to chess several times (pp. 376, 417–18, 494, 563). On the *Anubis,* inflamed by the beauty of a young girl, Slothrop wakes up to remember bits of a dream in which Alice's "White Rabbit's been talking to Slothrop, serious and crucial talk, but on the way up to waking he loses it all, as usual" (p. 468). His quasi-Carrollian attraction to children is a notable feature of his sexual preferences. Like Alice, he lives in a world of threat and of rules turned upside down, but unlike her, he does not strive to reach a position of authority. Her adaptability is a positive contribution to his behavior options, but her desire for power is negative.

Dorothy enters more frequently. The Zone, like Oz, is a psychic landscape, partly a projection of the protagonist's inner life.[18] Dorothy's famous line in the movie, "Toto, I have a feeling we're not in Kansas any more," is the epigraph for book 3, "In the Zone." As one of the constellation of hero-models, she first appears on the Brocken, where Slothrop thinks of his ancestress as "not, like young skipping Dorothy's antagonist, a mean witch" (p. 329). Slothrop is also exhorted to follow the yellow brick road in one of his dopester adventures in which the weirdness of the Oz landscape is a kindly version of the landscapes being experienced by the inhabitants of the Zone (pp. 596–97). Like Dorothy, he wishes upon stars and responds to rainbows. Dorothy's presence is perhaps strongest where it is implicit: when we think of her, we remember her desire to get back to Kansas, despite its dullness compared to Oz and despite the emotional shortcomings of her aunt and uncle. But there is no easy way from Oz to Kansas for her, and no way at all from the Zone to America for Slothrop.[19] The optimism and innocence of American fairytales makes Dorothy's return inevitable, but such popular mythology of the American sort has little power in the Zone, and love of America, Mom, and apple pie looks less innocent to Pynchon than to Baum. Slothrop plucks many feathers of memory, but "his fingers always brush by [. . .] America. Poor Asshole, he can't let her go. She's whispered *love me* too often to him in his sleep, vamped insatiably his waking attention with come-hitherings, incredible promises" (p. 623).

The heroes belonging to the savior configuration include Rocketman, Plasticman, and Plechazunga in particular, but they also include the many referred to in passing: Superman, the Specter, the Shadow, the Spirit, the Lone Ranger, Captain Midnight, Zorro, the Green

Hornet, and Hap Harrigan. Each one has a special, almost invincible strength or ability. Each exists outside the main patterns of society, often to be invoked as a semidivine force, rather than as husband, father, and neighbor. Each fights evildoers gratis, simply out of belief in law and order. Typically, each rescues the helpless from villains. Slothrop assumes such a role as Plechazunga, first in ritual, then in shambling earnest. Insofar as he is helping the preterite against forces of control, this seems like reasonable and even useful action, and Pynchon's positive pig symbolism colors this episode.

Rocketman, however, illustrates some of the dangers of such saviors. Within two hours of playfully assuming this guise, Slothrop is beguiled into undertaking dangerous forays on the ground that no ordinary person could succeed but that Rocketman could. Rocketman's famous "howdy" becomes known to Zone inhabitants of all nationalities. Tchitcherine will recognize him in Peenemünde; Džabajev knows him in Niederschaumdorf; Säure Bummer and Der Springer—upper echelon black marketeers—deal with him as a person to be reckoned with. Pig Bodine, after first thinking the pig-suited wanderer is a fake, drops all his other concerns to help Rocketman. Slothrop even finds graffiti devoted to himself in that guise. Slothrop naturally glories in all this attention and in the unwonted success he enjoys in his role. It stirs his albatross of self. But Rocketman is a machine/man hybrid. The very enjoyment of technology, the pleasure at creating and using it, is all too seductive, and Slothrop has no intellectual or moral standard by which to evaluate this marriage of human with machine.

We find similar warnings in Slothrop's partial identification with Plasticman, another human/technology hybrid. Plastic was used to condition Slothrop and helped to make him the piece of hardware he is. When he is on the Brocken, the faustian word *warum* is likened to "varoom, a Plasticman sound" (p. 331). As such, it is the answer given by a culture of rocket- and plastic-men to the faustian questions of meaning and value, no real answer but brute assertion of power. The contrast between a plastic answer and a genuine question is repeated when Roger asks Jeremy *why* the captured rockets must be fired. Jeremy's answer is what we expect of a man who "is every assertion the fucking War has ever made" (p. 177)—"Why? Damn it, to *see*, obviously" (p. 709). In other words, "because it is there" or even the childish "just because," an answer that helps explain why we live within the target areas of ICBMs today. The crude outlines of these heroes as saviors, the starkly simple nature of the wishes they represent, and the transparent ignorance of their juvenile adherents to the real psychological issues involved, are all important to our understanding of Slothrop, America, and even technological humankind in general.

The heroes as rebels—the third configuration, relevant to adolescents rather than children—crop up late in Slothrop's narrative, during the dissolution that accompanies his achieving oneness with the land through music. The Floundering Four (pp. 674–81) are an unlikely team who aid Slothrop in his mortal struggle with the Paternal Peril: "WAIT *that's a real gun*, this is a real bullet zinnnggg! good try, Pop, but you're not quite as keen as The Kid today!" (p. 674) Whether the threat takes the form of bullets, homosexual assault (in the Roseland and toilet-bomb fantasies [pp. 688–90]), or torture, the violence is mostly paternal aggression towards the hapless son, who daydreams miraculous rescues and artful dodges.

Byron the Bulb's story of rebellion (pp. 647–55) is an odd digression in the account of a drug dream recounted by a colonel getting his hair—and possibly his throat—cut. The lamenting harmonica blues in the background suggest that Slothrop is in the neighborhood. At first glance, the tale is unconnected to anything else. In the second part of *Faust,* however, there is an operatic interlude devoted to celebrating Euphorion, a symbolic amalgam of Lord Byron and the spirit of romantic poetry. Byron the Bulb dreams of overthrowing the system; Lord Byron devoted himself to the Greek war of independence. As Euphorion, he soars too high; while the chorus laments his icarian fall, he dies, but his aureole shuffles off the mortal shell and ascends as a comet. His voice, from the dark realm below, cries out, "Lass mich im dustern Reich, / Mutter, mich nicht allein!" (pt. 2, lines 9905–6). Byron the Bulb eludes the destructive forays of the System; like Icarus, he falls into the sea (reaching it, like Slothrop, via a toilet-bowl journey), and passes from hand to hand, screwed into socket after socket (*Mutter*). Like Lord Byron and romantic poetry, Byron the Bulb preaches rebellion against the system. Unlike Lord Byron, however, but like many rebels and romantic poets, Bulb Byron lives on, "knowing the truth and powerless to change anything" (p. 655). We are told that he will even learn to enjoy this frustration. In Byron the Bulb's case, paranoid fears of the father are projected onto the political system. The son lives, unable to secure real revenge against his father and even learning to enjoy his repressed existence. There is a fleeting reference to another immortal bulb, Beatriz, who perhaps, like her namesake in *Paradiso,* can lead rebellious Byron to love or to think he loves the Father, Phoebus, who moves the sun and other stars.

John Dillinger is another rebel. Just after Slothrop assumes the Rocketman identity, he formally enters black-market circles, where Dillinger is understandably a patron saint. One hangout has "oversize photos of John Dillinger, alone or posed with his mother, his pals, his tommygun" (pp. 368–69). Later, we learn that members of this underground use "B/4" as a code, it being Dillinger's old sign off: "Everybody in the Zone this summer is using it. It indicates to people how you feel about certain things" (p. 436). In the raid on Peenemünde to rescue Der Springer, Närrisch covers the retreat. In a melodramatic scene, he awaits his own end and thinks of Dillinger being helped through *his* death by the lingering movie-images of Clark Gable's tough-guy preference for electric chair over a life sentence (p. 516). As his name ("foolish," "crazy") and his references to the grail imply, he is somewhat like Slothrop as a holy fool, and like Slothrop can enjoy daydreams of heroic outlaw martyrdom, although in the crunch he lets himself be captured.

These early references to Dillinger set the stage for his final appearance in the story. Pig Bodine realizes in anguish that he is losing his ability to see Slothrop, the dissolving hero. With intense compassion, he tries to bridge the gap between them one last time:

"Here. Listen. I want you to have it. Understand? It's yours[. . . .] Look, I was there, in Chicago, when they ambushed him. I was there that night, right down the street from the Biograph, I heard the gunfire[. . . .] That's Dillinger's blood there. Still warm when I got to it[. . . .] He went out socked Them right in the toilet privacy of Their banks. Who cares what he was *thinking* about, long as it didn't get in the way? A-and it doesn't even matter why we're doing this, either. Rocky? Yeah, what we need isn't right reasons, but just that *grace*. The physical grace to keep it working. Courage, brains, sure, O.K., but without that grace? forget it. (p. 741)

Pig offers Slothrop grace, the grace of the outlaw who sets himself against the System. The romanticization of the bank robber is typical of the adolescent outlook. Moreover, as studies of Dillinger suggest, his rebellion against the system was very possibly vengeful retaliation against an unsympathetic father.[20] Bodine's indifference to Dillinger's sordid motives, his emotional affirmation of rebellion for its own sake, is purest adolescent emotion.

This array of youthful and adolescent heroes perhaps bothers readers precisely because Slothrop has not outgrown them. We are disconcerted that a rocketry expert reads Plasticman comics or that someone who has achieved a kind of mystic experience with nature should still be dogged by such flagrantly adolescent daydreams. These heroes so oversimplify the world that daydreaming their stories always protects the dreamer from responsibility and from difficult decision making. Their simpleminded approach to reality seems so far from Pynchon's own. We do not really want to be reminded of the childish and unsophisticated streak in Slothrop.

At times, it comes across as innocence, that well-known American trait. At other times, though, the innocence seems less harmless and more of a threat to the well-being of others. Insofar as Slothrop symbolizes The American or technological humankind, his childish streak is something we must reckon with when casting up our probable futures. Eastern cultures have certainly accused both Europeans and Americans of such cultural childishness. We may not see it easily when looking at our own culture, but we can recognize some of its drawbacks readily enough when they are embedded in a single individual.

Given the Janus-nature of most experiences in *Gravity's Rainbow*, however, we also see the problem of differentiating between the childish and the childlike when these traits are shown by some of the children of the book—Bianca, Ilse, Ludwig, even Gottfried—with their directness and flexibility; their openness to change, to love, to others. We are culturally conditioned to appreciate childlike behavior in children but call such behavior childishness in an adult. What makes us draw the line where we do? Pynchon undermines our assumptions and pressures us to reconsider that distinction by his distribution of this childishness among his various characters. He employs these childhood hero-patterns to the same effect. Whereas Faust and the wagnerian crew relate solely to Slothrop, Hansel and Gretel are part of the intermap system, and Dillinger is a hero to many in the Zone. From our cultural coign of vantage, we want to condemn this childishness in Slothrop but sentimentalize and laud it in children. Because of its presence in the intermappings, however, I suspect this simple division to be inadequate.

The Orphic Hero Pattern

Orpheus, as role model for Slothrop, emerges most clearly in the last book of *Gravity's Rainbow*. Orpheus is a complex figure, so Pynchon's precise reason for introducing him is not immediately obvious, especially since his name is not mentioned until we get to the very end of the novel.

The evidence for Orpheus's presence as a pattern is as follows. (1) Slothrop, toward the end of the book, suddenly becomes an instrumentalist, thus calling attention to his powers as a musician. His instrument, furthermore, is frequently called a harp, a colloquial term for the harmonica it in fact is. (2) For practical purposes the instrument is magical, it being the very harmonica he lost down the Roseland toilet bowl. Like various ovidian objects, like Slothrop himself, like Byron the Bulb, even like Orpheus's own severed head, the harmonica has disappeared down a subterranean waterway and appeared on another continent. (3) Slothrop achieves an unusual sense of oneness with nature, which, in the orphic context, reminds us of Orpheus's power over stones, trees, and the animals that gathered around him to listen, as unafraid as the insects and animals surrounding Slothrop (p. 623). (4) Slothrop's plucked albatross is a *sparagmos* or scattering of self, wrought in part through the violence of others. Significantly, the most violent description of this dismemberment (p. 712) mentions Slothrop's mother with a martini in the same sentence that details his scattering, a clear invocation of Orpheus's death at the hands of his own mother while she roamed the mountain in dionysian intoxication. (5) The precise relationship between Orphism and the cults of Apollo and Dionysus is disputed by classicists, but the view that has appealed most to later ages makes Orphism a compromise between the two antithetical impulses. Book 4 of Gravity's Rainbow has several references to Phoebus, to the apollonian dream and lyre (pp. 694, 754), and to Dionysus or to a related figure, Pan (pp. 656–57, 720).[21] (6) Orpheus's name appears in a subtitle, "Orpheus puts down Harp" (p. 754) and in the name Orpheus Theatre. (7) In a self-contained fantasy, an orphic pinball faces death at the hands of offenbachian Folies-Bergères maenads (pp. 583–85). And, finally, (8) there are many references to Rilke in *Gravity's Rainbow*, including a quotation from the *Sonnets to Orpheus*. I detail these allusions because Orpheus is alluded to only indirectly in connection with Slothrop. Other critics have noted the orphic influence, however, so lack of direct reference does not weaken the power of his invoked presence.[22]

The Orpheus myth, according to Elizabeth Sewell, falls into three parts. First, Orpheus enchants people, beasts, trees, and stones with his music; second, he penetrates Hades in an attempt to win Eurydice back, but undoes his unprecedented success by looking back too soon; and third, he is torn apart by maenads, one of whom is his mother. His head and lyre float down the river and come to rest on the island of Lesbos, where the head becomes an oracle. Sewell interprets the tale, saying that it

seems to say that poetry has power not merely over words and hence over thoughts, but also in some way over natural objects and their behavior, be they animate or inanimate; and to some extent, in conjunction with love, power over life and death as humans know and suffer them; that this power is almost indestructible and may turn, even in its own disaster, to something akin to prophecy.[23]

The writers to whom she and other critics have attributed a self-conscious orphic identity differ in their emphases. Emerson, for instance, saw his orphism in terms of the first phase of Orpheus's career and gloried in the power of language over nature and objects, a power demonstrated by its ability to make things meaningful, classify them, and put the universe in human terms. Others—Goethe, Novalis, Nerval, Mallarmé—have been inspired by Orpheus's descent into Hades, seeing in it the poet's descent into his own dark night of the soul, rewarded with the vision and authority to make declarations about our death-haunted world.[24] Dismemberment and fragmentation followed by a new form of creativity was Rilke's orphic inspiration.[25] Ihab Hassan, following Nietzsche, argues that literary form must periodically be rent with dionysian violence if writers in our repressed apollonian culture are to be able to sing at all; hence he identifies the condition of modern writers in general with the dismembered head of Orpheus.[26]

Pynchon invokes echoes of all three parts of the story but stresses the last. Slothrop's oneness with nature lets him communicate with trees (pp. 552–53) and lets him enjoy spending "whole days naked, ants crawling up his legs, butterflies lighting on his shoulders, watching the life on the mountain, getting to know shrikes and capercaillie, badgers and marmots" (p. 623). He descends into the underworld when he boards that floating Hades, the *Anubis* (named after the Egyptian jackal god who led the dead to judgment). When he thinks of rescuing Bianca, he is credited with a "Eurydice-obsession, this *bringing back out of*" (p. 472). Bianca's Eurydice-identity is strengthened when Slothrop feels on her corpse "lacing that moves, snake-sure" (p. 531), the original Eurydice having died from snake-bite. Like the Orpheuses of some romantic poets, Slothrop-as-Orpheus cannot resurrect Bianca, but he does bring back with him a vital truth about his own inner being—some Imipolex G—although he fails to recognize the full significance of the connection between this substance and himself.

The third phase of Orpheus's career emerges most simply in Slothrop's harmonica blues, heard here and there throughout the Zone. According to Hassan, the modern orphic writer protests authority and abstraction, and certainly those subjects exercise Pynchon. The prophesying orphic head disappears with Slothrop's final fade-out, to reappear on another continent as the Orpheus Theatre in which films apocalyptically dealing with death—Cocteau's *Orphée* and Bergman's *Seventh Seal*—have recently been shown. The orphic voice, this time in the cinematic medium, is trying to warn its audience of what is past, and passing, and to come.

The third orphic phase is also invoked when Pynchon alludes to Rilke's *Sonnets to Orpheus* with a quotation from part 2, sonnet 29 (p. 622). Rilke's lyric voice painfully hammers out his concept of the poet's role, Orpheus being the ideal pattern for humankind. Part of this argument is also developed in the *Duino Elegies*, some of which were written during the same brief burst of incandescent poetic activity. The rilkean angels that populate *Gravity's Rainbow* have by their nature reached the state humanity must strive toward, as Strauss argues:

Rilke's Angel is that being in whom the task of transformation has been accomplished: he is perfect and unified. The human task, however, devolves upon Orpheus—or, perhaps more accurately, on the Orphic poet, the poet-as-Orpheus. His task is to will the transformation and to perform its accomplishment. . . . he is divided [i.e. dismembered] and yet he is one, and so he guarantees the possibility of reassembling the shattered fragments.

The voluntaristic side of Rilke's Orpheus is important. The Angel is being, Orpheus is the will to be. (Strauss, p. 171)

Note that only the victim of dismemberment, an object rather than a subject, can provide the oneness. Strauss delineates the orphic task as the assimilation of the world to an interiorized world space, a Weltinnenraum. The original unity of the external world is shattered, but humankind can assemble fragments into an increasingly comprehensive whole within this creative inner space (see pt. 1, sonnet 16). The more one dissolves one's self into these impressions of external reality, and the more one becomes the object impressed upon, the better one will know reality.

A few of the Orpheus sonnets seem especially relevant to Pynchon. Rilke's hostility toward machinery that has been idolized rather than treated as servant is thematically similar to some of Pynchon's situations: "Knaben, o werft den Mut / nicht in die Schnelligkeit, / nicht in den Flugversuch" (pt. 1, sonnet 22).[27] Some of Weissmann's anguish for transcendence, some of his feelings about Gottfried and the rocket, are fueled by his youthful passion for Rilke, and we find his emotions echoed in part 1, sonnet 23. Pynchon's concern for the silences within the quartet parallels Rilke's fascination with "silence behind (or within) music" (Strauss, p. 149). Rilke

is a poet of transformation and of places where transformations take place. Rilke's Orpheus is certainly evi-
dent in *Gravity's Rainbow,* in part because of Rilke's
relevance to Germans for their idolizing the idea of transcendence, but Rilke's Orpheus is not favored to the
exclusion of all other Orpheuses; Offenbach's is invoked
(pp. 583–85), and the classical myth is generally relevant.

Slothrop may seem like an unheroic descendant of
Faust or Parsifal, but insofar as he assumes an orphic
identity, the disparity is less striking because he does play
music. He is, in fact, an artist, and in this role, his music
amounts to "striving subcreation"; such work creates a
rest in the "folksong Death," a breathing space in the
human mission to promote death (p. 720). That the
music may have some prophetic qualities of the third
phase in Orpheus's life is suggested by a series of equations set up by Pynchon.

He establishes that the modulated frequencies of the
sunset spectra (tinted by bomb debris) have information
for us (p. 642). He immediately shows hair being cut as
another set of modulated frequencies and likens the
separate hairs to tall towers about to be brought low by
the great shears from the sky. Shivers and incandescent
light are also commented upon as modulated frequencies that can communicate information. Consequently,
when "shiver-borne blues" from a harmonica are heard
during this scene, we associate those modulated frequencies with some sort of warning, one probably having
to do with the implications of Hiroshima. (Although we
never learn definitely that Slothrop is the harmonica
player, he does play the blues competently, and the only
other Zonal player mentioned is painfully unable to play
even a simple tune.)

Slothrop's warning may not even be a conscious or-chestration of doom, since his music is not heard again after he belatedly sees a headline announcing that bomb, but prophecy in music may not be conscious for the orphic Yardbird Parker either. Nonetheless, his thirty-second notes invoke the machine guns of the coming war, and even his most affirmative solos attest to the presence of "old Mister fucking Death he self" (p. 63). When Slothrop disappears, our focus shifts to the Or-pheus Theatre with its films about death. Because Sloth-rop so clearly is Orpheus in the Zone, the theater appears to represent or echo the prophesying orphic head that survived dismemberment and floated to another land to become an oracle. Naturally, for Western culture, the oracle takes a technological form—film—and Pynchon has already educated us on the correspondence between film's freezing action to still shots and the calculus of rocket trajectories.

Traditional Heroes and Pynchon's New Heroic Pattern

So how do these allusions to the array of Western heroes function in the novel? I suggest that Pynchon's new model for individual behavior emerges from an interplay be-tween such traditional heroic material and the inter-mapped episodes shared among the major characters in the novel. He does adopt or adapt some qualities from the old heroes: the openness to experience of Faust, the antiheroic bumbling of Tannhäuser and Parsifal, the childlike openness and directness of Hansel, Dorothy, and Alice, the willingness to help others of the super-heroes, the attitude of rebellion against the System of the adolescent heroes, and the oneness with nature and artistic response to experience and vision of Orpheus. He also, however, rejects the qualities conventionally valued in these figures: drive and ambition, intensity of emotional responses, successful acquisition of power over others, and a desire to enjoy that control. With the exception of Faust and Orpheus, who see deeply enough to be dissatisfied with the explanations, these figures believe in their various cultural systems of order. Even despite experience with evidence to the contrary, they apply closure, reduce their realities to an official rationale as swiftly as they can. We gradually learn to accept that such a response in us as readers is inadequate to Pynchon's postmodern reality. Similarly, for heroes in the text or for people in a postmodern world, the desire for control and lust for closure are self-deluding, dangerous to society, and grossly inadequate to the fragmented yet infinitely interconnected nature of the universe.[28] Pynchon can only accept marginal characteristics from the old-fashioned heroes and must carry out his construction of a new pattern with material used and interpreted in new ways.

Technically, Pynchon also estranges us from the known hero pattern by making his traditional figures part of an open system, a series of possibilities without any absolutes. It is as if each hero represents a square on a chess board, and Slothrop, by his moves, comes into the territory of each, one at a time. When in that hero's sphere of influence, his adventures in some way resemble those of the presiding figure, but no one figure emerges as the preeminent model, and the adventures themselves follow no very obvious logical sequence. We see contrasts and similarities but rarely feel any pressure on Slothrop to imitate any one closely. Only by embracing them all does he somehow assemble a life for himself that makes him the unusual literary character that he is, following no preestablished pattern. What we have in Pynchon's presentation of our culture's figures is yet another instance of his encyclopedic tendencies. The figures are indices of potentiality, fragments representing possibilities from which one can assemble a life.

Faust is particularly relevant to Slothrop because of his receptiveness to a wide variety of experience. Slothrop, however, does not strive to acquire new experiences in Faust's strenuous fashion; he flows with any passing current and undergoes a faustian range of experience without locking himself into the frantic faustian mindset. Many of Slothrop's adventures serve no logical purpose except to invoke Faust as Western cultural hero and to comment upon him. Slothrop's ascent of the Brocken with a witch seems to have been invented to make the allusive connection, since it does not advance Slothrop's quest, nor is it predictable from anything preceding it. Nor does Slothrop get enough spiritual illumination from the adventure to make it seem altogether natural to his story. Likewise, he serves his "Helen" (Greta Erdmann), but she does not advance him in any cause-and-effect fashion. As mother to Bianca, she influences a major adventure tangentially, but her role in the story seems to be to serve as experiential background. She broadens Slothrop's horizons with tales of making movies, and with her masochism. Were this a hero monomyth and he a standard monomyth hero, she would probably be a destructive temptress, a Morgan la Fée, and Slothrop would have to struggle mightily to free himself from her temptations and toils. But he does not. She is simply one of his experiences, and one of his chances to take care of someone who needs care. She embodies one set of approaches to life and Slothrop learns from exposure to them.

Bianca too seems to enter Slothrop's life because mythic referents demand such a figure, not because Slothrop is going to be transformed by love, as he might be in a traditional novel. Both Orpheus's Eurydice and Faust's Gretchen call her into being and determine her death. Slothrop experiences this and passes on. Figures like Plasticman, Alice, and Hansel get him into adventures, but really more to give us bits from which to construct our concept of his character than to advance him logically along any line stretching from beginning to end. From Hansel, we see his childish greed, which most obviously takes women as its object. Yet that detail in his character is hardly even judgmental, since more "adult" cultural outlooks were proving perfectly compatible with nonhuman behavior in the theater of war.

The wagnerian heroes add further fragments to the picture. Unlike the trip to the Brocken, Slothrop's tannhäuserian descent into the Mittelwerke can be justified on logical and thematic grounds; after all, his quest is taking him to all the stations of the rocket, all its historical sites. The hymns to love in limerick form, however, and the dwarfish work force and the allusion to Frau Holda or Venus all point to an obsession with technology and add to our sense that Slothrop as individual is no knightly hero. He, like Western humanity in general, is childish, ensnared in nonhuman or antihuman love.

Orpheus is the only figure with whom Slothrop seems to have a strong affinity. Apart from the Eurydice adventure, there is his oneness with nature and his activities as minstrel of the Zone. Slothrop actually does achieve a sort of artistry in this mode. His blues are heard and noted, wordless warnings associated with the bomb and its implications. And as rilkean Orpheus, he is the object bearing the impressions of all his varied experience.

The rilkean Orpheus takes the fragmented outer world and reassembles it in an inner space. In Rilke's mythography, the more fragments assembled, the closer the poet is to achieving the pure state of the Angel. Also, the more varied the experiences that the poet can transform, the better. (This openness to experience hinted at in Rilke has some parallels in the openness to experience encouraged by Gadamer in his concept of Erfahrung.) Slothrop's transformation of his experience into wordless blues may seem like an incomplete alchemy— but the imagery used by Pynchon to link modulated frequencies to warnings at least implies that these blues are not without content or meaning.

Slothrop comes into being as a character and assumes form to the degree that he is open to the kinds of experience these heroic figures represent. Their presence is not just a matter of literary source and influence. Pynchon invokes all of them for philosophical reasons. Take away these shadow identities and heroic referents, and Slothrop would be a featureless fugitive, an all-but-unidentifiable quester. Moreover, he gains his individuality as much by differing from these embodiments of the monomyth pattern as by echoing them; by assembling his own unique collection of fragments, which, in the new mythography, stays openended. If openness is a desirable personal trait in Pynchon's cosmos, then no closure would be possible in his aesthetic either, so the open fate of the main characters is appropriate.

These are some of the ways that Pynchon uses traditional heroes. They offer both similitude and contrast; we learn what Slothrop is both by how he resembles them and by how he differs. Obvious absences and lacks are as important as parallels and presences. There are no absolutes in this system, not even a clearly marked good and evil. The childish greed suggested by the Hansel parallels, for instance, is in its way childlike as well as childish, positive as well as negative.[29]

Pynchon uses monomyth heroes to construct Slothrop, but also uses him to discredit their modus operandi. None of the traditional heroes would be adequate to deal with Pynchon's postmodernist reality. Faust would have worn himself out chasing platonic ideals and trying to understand everything. In the long run, Orpheus might have grown tired of singing his warning to deaf ears, and put down his harp. Superman would have been helpless in a world where bad guys don't wear black hats, let alone a world in which primary reality is not material and predictable. Slothrop is an aggregate of possible responses to reality, and this configuration points ultimately toward the same kind of existence as that delimited by the intermappings.

If we back off from the figures borrowed from our cultural mythology and look at what Pynchon offers as their replacements in his mythology, we find some general patterns in these intermappings. Insight into the nonmaterial nature of reality is one common element. Slothrop, Enzian, Roger, Leni, Pirate, Tchitcherine, Pökler, and Katje all at some time see superimposed planes of reality; they all recognize the existence of a Them-reality, and sometimes other realities as well. Most of them act on this discovery. Once Slothrop becomes aware of Them-activity, he eludes surveillance and goes AWOL. Roger joins the counterforce. Katje and Pirate strive to secede from the System, and see the importance of trying to be kind. Tchitcherine and Enzian have troubles with the insight, Tchitcherine because he sees no very effective way to secede from the Soviet structure, and Enzian because he wants to integrate his insight into his people's quest for a new Text for their lives. But in most instances, the characters give up the consolations and security offered by a purely material universe and reorder their lives to accord with their insight. This immediate response is heroic in its way, because shedding one's cultural outlook is not easy, but they meet this demand for transformation without hesitation or fanfare. On the surface, the change makes little difference to their lives, because these are in flux anyway on account of the war, but by entering the new reality, they destroy their chance of fitting back into the prevailing system ever again.

Accepting new levels of reality, especially nonmaterial reality, enjoins on them the acceptance of openness. If any of our cultural rules for confining chaos—assumptions such as those concerning cause and effect or the purely material nature of reality—prove perspectival and human rather than absolute, then our other rules are undermined as well. These main characters learn to live without planned futures, without livelihood, without stable identity. They don't even know what these other levels of reality may be, having only glimpsed them as possibilities. Some of the additional realities are political and social (technology as a force transcending nations and dictating their policies); some pertain to the Other Side. What the characters can do in light of their insights is to stay relatively detached from the world. They can try to be kind; perhaps they can also try to be creative. If they lose their flexibility and commit themselves unyieldingly to something—as Enzian apparently does to his rocket—they are likely to harm themselves and others.

Not only must they be flexible, they must not exercise control over others. One characteristic of traditional heroes is that they usually end up ruling others. Pynchon's main figures try to avoid such control, and even Enzian is an unwilling leader. Pirate started as a controller of fantasies, but toward the end, he tries to opt out of that activity. Roger has been identified with the uncontrolled probabilistic area between 0 and 1, rather than with the binary digits and their pointsmanesque claims to behaviorist control. Pig Bodine manages to help others but leads a rootless existence in which he appears to exercise little control over anybody. Pökler mentally secedes from the power games of the rocket group, when he comes to value his child above the rockets.

Pökler also acknowledges some sense of responsibility toward Camp Dora when he leaves his ring on the woman's finger, and this too is a common element in Pynchon's new hero figures. Pökler, Katje, and Roger all recognize some form of guilt or complicity or responsibility. Slothrop's values, insofar as they warn wordlessly of Hiroshima and its implications, show his sense of involvement taking an artistic form.

Sequentially, the new hero pattern that Pynchon proposes shows an initial equilibrium where the protagonist is more or less at one with society. Then the hero is exposed to other levels of reality and accepts this radical transformation of the cosmos. He or she learns to be open, to glide along the interfaces of greater powers, to be flexible, to put aside the more compulsive sorts of fear, and to show at least a minimal sense of responsibility and kindness.[30] Most of those who achieve such psychological openness are not betrayed into a fictional closure by Pynchon. We do not know how those still alive will do in later years. Whereas the traditional hero monomyth shows the hero integrating into society, this new pattern shows the individual integrating with chaos and accepting uncertainty. Where the traditional hero monomyth shows reconciliation with the system, Pynchon shows abdication and avoidance and withdrawal. What his heroes accept is limited to personal relationships, Counterforce gestures, and creative endeavor.

To readers conditioned by the millenia-old hero monomyth, such an alternative seems shiftless and spineless, literally unheroic. We tend to blame Slothrop for not doing more, for not saving Bianca, for instance, although after he falls overboard, he could hardly have protected her even had he previously resolved to do so. We may not approve of his lack of fervor at the birthplace of the rocket, but would we have been any more responsive, particularly when engaged on a dangerous raid? Because he does not commit himself to a passionate and exclusive love affair, some readers condemn him for accepting indiscriminate sexual solace, though few would refuse those gratifications, given Slothrop's opportunities. When he meets a woman with evil-seeming elements in her character—Greta Erdmann, for instance—we expect him to struggle against her, but he is as kind to her as to anyone. Slothrop does little moaning or groaning about how difficult he finds his open life in the Zone, though the occasional tear and the pain of plucking the albatross of self suggest that it is not always easy.

We associate heroes with progress, and clearly Pynchon's characters are not likely to make technological advances or create a new form of advanced society. Indeed, Pynchon's hint as to what kind of society is most valid strikes the majority of readers as regressive, since his major figures thrive best in the personal level of wheelings and dealings in the black market. In such an Ur-Markt, Slothrop is surprisingly active and effective; he bargains his way to information on Jamf and to acquisition of Imipolex G without any real money at all, and more important, he survives. Pig Bodine and Gerhardt von Göll are likewise effective in this milieu. As alternative to the closed systems we know today, Pynchon offers us the radical decentralization of the Zone, where all barriers are down.

The fragments that Slothrop assimilates from the lives of Faust, Orpheus, Plasticman, and some of his other heroic shadows, when brought together in his individual blend, would make him a suitable figure for an open world. He is a survivor, after all, but one who survives without destroying weaker competitors. If we wipe out life with nuclear warfare, then no pattern of behavior will be relevant. If the current economic and technological system is destroyed by war, catastrophe, or revolution, Slothrop's way might come into its own, at least for a while. As readers, longing for heroic solutions to the System's problems, we want to berate Pynchon for not giving us a "real" hero, one who could save us and our way of life. But Pynchon gives no indication of wanting to save the System and with it our way of life. The closed system, based as it is on an obsessive fear of death, has prevailed because it supports the survival of strong individuals. Its attitudes and assumptions, however, when applied on a national and international level, are probably not compatible with survival of the species, or at least not with both survival and freedom. Pynchon seems to be exploring attitudes and patterns of behavior that would be compatible with survival of humankind, if not, always, of the individual.

5

Chaos and Cosmos Integrated

a film we have not learned to see

GRAVITY'S RAINBOW breaks down systems, myths, and structures, and returns us to uncertainty and chaos: this is the point of Pynchon's exploit—or so many critics have argued. My insistence that there is a mythology, and that Pynchon uses it without undercutting it, appears to contradict this orthodoxy and may seem like a timid attempt to deny the magnificently total negativity of Pynchon's endeavor. On the face of it, mythology and Pynchon's penchant for dismantling traditional structures are incompatible, but, as I shall try to demonstrate, Pynchon does integrate them. Thus combined, they create the muffin-crater interplay of values central to the effect of the novel.

As a preliminary to my argument, let me quote from Betty Edwards, an artist whose theories unite drawing with L(eft) and R(ight) modes of perceptions and with creative thought of any sort, not just artistic. She discusses several optical illusions, including the one containing two faces or a chalice and the one containing a duck or a rabbit, and makes the following observations:

> In nearly every group I've worked with, a certain percentage of individuals are simply unable to "find" one image or the other, both of which are there, of course, right in front of the eyes. This is an almost painful experience of the brain's yearning for closure. . . . It seems to me that premature closure is one of the greatest roadblocks in both the process of drawing and the creative process itself. . . . How, then, to throw a glitch into the system to achieve an open, not a closed, mind and the unity of vision (L-mode *and* R-mode) necessary for Saturation?[1]

Our yearning for closure evidently operates in more activities than literary criticism, and it can obstruct both the mental integration of different kinds of perception and creativity itself. I shall be arguing for an approach to *Gravity's Rainbow* that encourages a kind of reading that holds two sorts of perception in balance. When we find the standpoint from which the two perceptions— postmodernist and mythological—can be integrated, we will have exercised a kind of creativity as well.

Pynchon's Postmodernism and Its Implications for Readings

In grouping together as postmodernist the critics who focus on Pynchon's destabilizing techniques, I am blurring several distinctions. According to some of these critics, the world of order has simply disintegrated, and Pynchon just reflects what he finds; for others, his act is more a conscious destruction of our cultural and readerly assumptions; yet others see his tactics as deconstructive, as tracking our cultural discourses to their contradictions and as playful engagement with the absences behind our falsely absolute presences. Many readings combine more than one of these suppositions. Nineteenth-century reality, solid and mechanistic, has disintegrated, though one might not realize it from reading in the conservative Anglo-American novelistic tradition. In that sense Pynchon reflects philosophical, scientific, and social changes outside of literature. And there is a zestful force to his treatment of readers: postmodernist bullying, if you like, although readers have the options of closing the book to escape or of adopting so flexible a stance that there are no longer any rigid expectations to be shattered by authorial blows. And Pynchon does portray and embody in his many plots the ways in which systems of meaning and interpretation undo themselves, and he does tease us into trying to impose interpretive schemes, only later to prove them inadequate.

The centrifugal, fragmenting effect of Pynchon's writing has attracted admiring attention in part because his technological knowledge gives a scientific aura to matters normally considered humanistic. Given the value placed on science and technology in our society, Pynchon gets deserved credit for being able to bridge this cultural gap:

To a populace that has lived for some 50 years and more with quantum mechanics, and which is finally beginning to feel on a cultural level the effects of that system of regarding reality, these assumptions on which the realistic novel rests are no longer acceptable. Part of the crux of the Einstein/Bohr debate is whether or not reality exists independent of observation, and at present the weight of the evidence rests with those who argue with Bohr that it does not. Moreover, even if it does, the Heisenberg Uncertainty Principle assures us that it is not even theoretically possible to achieve a complete knowledge of reality—that in ascertaining one thing we must inevitably sacrifice knowledge of another. And deterministic causality, challenged as far back as Hume, has fallen prey to statistical probabilities. When we add to these the idea of complementarity, which allows for the harmonious co-existence of mutually exclusive opposites; the idea of a curved space and non-linear time; and Relativity Theory, which rejects the validity of an absolute frame of reference (another impediment to achieving absolute understanding of "the way it really was"), the foundations upon which the traditional realistic novel rests crumble. (Schwartz, p. 166)

Another critic states that "Pynchon not only bases his thematic analyses of human society and psychology on the concepts or 'themes' of today's science, but he also renders into literature its most challenging epistemological and methodological problems." The critic goes on: "Most of what is distinctive in Pynchon, even his radical ambivalence, reflects some development in modern physics" (Cooper, pp. 110–11). Westervelt and Pyuen also tie Pynchon's abnormal portrayal of reality to the concepts of contemporary physics and warn us against applying newtonian interpretive methods to a postnewtonian text. These readers all make a good case for Pynchon's scientific postmodernism.

The affirmation of uncertainty within the text and the joyful destructiveness of Pynchon's endeavor have also been argued on philosophical, nietzschean lines. According to Nietzsche, we kill reality by analyzing sense data, by reducing it via metaphor to dead and totally inadequate signs. From reality to image, and from image to word, we introduce such distortion into our input that no absolute knowledge is possible. Weissmann's reference to the Western "order of Analysis and Death" (p. 722) echoes such nietzschean concerns. By giving us contradiction and fragmentation and fantastic, kaleidoscopic texture, Pynchon reminds us that there is far more to reality than analysis can ever tell us.[2]

Pynchon's deconstructions are many and varied, so I will only describe his general effect here. His way of disarticulating our cultural and readerly systems is approachable by means of Wolfgang Iser's concept of blanks and gaps. Iser points out that modern literature transforms expected functions into blanks. In other words, anything that might arouse definite expectations—be it conventions of genre or developments within the story line—is negated, and a gap in connectedness results. Gaps, such as shifts in point of view or the conflicts between surface statement and irony, exist in most fiction; they are necessary for any sort of reader participation. But multiplying the blanks as Pynchon does ultimately negates one normal function of the text, namely, "to provide the framework for the communication of a message—and instead it serves to turn attention to the process of communication itself."[3] Iser goes on to speak of *Ulysses*, but what he says is just as applicable to *Gravity's Rainbow*: "The reader is made aware of the basic features of his mode of perception: porous selectivity, dependence on perspective, habitual reflexes. In order to orient ourselves, we constantly and automatically leave things out, but the density of the repertoire in *Ulysses* prevents us from doing this. Furthermore, the successive changes of style, each restricted to its own perspective, indicate the extent to which perception and interpretation depend upon the standpoint of the observer" (Iser, p. 84).

Radical uncertainty, whether scientific, philosophical, or deconstructive, is unquestionably a major feature of Pynchon's world, but what import does such uncertainty have for his readers? To what extent does this uncertainty govern and limit our possible responses? Does the uncertainty logically bar all kinds of order-seeking endeavor by Pynchon himself or by his readers? More specifically, does it rule out mythology?

Take the issue of linking Pynchon's general philosophy to that of contemporary science. Do the uncertainties of contemporary science militate against any sort of systematic reading, a stand implicit in some science-oriented criticism? I think not. Heisenberg's uncertainty principle has no direct bearing on our struggles with the text, although some readers feel cowed by the prestige of science or thrilled to find it relevant to the humanities. The problem in science-oriented readings arises when one considers levels of reality and the applicability of principles from one level to another. Heisenberg's uncertainty principle applies at the subatomic level but does not translate directly to the level of human activity. Our use of it there is pure metaphor and has no logical validity. In making his world so uncertain, Pynchon has not created a postnewtonian cosmos, but rather a fictional analogue to that world, one in which characters and readers must deal with uncertainties as radical as those of physics. His creation remains an analogue, however, not a scientific reality. Hence, I would argue, Pynchon's scientific concerns do not form a valid barrier to his using various kinds of ordering structure. Science is one of Pynchon's metaphors, not his starting point for examining reality.[4]

Nor does the philosophical negativity in *Gravity's Rainbow* necessarily bar some kinds of order, including mythology. Readers who argue from such philosophical principles are indubitably right that Pynchon explodes various "myths"—in the sense that term is used for systems that characters impose on experience when trying to wrest order from chaos. Cause-and-effect relationships, transcendence, revolution, consecration of a nation, love—each is subjected to the corrosive acid of his vision. Our inability to arrive at any correspondential knowledge—our inability to escape the confines of perspectival and human knowledge—is theoretically true, of course, but such inability is not that significant on the level of quotidian experience. We may not really know what is "out there," but our vision and conceptualization, however faulty, let us predict, avoid, and survive many perceived problems—so we do not worry about the gap between reality and our perceptions. We can be made to learn or relearn that our everyday reality is not demonstrably true, and that the relationship between language and reality is arbitrary, but such theoretical unknowability and arbitrariness make relatively little difference to practice and survival.

Central to the problem of reading *Gravity's Rainbow* is the value one puts on human life and human problems of survival. A fully deconstructive perception of reality is only partly thinkable and, more to the point, is not tenable as a philosophy of everyday action and survival. One needs arrangements, as Geli observes, when facing total freedom or free play. Insofar as the mythic structure I have discussed has a center, that center is human life and survival, not because humankind "deserves" to survive on account of inherent dignity, purpose, or beauty, but because most of us individually do not wish to be exterminated when cosmic DDT is applied to rid earth of its vermin. In theory, individuality is problematic on philosophical, psychological, and sociological grounds, but in practice this seldom prevents a member of the human species from trying to save his or her own skin. Pynchon does not offer a totally deconstructed universe, and whether such an endeavor is even possible remains doubtful. Practical living as we know it is not compatible with undoing all hierarchy and refusing to privilege either side of an opposition with valorization based on presence. Pynchon does not, it is true, offer us Order, and in that respect he reflects the postmodernist outlook. As Hite points out, however, he does leave open the possibility of multiple local orders. He certainly shows his characters creating or using their own systems in order, blindly or self-consciously, to deal with experience. This practice seems to be part of the human condition, and Pynchon cannot be entirely exempt from the force of this need.

Postmodernist critics could likewise object that the mythological approach rests on the dubious assumption of something "being there" in the text. We might recast this problem and locate both text and possible meanings vis-à-vis readers. The ontological status of the mythology on whose behalf I am arguing cannot be proven. If it works, though, as a useful framework for many readers as they read or discuss the text, then it has at least a functional or provisional validity. Usefulness in this sense would mean that awareness of the mythology reduces some of our anxiety in interacting with the text, that it establishes some values through which we can relate to the many levels of the narrative, and ultimately that it can help us assimilate an experience of "meaningfulness," whether or not we are able to express the latter in a coherent statement. But should this particular text rather foster an experience of meaninglessness? Perhaps our anxiety ought not to be reduced. Such questions run into logical objections. Once the "experience of meaninglessness" is conceptualized, it becomes a meaningful procedure. In addition, anxiety will be reduced during subsequent readings whether a mythology is sensed or not. Using the mythology reduces free play somewhat, but so does any critical discussion. If one keeps the mythological perspective in a dynamic balance with a poststructuralist perspective, one is not desperately applying closure to rule out the frightening parts of the text, and there are genuine virtues to such an integration.

Molly Hite's formulation that there is order but not Order is one way of narrowing the gulf between postmodern and more traditional readings. Several critics have discovered isolated orderly patterns. Ozier's study of mathematical images and the calculus of transformations is one such work. So are the studies by Hayles on cosmology; by Cowart on blackness, victimization, and music; by Wolfley on anal imagery; and by Hite on "Holy-Center-Approaching." Most such image clusters project values. Indeed, critics working with very different assumptions agree fairly closely on the presence of certain values in the text and accept that Pynchon attributes some kind of positive quality to these patterns of behavior. Even when overwhelmed by Pynchon's ability to decompose reality into fragments, many readers would agree that kindness is foregrounded as one of humanity's more helpful emotions; that control is evil; that an ecological sensitivity to earth's fruitful processes is valorized; that Pynchon insists on some form of non-material, nonempirical reality; and that he seems to approve of people's accepting both their own preterition and the necessity of their own deaths as parts of relinquishing control.

I see no signs that these values are undercut with irony. True, they are not offered as a grand solution to our social problems, but then society could not relinquish its networks of control without ceasing to be society. Pynchon is not offering his ideology as salvation for the status quo, but he is making some claims for it apart from society. His ideology, furthermore, is widely, if not unanimously, recognized as coming across in the text, even when some form of disintegration or decomposition is being claimed as the text's main objective.

If we ask how these positive values are communicated, we find that they emerge mostly through redundancy, as indeed values emerge in mythology. Repetitions bring both the basic problems and any proffered answers to our notice. From this emergence of something fairly widely agreed upon, I would like to argue that values and value structures are not necessarily bound to the same level of the text as Pynchon's fragmentations of reality. Chaos and order can work simultaneously at different levels or as different discourses within the text and can even complement each other, as I shall try to demonstrate. The positive values can exist despite messages of uncertainty. When humans live in relative chaos, they both need and create values to fit such circumstances. Indeed, the human needs will call forth values to handle the disorder. The values may or may not be admirable, seen from the outside, but their presence is not barred by postnewtonian science, or by philosophy, or by postmodernist criticism.

The Nature and Suitability of Pynchon's Mythology

Pynchon's scientific concerns create a fictive analogue to a more theoretical level of the universe than we usually deal with, where a pseudoheisenbergian uncertainty contributes to the fragmentation of reality. Likewise, his interest in semiotic systems, in the centrifugal impulses in language, and in nietzschean philosophy also contribute to the density and complexity of this same chaos. How, then, can a simply ordered, conventional mythology interrelate to the artfully constructed morass of conflicting data that makes up his fictive world?

One way the two interrelate is through Pynchon's new pattern for the individual, which is literally tailor-made to the chaotic conditions within his fictive cosmos. The pattern consists of the protagonist starting more or less at one with society. Then he or she is exposed to other levels of reality, especially a Them-reality, the very existence of which makes nonsense of all the neat systems and pat assumptions that had served the protagonist as a member of society. All of society's imposed closures are thrown open. This experience demands a transformation in the character's prior interpretation of reality, and the new hero makes such an adjustment. He or she learns to be open, to glide along the interfaces of greater powers, to be flexible, and to shed various sorts of fear—especially the compulsive fears associated with preterition and death. The individual also learns to make personal arrangements, and—often as the aftermath of disappointed love—learns to show kindness and to feel a sense of responsibility. Instead of reintegrating into society, the new style of hero integrates into chaos, more or less by allowing the ego to disintegrate. He or she will live with openended reality and with uncertainty.

Thus part of Pynchon's mythology at least does not contradict the message of disorder; it shows us how to live with that chaos. Although its values go against our darwinian notions of survival behavior and deny our worship of technological progress, they may promote survival when claws and teeth have been replaced by ICBMs. They would certainly improve chances for survival of the species, if not of the individual, were they to be generally adopted. They let humans interact with their environment in a relatively nondestructive fashion. They encourage freedom from major kinds of stress—those arising from fear of death and from attempts to control the future—and might even promote happiness of a low-keyed and nondemanding sort. Pig Bodine is happy during his last appearance. He may seem more a pig satisfied than Socrates dissatisfied, but Pynchon appears to honor him for it.

The key to another way that Pynchon's mythology and chaos interrelate lies in the prophetic element commonly found in the former. The mythology, through its stories, gives instruction, advice, and warning of apocalyptic futures that will follow if we do not change our values. As we know from practical experience, nothing, no matter how chaotic or disturbing, prevents us from feeling that we can give advice and warning. The actual warning may prove inadequate or mistaken, but there is nothing about chaos that blocks that mode of expression, either

in practical activity or in fiction about chaos. Unknowability and uncertainty did not keep Nietzsche from offering analyses and warnings; they do not keep Pynchon
from similar activities. So this element in the novel is
also immune to the strictures of poststructuralist criticism.

Another factor contributing to the mythology's ability
to interrelate with uncertainty is the symbolic nature of
mythology. Mythology is not meant as realistic description or analysis of reality. There need be no scientifically
demonstrable correspondence between the myths and
the fictive universe. Mythology addresses itself via artifice and metaphor and analogy to human values and
problems, and those do not disappear entirely when a
postmodernist discourse replaces humanist or modernist assumptions. Even if reality is uncertain, there are
always human problems to be addressed, and no theoretical difficulties in communication or failures in systems of order will keep us from trying, however
imperfectly, to discuss these problems.

Pynchon's use of his mythology differs from the uses
made of various "myths" by his characters in that most
of them adhere blindly to a belief, whereas he uses his
ordering structure self-consciously, fully aware of its being
an arbitrary means of imposing system in order to talk
about human needs and values. It is his own creative
paranoia at work. Pointsman believes fanatically in
stimulus-and-response explanations of behavior and a
world explicable in binary terms; Weissmann and Gottfried and Franz Pökler burn with rilkean desire for transcendence; Enzian binds himself to his people in their
service to the rocket as Holy Text. But Pynchon, by
showing such myths exploded again and again, suggests
that such passionate adherence is willful self-delusion.

Humankind, unable to bear antiparanoia for long, creates myths and mythologies—which is well and good,
possibly even creative, a form of personal arrangement—but then makes the mistake of believing them.

Another factor that links Pynchon's mythology to his
fractured reality is the process of creativity: making the
myth in order to handle the reality relates the two, if
only functionally. His embedded comments on Orpheus
and on music appear to valorize striving subcreation;
the orphic activity creates local order in the form of
music and broadcasts prophetic warnings through the
kind of music involved. That activity also helps the creative being become more open to the Other Side, to
alternate realities, as we see in Slothrop's case. In sum,
there are many reasons for feeling that a mythology can
interrelate with a complexly conceived uncertain universe. The myth is a comment upon, and therefore at
a different level of discourse from, that fragmented and
contradictory reality.

Pynchon works with a semifamiliar mythology, one
loosely echoing the biblical origins-to-apocalypse structure known to our culture. It grows out of his own concerns and insights, out of his 1960s sense of Western
civilization, his feeling that humanity and the machine
are moving toward an unhallowed match. The "myth
explains not so much what to think about events and
objects but in what direction and with what degree of
force to think. . . ."5 Pynchon can direct us toward the
crisis he foresees, despite the thoroughness with which
he shatters our assumptions about reality, because he is
dealing with human action, values, and needs, not just
with the nature of reality as viewed by science or philosophy. Even if all else is rendered uncertain, human

demands and desires can still be felt and can push the reader to seek a sense of meaning; Pynchon has not so fragmented the human realm that such meanings are unavailable. Shuffling the deck of postmodernist reality, Pynchon does not seem to have abandoned all frameworks, and this human frame of reference, this concern for ultimate survival if nothing else, is one he has retained, however counter to the spirit of what critics identify as his postmodernism.[6]

There is no necessary incongruity between Pynchon's philosophic position and his using a mythology for symbolic commentary. Why, then, has the organizing force of the mythology been so overlooked by his admirers?

Reader Response

In trying to assess how contradictory elements interrelate, we must remember that the concerns and responses of readers change as they grow familiar with the text of *Gravity's Rainbow*. Interpreters who stress the radical fragmentation of everything and the total postmodernism of Pynchon dedicate themselves to preserving the reader's reaction to a *first* reading. The first approach is the one in which the text seems so determinedly and wantonly destructive of all novelistic norms. The reader's feelings include acute anxiety, a "paranoid" desire to connect anything that seems remotely connectable, frustration that no connections work really well, and considerable resentment. The anxiety stemming from not feeling in control causes many readers to put the book down unfinished. On first contact, one feels helpless at the near-total decomposition of the narrative, and fragmentation strikes one as the book's overriding characteristic. In Iser's terms, we find an overwhelming density of blanks and all our expectations negated. Interpreters preserving this first impression focus on the surface texture; on the changes in style and tone and narrative voice; on the intermapping; on the dream-, drink-, and drug-generated hallucinations; and on the sheer variety of materials that go into making Pynchon's world.

Gravity's Rainbow, however, invites rereading. During subsequent perusals, the reader is likely to feel triumph at piecing fragments together into larger patterns, pleasure at remembering characters and places and at being now able to connect them to major plot lines. The triumph is uneasy, for some of the patterns, such as the "impossibility" of Imipolex G being the mystery stimulus or the lack of causal correspondence between girl and bomb maps, remain flawed by contradictions. Not all patterns are thus marred, to judge from studies of themes and imagery, but enough are imperfect to rob readers of the expected satisfactions offered by most literary texts. The reader is very active at this stage, always comparing and matching parts of the story, looking for links, an active quester after the grail of meaning.

As the quest fails to produce global meanings and our modernist expectations are frustrated, though, yet another response may supercede. Readerly anxiety largely disappears. We no longer worry that we cannot tie everything into a neat system. We feel increasingly comfortable with the text and move from one episode to the next, focusing on each as it comes. We know who the characters are, what the White Visitation or PISCES is, and do not need to fumble for our coordinates just to

follow what is happening. We can simply enjoy the slap-
stick, the weird fantasy, the realistic detail, the changes
in narrative register, and the deliberate mysteries. We
reach a state corresponding to that of Pynchon's new
style of hero. Like Pynchon's heroes facing their fragmented cosmos, we learn to survive through flexibility
and through not demanding too much control. We learn
to accept uncertainty, make personal arrangements of
local order, and go with the flow.[7]

As familiarity increases, the text starts to establish links
in each reader's mind to the broader literary tradition.
Borges, discussing Kafka, points out that "every writer
creates his own precursors,"[8] and paradoxically that is
true, at least for readers acquainted with the literary
tradition. The reading process more or less inevitably
becomes echoic and evokes literary chains of associations. In the case of *Gravity's Rainbow,* literary and cultural relationships establish themselves to *Faust,* to *Moby-
Dick,* to *Ulysses,* to Wagner, and to the Bible, as well as
to the films of Fritz Lang and to *King Kong.* In some
cases, the association is explicit; in others such as *Faust,*
it is implicit. Other links will be more arguable—their
influence felt more as a matter of reader sensation than
provable presence—but whether Pynchon was influenced by any one text or not, beyond a certain point, is
not the issue and does not matter. It is the nature of the
reading experience to attach the text one is currently
reading (in this case, *Gravity's Rainbow*) to texts previously read. Making such attachments is part of the process by which a text comes to seem meaningful and
worthwhile to each reader. Through this intertextual
identification of resemblances and distortions, echoes
and literary challenges, readers make the new text part

of their inner horizon, to be applied in turn to new novels and experiences. Part of our sense of the text's meaning comes from our establishing such individual linkages. Like repetitions within a text, echoes to further texts do not constitute a meaning identifiable by logic, but they certainly create the subjective sensation of meaning in the reader, which is part of our overall experience of meaning, and we find that this sensation reinforces our feeling that we understand a piece of literature. Whether we use a mythology or not, this process inevitably takes place.

Even where connections and patterns are disturbed by an inherent contradiction, we quickly learn to make allowances; in *Gravity's Rainbow,* we accept Slothrop's infant conditioning as probable if not provable and as symbolically true if not personally accurate—Freud has accustomed us to *that* form of semitruth. Readings that insist on the destruction of pattern in Pynchon's novel largely ignore such insistent sensations of meaning and appropriateness. Whether these patterns of connectedness and literary echoes and thematic structures are totally consistent or not seems to be less important to the reading experience of this difficult text than critics assume. Even broken and imperfect patterns are capable of evoking the feelings that accompany our finding a sense of meaning, and they still can create a network of associations that makes part of the reading experience of this difficult text entirely normal. The reader's sense of knowing what is going on, or what the text means, may be looser and less expressible than would be the case with a realistic novel, but in the end, after several readings, this particular literary experience is much like other such experiences. To say that not just reality but

Gravity's Rainbow as well is radically uncertain asserts as theory something that does not stand up well in practice.

This stage of familiarization, and of creating links both within the text and to the literary and cultural tradition, seems to me natural and inevitable and desirable, but one might ask whether this sense of comfort with the text is more correctly deemed a form of bourgeois possessiveness? Or at least academic consumption? Is this a matter of taking the text over and remaking it in one's own image? Is it a parasitic process? A process of mutilation? Richard Poirier warns us particularly against academic consumption:

Unless academic writers and teachers are extremely careful they will do to him [Pynchon] the damage already done to Joyce and Eliot.
Put simply, the damage consists of looking at the writing as something to be figured out by a process of translation, a process which omits the weirdness and pleasure of the reading experience as it goes along. . . . The damage consists of treating each of the formal or stylistic or allusive elements in a work as a clue to meaning, a point of possible stabilization.[9]

Poirier's warning might seem significant when we remember that the fragmented first reading is what is changed by subsequent encounters. Any reading that denies the sensation of fragmentation will inevitably seem antipostmodernist or academic or newtonian or bourgeois.

Of course, if we read the text only once, the disruptive and disquieting features will retain most of their pristine force. The sense of near-total otherness will be our strongest response to a kind of defamiliarization that does not just slow down our regard until it sees the stoniness of the stone, but pulverizes the stone itself.[10] Subsequent readings are what do most to make the text more open to us and make us more open to the text. Can a piece of literature, especially as long a piece as *Gravity's Rainbow*, sustain the effect of permanent shock and defamiliarization over subsequent readings? Probably not, since part of that effect derives from ignorance of what is coming, from surprise. Genuinely random gibberish might resist familiarization, but would not retain readerly interest for 760 pages. What keeps us going back to *Gravity's Rainbow* despite its difficulty is the richness of its material, and part of that richness consists of the complexity of the patterns and connections, even if and possibly because they resist easy closure. Ultimately, it seems to me, the totally postmodernist *Gravity's Rainbow*, though valid for a first reading and a treasured part of our total experience of the work, must make room for others, unless the novel, like toilet paper, is to be used only once and discarded.[11]

This suggests that at least three quite different kinds of reading are called for. The first is the fragmented vision promulgated by various postmodernist critics. The second would include the perspectives that provide a sense of limited, local order, including among many possible approaches my straight mythological analysis. The third would be the viewpoint from which both these perspectives can be held in balance, from which some kind of integration can be made. Interpretations of the second sort, those seeking order, have been partly avoided out of deference to the first by many academic readers, because the first is superficially the more attractive: it promises novelty for commentary. Deconstruction as a critical discourse is less well-worn than myths or themes.

The more significant novelty seems to me, however, to reside in the third sort of reading and in the mental mechanisms by which we as readers can learn to balance and integrate the approaches, for the first reading is the most limited of the possibilities. Once we finish tracing systems of order to their internal abysses, there is nothing more to say.

Retaining both readings requires that mental state, described at the beginning of this chapter, in which we circumvent the brain's longing for closure enough to let two modes of perception resonate with and against each other. Trying to reach this state for reading *Gravity's Rainbow* seems appropriate, because observing the human desire for order in its struggle with an uncertain reality is partly what *Gravity's Rainbow* is about.

The myth Pynchon uses helps him and us handle the chaos. The new hero-myth he offers tells us how one should try to live with chaos, and the attitude espoused by that hero-myth is analogous to that of the third stage of reading. The new hero, in addition to having mythological functions, becomes a model for the ideal reader. Moreover, though Pynchon foregrounds the forces that dismantle order, *Gravity's Rainbow* can only exist because of both of those impulses within his own mind: the intuitive, nonlinear mode that dissolves assumed patterns into "meaningless" (that is, nonrational) forms, and the rational, linear, analytic mode that organizes the extraordinary mass of detail. Combined, these impulses create the artistically satisfying whole. In the hero, they nurture both flexibility and the ability to make personal arrangements. In the reader or critic, they produce a reading, an interaction between text and reader, richer and more full of the sensation of meaning, even more creative, than either mode alone can produce. The state of mind that permits the two modes of perception to coincide is playful and revels in the permutations without trying to pin them rigidly down. It encourages a barthesian jouissance in the open and relaxed reader, who can accept Pynchon's entire circus of effects without needing desperately to control them.[12]

Thomas Pynchon as Mythographer

Because Pynchon's fragmentation of reality is not as absolute as has been assumed, the contradiction between this postmodernist technique and the use of a mythological structure proves to be more apparent than real. Meaning structures may function, even when one aim of the work is to disorient us and deny our frameworks for dealing with reality. Not only do readers adapt to probabilistic interpretation, they also adapt to the mythology as a symbolic way of talking about the cosmos, history, and humankind's predicament.

Symbol, not scientific analysis, is the key here. One can integrate the silences with the music, the muffins with the craters, partly by identifying each with an earlier or later stage of familiarity with the text, but mainly by recognizing the symbolic nature of the mythology. It is a self-consciously artificial structure for discussing reality when other, more direct, analytic means have been undermined and exploded. Pynchon is not just presenting fragments; he is commenting on them and on how humanity can interact with reality, by means of the new hero-myth. Practically any sort of discussion requires a means of imposing order: one cannot comment (in any normal sense of that word) on chaos purely by means of chaos. The mythological symbolism lets Pynchon present the fractured reality, comment upon it, and suggest better ways of relating to it. His artifice remains apparent: the significant geography, the highly ritualized wedding between Gottfried and the rocket, the apocalyptic glimpses of possible futures—from these we know we are not dealing with a realistic attempt to analyze reality but with an indirect mode well served by the mythology.

In building a new hero pattern as he does, Pynchon gives us not only a model for the individual in a fragmented reality, but also a model for the individual as reader of this text. One obvious quality demanded of both reader and pychonesque hero is flexibility. The rules of the game change frequently for Slothrop, and his survival depends on his ability to change as rapidly. So too for readers: flexibility is required if they are to survive the rather brutal battering given the traditional rules of fiction. Implicit in that flexibility is the reader's acceptance that he or she will never control this text in accustomed fashions.

Another quality demanded can be called interactivity. Indeed, Pynchon's realities are assimilable only by those who mingle themselves with the events at various levels, and they depend upon the reader/actor's creative participation to become fully real. The subtle levels at which Pynchon's characters interact with their world can be seen in Jessica's awareness of her own relationship to snowflakes. They fall on her eyelashes, and she notes the fugitive prismatic effect of light through those crystals, visible only through squinting eyelids: "purple and orange creatures blooming on her long lashes" (p. 58).

Slothrop, while being crammed with rocket information, is simultaneously sensitive to equations for rocket yaw, to the influence of the spirit Roland Feldspath, and to the qualities of his own reverie ("one where the colors are more primaries than pastels" [p. 237]). Characters interact with reality via hallucinations and drugs, partly experiencing and partly creating what they experience: when sniffing gasoline, the Herero, Pavel, hallucinates what appear to be Herero rather than European figures, such as the Moss Creature, the Water Giant, and a host of minute Pygmies (p. 523).

Because of the preponderance of iserian blanks, the reader too must create in order to experience. Colors, for instance, demand interactivity from the reader, for alizarine, bittersweet, taupe, and the color of boiled shrimp force us to delve into memories to fill in the hues. The persistence of vision—the way the eye of the observer interacts with a series of still frames to produce the illusion of motion—is one of Pynchon's favorite images for how reality as experienced differs from its theoretical nature. Greta Erdmann interacts so thoroughly with her silver screen audience that her *Alpdrücken* orgy begets children for the onlookers.

The more the reader is immersed in the text, especially during subsequent readings, the more participatory the relationship. We integrate from the fragments to patterns. We make connections, some invited but others made at our own discretion, out of our own experience. Because so much depends on the reader, multiple interpretations of local order are inevitable and appropriate. Insofar as Pynchon upholds creative interaction with the universe our creative interactions with his text are exercises of that function. Readers who return to the novel are the ones most likely to resist being crushed by the power and weight of the text and to resist being controlled by it; they will learn to glide along its interfaces, interacting to some degree as they choose or wish to do and, above all, will shed some of the initial anxiety.

Pynchon is not alone in focusing on flexibility and interactivity, both for his characters and his readers.[13] Several contemporary authors, all of whom have produced mythographic works, focus on these same qualities. Günther Grass, in *The Flounder* for instance, expresses the need for flexibility as he traces the narrator's experiences down through the ages, from prehistoric bog people to modern Germany and Poland. The narrator, while participating in the battle of the sexes throughout this span of history, must adapt with each generation to the ebbs and flows of power if he is to maintain his identity at all. His modern wife, Ilsebill, is pregnant and feminist and not easy to live with, but he does his best to be considerate and raise his consciousness. Interactivity takes the form of eating in Grass's epic. People interact by means of food, showing affection or hatred, respect or contempt. It is the weapon in the ongoing gender battle, the medium of exchange, the instrument of vengeance, the consolation in sad times, the celebration, the sacrament that binds one to life, and the surest bond between the narrator and the series of cooks who are his partners down through the ages. The narrating consciousness sees the world through the beauties of food and deals with reality through what and how he eats. Feastday geese or thin potato soup in times of famine—these are what make his world. The narrator is most thoroughly alive when interacting with food, and reality for him depends on what he is eating in that particular lifetime. Insofar as readers share Grass's interest in food, they too will interact—physically, even—to his loving descriptions of food.

Italo Calvino also upholds interactivity and flexibility as prime virtues in *Cosmicomics* and *t zero*. He too uses a narrator whose existence transcends mortal span: Qwfwq was conscious prior to the Big Bang yet is also present in a Manhattan of skyscrapers and transistors; in between, he has seen the condensation of matter, the first light, the first color, the first reptiles to evolve into land animals—and has actually been the last dinosaur. He was also the first mollusk to produce a colored shell (despite blindness), and he participated in many other such evolutionary events. Throughout these mythological fables, Calvino's narrator embodies the principle of flexibility: metamorphosis and change are sacred values in this cosmos. Indeed, they are the mediating terms that emerge from a structuralist study of that cosmos's binary oppositions.[14]

Over and over, Calvino poses the question: What can cartesian awareness do to keep itself from feeling annihilated by the silent spaces of the universe which science has given us? Qwfwq goes through galactic years (two hundred million of our years); he lives with light-years as everyday measurements of his world. For our fragile egos not to be dwarfed into insanity by the contrast, we have to find ways of measuring the universe in smaller, human terms. This Qwfwq ultimately does through the key human emotions or actions of attraction, repulsion, rivalry, and the creation of things new to the universe. In other words, Calvino's answer to his central question is interactivity. One interacts with reality. Why be passive when one can play with the universe?

Qwfwq shows us that we need the willingness to interact zestfully and the flexibility to change. Qwfwq, indeed, mutates through many forms as he changes to meet newly emergent realities.

Calvino is obviously working in a mythological vein when imagining the first light, first life on land, and the like. (There is no apocalypse because metamorphosis and change are offered as an answer to death, and apocalypse is a projection of individual death on the world.) Grass's narrative is mythological in that it attempts to fill the gap between origins and what we are now, and his principal male characters, the eternal narrator and the equally eternal Flounder, would appear by that token to be quasi-divinities in this mythic history.[15] The great struggle and the shifts in the balance of power between the sexes form the mythological history. The long, interspersed trial of the Flounder gives us a central symbolic action. The sadness of the narrator at the end, his feeling that women have overlooked, overstepped, and passed men by, shows the death of an old order and birth of a new, not so much with a bang as a whimper. Both writers, seeking to get beyond the realistic to more fundamental and wide-reaching issues, turn to myth, and both offer us patterns suggestive of how we can or should interact with the realities they define. Both hail flexibility and interactivity as crucial to happiness and survival. (We have only to look at the Bible to realize that flexibility and interactivity are not the inevitable messages of mythological literature. One does not develop a chosen people through either mode of behavior.)

In *Cosmicomics* and *t zero*, Calvino may not demand that his readers imitate his protagonist in order to carry out the act of reading, but he does make such a pynchonesque demand in *If on a winter's night a traveler.* The first and second Readers, characters in the novel, are also surrogates within the text for the readers outside of it. The quests of first and second Reader allow Calvino to identify the qualities he desires in his readers. The second Reader, in particular, seems an ideal audience because of her flexibility and her willingness to interact with so many kinds of writing. Writing for such a reader is a quasi-sexual courtship and consummation. This second Reader is not ignorant or easily pleased, but she meets novels on their own grounds and attempts seriously to understand what the works are trying to do, rather than force what she reads to pass through a distorting filter of prejudices, personal preferences, and expectations. Again, flexibility and interactivity are prized, and are called for both from the characters of the story and from the readers of that novel.

By drawing attention to such parallels between Pynchon and other contemporary authors, I do not mean to lessen his claims to importance or originality. Rather, I wish to make four points. (1) The qualities upheld by his new hero and new myth are attracting serious attention from other writers who do not share Pynchon's ideological biases from the American 1960s. Readers distrustful of this sixties slant may be more willing to listen if others as well are turning in the same direction. (2) By recognizing Pynchon's interrelationships with other writers, we deepen our ability to respond to his text, simply because these give us new levels on which to interact with it. Since Pynchon's insistence on multiple realities implies an aesthetic favoring multiple levels or kinds of interaction, our improved ability to build connections is central to our reading endeavor. (3) His establishing parallels between the new type of hero and the reader of his text reminds us of the participatory role of the reader in contemporary fiction. Not only must the orphic poet assemble the shards of reality into a new reality within his own interior space, the reader must perform an analogous act to create the text from the assemblage of blanks and fragments. Calvino explores this point by making up *If on a winter's night a traveler* from fragments of novels; Pynchon makes a text so splintered that any reading of it will be unique and individual to a greater degree than usual. And (4) these writers, when they work in mythic modes, are usually commenting on what humankind should be. They offer hero patterns, their own sense of what humanity must do or become if it is to live with newly defined or evolving or multiplying realities.

Mentioning the experiments of other writers is one way of putting Pynchon's use of mythological material in context. But there is at least one further context that sheds light on Pynchon's affinity for his quasi-biblical device, and that is the mystical streak in Pynchon's writing. According to one source, Pynchon was still a practicing Catholic while in college.[16] Whether he was such during the writing of *Gravity's Rainbow* is not writ large upon the text, but his insistence that there is something, some sort of reality, beyond material reality is very much in evidence.

I detect no recognizable theological dimension to this position as he presents it, but do find passionate dedication to the proposition of nonmaterial realities. He creates multiple alternative realities, and several times brings back the dead to comment on the blindness of the living to the true nature of reality. Colors, for him,

as for Goethe, seem to invoke another order of existence. So does music—so much so that his many lyrics
and references to Orpheus have been taken to establish
a strong streak of orphic mysticism in the text:

> What makes *Gravity's Rainbow* an Orphic text, then, are . . .
> the adoption of Orphic tropes and precepts—life as sleep
> disturbed by dreams; Eros as a first principle that is at once
> life, love, sleep, and death; a soniferous aether to solve the
> problem of how all things are separate yet one; history as a
> progression from undifferentiated mass through individua-
> tion and back again to unity; our current age as a fall into
> time presided over by Ananke and Night; the twofold nature
> of being as a struggle between the Titanic and Dionysiac; the
> belief in life after death as a negotiable transformation; the
> primacy of the text in explicating esoteric mysteries; music
> and dance as vehicles of worship and images of the liberated
> self; and, finally, belief in Dionysiac enthusiasm as a way back
> to the original erotic unity. (Bass, p. 43)

Another proponent of religious orphism, Dwight Eddins, argues that the author-persona presents us with
orphic naturalism as a religion and opposes to it various
strains of Gnosticism, whose tenets, including that of
transcendence, can be held responsible for the activities
of Them and Their destruction of earth. In this reading,
Gravity's Rainbow becomes the sacred text often mentioned by characters in the narrative.

I would not limit Pynchon's mystic concerns solely to
the orphic and gnostic traditions. At least as much of
his interest in Orpheus seems to depend on Orpheus as
a mouthpiece for attitudes towards art and creativity, on
Orpheus as conventional representative of the poet,
whereas his mysticisms range from spiritualism and
theosophy to rilkean transcendence, "electromysticism,"

the Kirghiz Light, and, in earthier form, to Pan and Walpurgisnacht. He also seems to draw on various Eastern traditions.

Something like the Buddhist "pure light of the void" recurs as a form of the ultimate in the text. Nora Dodson-Truck faces "the Outer Radiance" and "each time has taken a little more of the Zero into herself" (p. 150). Slothrop realizes that he already knows such light when he is temporarily blinded by the phosphorous flare. He "feels a terrible *familiarity* here, a center he has been skirting, avoiding as long as he can remember—never has he been as close as now to the true momentum of his time" (p. 312). In that "white moment" he feels "vain and blind tugging at his sleeves *it's important* [. . .] *look at us*," but then his awareness only registers, in a passage replete with interactive detail, "*g*-loads, and the blood of his eyes has begun to touch the whiteness back to ivory, to brushings of gold and a network of edges to the broken rock" (p. 312). The Kirghiz Light manifests itself in "a place which is older than darkness, where even Allah cannot reach"— the latter obviously a Moslem rather than Buddhist rendition of this radiance. Pan too is a way to the "luminous spaces" beyond good and evil (p. 720). Blicero recognizes radiance as his outmost goal (p. 724). The void appears as a dark void to Pökler (p. 578), as wind to the spirit Roland Feldspath (p. 30), and as both dark and light on Snake's hide (p. 342). The account of crossing a cusp (p. 664) to a world that looks the same but isn't echoes accounts of satori.[17]

One can indeed argue that Pynchon offers a fifth future, one apart from the four versions of immachination. This fifth is Slothrop's dismantling of the ego, his narrowing of bandwidth to the present, his renunciation of control and his rainbow vision. Various critics have noted the presence of this mystical option, but few can accept it. such a thorough renunciation of control and individuality strikes at the very root of Western consciousness, so their descriptions include some kind of reservation or disclaimer:

Only Slothrop achieves transfiguration. He may or may not be illuminated by radiance when he sees the rainbow, but he has lost his self in the All of the universe and will break the cycle by surviving as a "Rolling Stone." Stones have a low-frequency perception, however, and do not function charismatically. To be subsumed by the All, without being able to maintain the integrity of the self, is to lose the joy of paradox, according to which the self can be part and whole. (Slade, "Escaping Rationalization," p. 36)

James W. Earl describes the problem as we see it from within the system:

This is the particular theme we have been developing in *Gravity's Rainbow:* first, that rational analysis, as the modern world's characteristic mode of life, has stolen man's freedom by seducing him intellectually into a "stone determinacy" at every level of his being; second, that we can return to our freedom, but only individually and alone—only at the cost of relinquishing society, because society cannot see its own enslavement to reason, does not understand its dangers, and so pushes it upon us aggressively, wrongly, and mortally, even if innocently; and third, that our solitary return into freedom is experienced both by society and ourselves as a dissolution—a loss of the self that is, paradoxically, an act of identification with the world and of all of those who constitute the very society we cannot belong to. (Earl, p. 244)

And to many critics, Slothrop is simply a failure. Like his acquaintances in the Zone, these readers gradually lose their ability to see him. His values and life-style become invisible to them. Their cultural predispositions and mental filters keep them from registering his discourse as anything but noise.

A few readers have noted Slothrop's dismemberment of ego as a spiritual advance from non-Western or mystical perspectives, and can grant him, therefore, a kind of success.[18]

Certainly Slothrop is a casualty in "reality"—a spaced-out, unidentified amnesiac if he is present on the physical plane at all—but the centrality of the Zone in the novel demonstrates that "reality" does not define the full extent of significant experience. (Kappel, p. 249)

Readers able to divorce themselves from Western bourgeois values argue that Pynchon is upholding nonrational knowledge and a nonlinear organization of reality (including nonlinear time), that he is even creating in *Gravity's Rainbow* a mandala, with all opposites balanced, the void at the center—radiant, beyond good or evil and beyond human understanding.[19]

How seriously readers take this fifth possible future—this dismantlement of Western individualism and the ego—will depend on each reader's own responses. Most readers will reject it as impractical or unrealistic, and so it is, by Western definitions of reality and by bourgeois standards of work and achievement and security and control. If the Western standards are under attack, however, they are not the most suitable means of weighing and judging this option. This mystical option is an extension of Pynchon's myth of the new hero, and to weigh its validity, we must again make a distinction between survival of the individual and of the species. One gains something from at least trying to envisage what such a future would entail. Slothrop's experience may make more sense if we look at the Zone symbolically. As Malekin notes, all our provisions for life are impermanent, as are our bodies. Our bureaucracies are without ultimate essence. Like Geli, we lie under rigged canvas in the rain, metaphorically speaking, and we all have to struggle to maintain such shelter. Malekin adds that perhaps Slothrop remains in the Zone because it "is a cusp of time if viewed from a linear-time point of view, but a state of reality if seen from outside."

Whatever Pynchon's personal beliefs may be, he seems devoted in this text to the proposition that material reality is not ultimate, indeed that it is not even a consistent, well-tailored veil of illusion. It is patchy, irregular, and so perforated with rents that further realities can be glimpsed from almost every vantage point, if we only knew how to look or even just knew how not to blinker ourselves. After all, the Titans "are all the presences we are not supposed to be seeing—wind gods, hilltop gods, sunset gods—that we train ourselves away from to keep from looking further" (p. 720). From the epigraph of book 1, in which Wernher von Braun asserts his belief in spiritual existence after death, to William Slothrop's hymn on the final page, with its faces in mountainsides and souls in stones, Pynchon points beyond the material reality to other forms of sentience and existence, without ever promising us transcendence.

Someone open to the concept of mystical experience should have no trouble reconciling a chaotic world with the kinds of symbolic order offered by a mythology. Far from having to strain to understand a chaotic universe, the mystic would be at home with the idea, given that many strains of mysticism view reality as variously inconsequential, unreal, flawed, fallen, and in any event, as received through inadequate sense organs. That we cannot really expect to understand reality is often a given. That we should still be concerned with how best to live within its constraints is also a given. That one might use mythology as one means of talking about the human condition within it is traditional. No contradiction need arise.

Thinking of Pynchon's concern with Orpheus within this text, and of his narrative voice as an orphic voice, may help us to see how some of the many strands of this text come together. Orpheus reached a oneness with nature through his music; he used his music to try to turn back time and death; and he prophesied. Pynchon touches lightly on the first, but he explores the theme of death throughout the narrative, and his apocalyptic vision constitutes a prophetic strain central to the novel. Nineteenth- and twentieth-century orphic artists have seen Orpheus as using his power to probe the limits of art in relation to reality, and this Pynchon certainly does. Orpheus fails to rescue Eurydice but gains from that experience with death the authority to speak. Pynchon too fails to rescue us and find salvation for our culture, our beloved technology. The failure in both cases is practically inevitable, but overall failure does not discredit any piece of wisdom that may emerge from the enterprise. Orpheus as founder of a religion gave humanity a new picture of its relationship to reality. Without making his results into a religious cult, so has Pynchon: he gives us a deconstructed view of our relationship with our pluriverse of multiple realities, a specific warning against immachination, and a new hero-myth as guide for individual action.

Were deconstructive contradiction or philosophical and scientific uncertainty all that Pynchon could envision, he would, logically at least, not have written *Gravity's Rainbow*. That act of creation is a constructive assertion, which by its existence testifies to the possibilities both of creation and of at least limited interpretation. Such a positive assertion can be made in the minimalist mode of Tertullian's "credo quia impossibile" (this is John Barth's attitude in *Chimera*), or one can take the human condition to be worth comment and readers to be worth warning against foreseen danger.

The novel's very title—with the same sort of condensation of meaning present everywhere in the text—suggests Pynchon's concerns: science, trajectories, inevitable declension toward the grave, and seriousness, but also the interplay of light with matter and with the observer resulting in color, a bridge to other realities, and even a mythological covenant by which another reality penetrates our own—a promise of protection, and a warning of the fire next time. The rainbow will reappear as a stout rainbow cock driving into Earth's green valley. It will surround shadows cast from the Brocken, adorn Katje, accompany Pan. It is a floating signifier; no one appearance or use is definitive, no one rainbow is presented as possessing "meaning" applicable throughout the text. What we make of it will depend on what we can relate it to. Its effects will be the richer as our minds are rich in associations; stirring to the degree that we interact with it. Like the rest of the text, it resists fixed

interpretation but demands from us the effort to inter-
pret and to interact with it. To ignore the intertextual
mythological associations is virtually impossible and
would constitute a turning away from the hilltop and
sunset gods, our avoidance of whom Pynchon deprecates.

Pynchon is certainly a postmodernist writer by most
definitions of that term. In McHale's sense, he desta-
bilizes our ontology. In accordance with Lyotard's definition, his postmodernism "denies itself the solace of
good forms, the consensus of a taste which would make
it possible to share collectively the nostalgia for the un-
attainable" and "searches for new presentations, not in
order to enjoy them but in order to import a stronger
sense of the unpresentable" (Lyotard, p. 81). *Gravity's
Rainbow* is also postmodernist in the sense that it calls
attention to gaps and absences; it denies the assumptions
of organic form, cause-and-effect relationships, origins,
mechanistic answers, people as entities, and systems of
organization as inherently valid. We miss half the richness and power of *Gravity's Rainbow,* however, if we find
it no more than the promulgation of absences and contradictions and uncertainty, no matter how potently it
presents such a vision. For the reader who works through
the text sufficiently to get beyond disorientation, *Gravity's Rainbow* should imply an author who has achieved
a vantage point on the far side of the abyss into which
all conventional meaning has disappeared. This author
does not ignore the void; he works through it and with
it, to give us something ultimately positive, a way of
interacting with that void, of incorporating it into our
lives. What he gives us is rich and splendid, kaleidoscopic
and complex, a labyrinth of infinite regresses that fas-
cinate indefinitely.

Notes

Bibliography

Index

Notes

1. Separating Cosmos from Chaos

1. E. H. Gombrich, *Art and Illusion: A Study in the Psychology of Pictorial Representation*, 2d ed., Bollingen Series 35, no. 5 (Princeton: Princeton University Press, 1969), 5.
2. Quotations come from *Gravity's Rainbow* (New York: Viking, 1973) and will hereafter be cited parenthetically by page number alone. This passage is found on 713.
3. This loose definition of postmodernism derives from several sources, chief among them Brian McHale, both in conversation and in his article "Modernist Reading, Post-Modern Text: The Case of *Gravity's Rainbow*," *Poetics Today* 1 (1979): 85–110. McHale has a book forthcoming on postmodernism. "Stabilizing" and "destabilizing" are his useful terms.
4. For a good description of major themes and a summary of criticism, see Charles Clerc's Introduction to *Approaches to* Gravity's Rainbow, ed. Charles Clerc (Columbus: Ohio State University Press, 1983), esp. 22–23.
5. Charles Russell, "Pynchon's Language: Signs, Systems, and Subversion," in *Approaches to* Gravity's Rainbow, 272, 252. Also stressing uncertainty is Thomas H. Schaub, *Pynchon: The Voice of Ambiguity* (Urbana: University of Illinois Press, 1981).
6. Molly Hite, "'Holy-Center-Approaching' in the Novels of Thomas Pynchon," *Journal of Narrative Technique* 12 (1982): 123, 128. Hite develops this perspective in greater detail in her book *Ideas of Order in the Novels of Thomas Pynchon* (Columbus: Ohio State

University Press, 1983). A variation of this vision is that of John M. Muste; when analyzing Pynchon's mandalas, Muste notes that at "the center of the mandala rests that infuriating empty circle, that refusal to impose meaning or to confirm either our fondest wishes or our direst fears. We are left with the silence, the void, the sterile nothingness; we are left also with unlimited possibility" ("The Mandala in *Gravity's Rainbow*," *Boundary 2* 9 [1981]: 178).

7. McHale, 106. Another critic, Linda A. Westervelt, says that Pynchon "manipulates the reader to construct a series of responses to the wrong questions" ("'A Place Dependent on Ourselves': The Reader as System-Builder in *Gravity's Rainbow*," *Texas Studies in Literature and Language* 22 [1980]: 86). For another reading that focuses on Pynchon's deconstructive techniques, see Bernard Duyfhuizen, "Starry-Eyed Semiotics: Learning to Read Slothrop's Map and *Gravity's Rainbow*," *Pynchon Notes* 6 (June 1981): 5–33. Volume 14 of *Pynchon Notes* (February 1984) is devoted to deconstruction and *Gravity's Rainbow:* the volume contains Louis Mackey, "Thomas Pynchon and the American Dream"; Joel D. Black, "Pynchon's Eve of De-struction"; Terry Caesar, "'Trapped inside Their frame with your wastes piling up': Mindless Pleasures in *Gravity's Rainbow*"; Stephen P. Schuber, "Textual Orbits/Orbiting Criticism: Deconstructing *Gravity's Rainbow*"; and an introduction by Bernard Duyfhuizen. The only article to take full advantage of radical deconstructive style, with its associative modes of thought, is that by Pierre-Yves Petillon, "Thomas Pynchon et l'espace aléatoire," *Critique* (France) 34 (1978): 1107–42. Petillon's article has been translated and appears in *Pynchon Notes* 15 (Fall 1984): 3–46.

8. Brian McHale discusses these vagaries of the narrative voice in "'You used to know what these words mean': Misreading *Gravity's Rainbow*," *Language and Style* 18 (1985): 93–118.

9. Marcus Smith and Khachig Tölölyan, "The New Jeremiad: *Gravity's Rainbow*," in *Critical Essays on Thomas Pynchon*, ed. Richard Pearce (Boston: G. K. Hall, 1981), 180.

10. See Edward Mendelson, "Gravity's Encyclopedia," in *Mindful Pleasures: Essays on Thomas Pynchon*, ed. George Levine and David Leverenz (Boston: Little, Brown, 1976), 161–95.

11. See Lawrence C. Wolfley, "Repression's Rainbow: The Presence of Norman O. Brown in Pynchon's Big Novel," *PMLA* 92 (1977): 873–89. See also Geoffrey Cocks, "War, Man, and Gravity: Thomas Pynchon and Science Fiction," *Extrapolation* 20 (1979): 368–77.

12. For a detailed analysis of the various paranoias, see Mark R. Siegel, *Pynchon: Creative Paranoia in* Gravity's Rainbow (Port Washington, N.Y.: Kennikat Press, 1978).

13. Roland Barthes, *Mythologies,* trans. Annette Lavers (London: Granada, 1973). Sanford S. Ames relates Pynchon's endeavor—the revelation of an oppressive ideology—to the parallel effort of Deleuze and Guattari in *Anti-Oedipus: Capitalism and Schizophrenia.* See Ames, "Pynchon and Visible Language: Ecriture," *International Fiction Review* 4 (1977): 170–73.

14. Hough's remark is cited by William Righter in *Myth and Literature* (London: Routledge and Kegan Paul, 1975), 72.

15. Eric Gould, *Mythical Intentions in Modern Literature* (Princeton: Princeton University Press, 1981), 6.

16. Northrop Frye, *The Secular Scripture: A Study in the Structure of Romance* (Cambridge: Harvard University Press, 1976), 9, 14.

17. Northrop Frye, *Anatomy of Criticism: Four Essays* (Princeton: Princeton University Press, 1957), 55–56.

18. Pynchon's own religious background is Catholic, according to Jules Siegel, his college roommate: see "Who Is Thomas Pynchon . . . and Why Did He Take Off with My Wife?" *Playboy,* March 1977. Siegel says that Pynchon's father is descended from Puritan stock, but that his mother is Catholic (122).

19. Italo Calvino, "Myth in the Narrative," in *Surfiction: Fiction Now . . . and Tomorrow,* ed. Raymond Federman (Chicago: Swallow Press, 1975), 79.

20. Brailoiu's investigation is described by Mircea Eliade in *The Myth of the Eternal Return; or, Cosmos and History,* trans. Willard R. Trask, Bollingen Series 46 (Princeton: Princeton University Press, 1971), 44–46.

21. Claude Lévi-Strauss, *Tristes Tropiques,* trans. John Weightman and Doreen Weightman (Harmondsworth: Penguin, 1976), 70–71.

22. See Kathryn Hume, "Visionary Allegory in David Lindsay's *A Voyage to Arcturus," Journal of English and Germanic Philology* 77 (1978): 72–91.

23. See Edmund R. Leach, "Genesis as Myth," in *European Literary Theory and Practice: From Existential Phenomenology to Structuralism,* ed. Vernon W. Gras (New York: Delta, 1973), 317–30. See also Claude Lévi-Strauss, "The Structural Study of Myth," in *Myth: A Symposium,* ed. Thomas A. Sebeok (1955; reprint, Bloomington: Indiana University Press, 1965), 81–106.

24. Paul Ricoeur, *Interpretation Theory: Discourse and the Surplus of Meaning* (Fort Worth: Texas Christian University Press, 1976), 61.

25. Northrop Frye schematizes such cosmic symbolism as it appears to be relevant to literature in *Anatomy of Criticism*. Mircea Eliade examines some of the standard beliefs attaching to mythic universes: the concept of sacred versus profane time, the world center or *axis mundi*, the myth of the eternal return. His clarification of the symbolism of initiation rites sheds some light on Slothrop's wanderings without identity in the Zone. See Eliade, *The Myth of the Eternal Return*, and Mircea Eliade, *Rites and Symbols of Initiation: The Mysteries of Birth and Rebirth*, trans. Willard R. Trask (1958; reprint, New York: Harper and Row, 1965).

26. Claude Lévi-Strauss, *The Raw and the Cooked*, trans. John Weightman and Doreen Weightman (New York: Harper and Row, 1970), 3.

27. The parallels to *Ulysses* and its reception are instructive. T. S. Eliot undertook to defend *Ulysses* from critics like Richard Aldington, who saw Joyce as "a prophet of chaos" and wailed "at the flood of Dadaism" that would ensue. If for Dadaism we read Derridadaism, the parallel is clear. Then as now, some readers rejoiced rather than wailed over this destabilizing effect. See Eliot, "Ulysses, Order, and Myth," *The Dial* 75 (November 1923): 480–83.

2. The Mythological Cosmos

1. Many of Pynchon's London details have been traced by Steven Weisenburger and Khachig Tölölyan. See respectively "The Chronology of Episodes in *Gravity's Rainbow*," *Pynchon Notes* 14 (February 1984): 50–64; and "War as Background in *Gravity's Rainbow*," in *Approaches to* Gravity's Rainbow, 31–68. The importance of such detail is discussed by Alfred MacAdam in "Pynchon as Satirist: To Write, To Mean," *Yale Review* 67 (1978): 555–66. John Brunner disparages the book for what he sees as inaccuracies in this London setting. It is true that Pynchon has an Englishman ask for applesauce rather than stewed apples— and Brunner finds other such genuine lapses—but to claim that Pynchon has given us "a complex and incontestably science-fictional retrospective parallel world"—in other words, a London alternative to the real one—seems to me to put too much weight on minor errors. Brunner also accuses Pynchon of ignoring the

fact that most V-2s fell short to the east, but on pages 171–73 of *Gravity's Rainbow*, we find Pynchon's recognition of this anomaly. See Brunner's "Coming Events: An Assessment of Thomas Pynchon's *Gravity's Rainbow*," *Foundation* 10 (1976): 20–27. For a more thorough list of Pynchon's minor errors, see Bertram Lippman, "The Reader of Movies: Thomas Pynchon's *Gravity's Rainbow*," *Denver Quarterly* 12 (1977): 1–46.

2. Pynchon also associates the Kirghiz Light with the North, possibly because it is six days' ride north of Tchitcherine's territory.

3. Thomas Schaub constructs a mandala embodying some of these values. Although he puts Berlin at the eastern point and London on the western, his organization is not primarily geographic. North, direction of whiteness and the toilet bowl, opposes south, direction of blackness and coal-tars. Rainbow, rocket, benzene ring, and serpent adorn the perimeter. At the center he locates Grid, Ego, and History. See Schaub, *Pynchon: The Voice of Ambiguity*, 56.

4. Kathryn Hume and Thomas J. Knight discuss this aspect of the Roseland toilet vision in "Orpheus and the Orphic Voice in *Gravity's Rainbow*," *Philological Quarterly* 64 (1985): 299–315.

5. There is also a chronological dimension for this cosmos. Each book is associated with a season (winter, spring, summer, autumn). For details of this timetable, see Tölölyan, "War as Background." For an analysis that links many events to specific dates by reference to the London *Times* and to holy days, see Weisenburger, "The Chronology of Episodes."

6. This quasi-allegorical connection between World War II and "the world's present predicament—the system of global terror dominated by ICBMs" is brought out by Smith and Tölölyan, 169.

7. Dionysian themes are discussed by Raymond M. Olderman in "The New Consciousness and the Old System," in *Approaches to Gravity's Rainbow*, 199–228; Peter A. Brier in "Caliban Reigns: Romantic Theory and Some Contemporary Fantasists," *Denver Quarterly* 13 (1978): 38–51; and Douglas Fowler in "Pynchon's Magic World," *South Atlantic Quarterly* 79 (1980): 51–60.

8. Kathryn Hume and Thomas J. Knight discuss music as prophecy and Pynchon's thematic variations on the concept of modulated frequencies in "Orpheus" and in "Pynchon's Orchestration of *Gravity's Rainbow*," *Journal of English and Germanic Philology* 85 (1986): 366–85.

9. Rilke's Tenth Elegy angel is particularly influential. John O. Stark says that Pynchon "includes echoes of Rilke's elegy so often throughout this novel that it sometimes seems like an expanded

version of that poem" (*Pynchon's Fictions: Thomas Pynchon and the Literature of Information* [Athens: Ohio University Press, 1980], 151). For other criticism linking *Gravity's Rainbow* to Rilke, see David Cowart, *Thomas Pynchon: The Art of Allusion* (Carbondale: Southern Illinois University Press, 1980); Alan J. Friedman and Manfred Puetz, "Science as Metaphor: Thomas Pynchon and *Gravity's Rainbow*," *Contemporary Literature* 15 (1974): 345–59; Siegel, *Pynchon*, 89–93 and *passim;* Lance W. Ozier, "The Calculus of Transformation: More Mathematical Imagery in *Gravity's Rainbow*," *Twentieth Century Literature* 21 (1975): 193–210; and Dwight Eddins, "Orphic contra Gnostic: Religious Conflict in *Gravity's Rainbow*," *Modern Language Quarterly* 45 (1984): 163–90.

10. Douglas Fowler in *A Reader's Guide to* Gravity's Rainbow (Ann Arbor, Mich.: Ardis, 1980), appendix 3, 273, points out that Imipolex G was apparently developed in 1939 (see *Gravity's Rainbow*, 249–50) and therefore could not itself be the stimulus used in Tyrone's babyhood in the 1920s. But Slothrop himself says, "though according to these papers it would have been too early for it . . . he knows that what's haunting him now will prove to be the smell of Imipolex G" (*Gravity's Rainbow*, 286).

11. Robert L. Nadeau argues that Pynchon builds an elaborate game, suckering readers into postulating suprarational connection between Slothrop's sexual adventures and the rocket falls. Because the time dimension is not predictable, we have no grounds for assuming anything but chance correspondence between the two series of events. See Nadeau, "Readings from the New Book of Nature: Physics and Pynchon's *Gravity's Rainbow*," *Studies in the Novel* 11 (1979): 454–71. Bernard Duyfhuizen also challenges the existence of any meaningful connection between Slothrop's sexual adventures and the rocket falls in "Starry-Eyed Semiotics."

12. Northrop Frye discusses the archetypes associated with animal, vegetable, and mineral levels of creation in *Anatomy of Criticism*, 141 ff.

13. For discussions of Pynchon's interest in pigs, see John C. Calhoun, "The Concept of Revolution and Its Influence on the Genesis of Art in the work of Thomas Pynchon," *Perspectives on Contemporary Literature* 2 (1976): 40–52; also, André le Vot, "The Rocket and the Pig: Thomas Pynchon and Science-Fiction," *Caliban XII*, n.s. 11 (1975): 111–18.

14. Several critics have noted Pynchon's sensitivity to people, substances, and objects discarded by The System. References to his poetry of detritus occur in Tony Tanner, *Thomas Pynchon* (Lon-

don: Methuen, 1982), 21; Peter L. Cooper, *Signs and Symptoms: Thomas Pynchon and the Contemporary World* (Berkeley and Los Angeles: University of California Press, 1983), 85–92; Caesar; and F. S. Schwarzbach, "Pynchon's Gravity," *New Review* 3 (June 1976): 39–43.

15. Alan J. Friedman gives the figure for the number of times crystals appear in "Science and Technology," in *Approaches to* Gravity's Rainbow, 96–97; see also Friedman and Puetz, 349.

16. Lance W. Ozier, 203. Another critic to discuss the rich and varying role of points and transitions in Pynchon's cosmology is N. Katherine Hayles, in "Cosmology and the Point of (No) Return in *Gravity's Rainbow*," *Markham Review* 12 (1983): 73–77; see also her book *The Cosmic Web: Scientific Field Models and Literary Strategies in the Twentieth Century* (Ithaca: Cornell University Press, 1984).

17. Pynchon develops this idea of sense data as wave phenomena in *The Crying of Lot 49* (1966; reprint, New York: Bantam, 1967), 96.

18. Siegel explores this aspect of paranoia in his book *Pynchon: Creative Paranoia in* Gravity's Rainbow.

19. See Olderman, "The New Consciousness," and Tölölyan, "War as Background."

3. Mythological Actions

1. Frye, *The Secular Scripture,* 9.

2. Rosemary Jackson discusses the two functions covered by the word "express," namely, to "tell of" and to "expel" or "drive out." Both come into play in her definition of fantasy, and both seem relevant to Pynchon's mythological mode of working. See her *Fantasy: The Literature of Subversion* (London: Methuen, 1981), 3–4. For Leach, see "Genesis as Myth."

3. Tanner, 81–82.

4. This theme is emphasized by V.'s acquiring more and more prosthetic replacements for flesh and blood, until she seems more clockwork than human. Another character in the novel, Bongo-Shaftesbury, has a mechanical arm and frightens Victoria Wren's younger sister with it. "The Rock," ultimate emblem of the inanimate in the novel, is the pervasive spiritual trap for humans; men and women give up their animation and become rocklike in order to escape suffering. The transfor-

mation of bodies into electromechanisms is treated as a form of creeping petrifaction. *V.*, Pynchon's first novel, was published in 1963. In his disquisition on the Luddites, Pynchon makes the following m/antic prediction: "If our world survives, the next great challenge to watch out for will come—you heard it here first—when the curves of research and development in artificial intelligence, molecular biology and robotics all converge" ("Is It O.K. To Be a Luddite?" *New York Times Book Review*, 28 October 1984, 41).

5. John Gardner, *Grendel* (1971; reprint, New York: Ballantine, 1972), 61.

6. Mendelson, 164–65. Mendelson thus emphasizes the creation of a new culture; Mark R. Siegel emphasizes instead that Pynchon's apocalypse is the destruction of culture (rather than of the world). See Siegel, "Creative Paranoia: Understanding the System of *Gravity's Rainbow*," *Critique* 18 (1976–77): 39–54. Jean-François Lyotard comments on our information society: Where · "knowledge is and will be produced, in order to be sold, it is and will be consumed in order to be valorized in a new production. . . . Knowledge ceases to be an end in itself, it loses its 'use-value'" (*The Postmodern Condition: A Report on Knowledge*, trans. Geoff Bennington and Brian Massumi [Minneapolis: University of Minnesota Press, 1984], 4–5).

7. Russell Hoban, another novelist interested in how we create our myths, emphasizes this image of infanticide as appropriate to our era in *Riddley Walker* (1980). He replaces our story of Cain's fratricide (the first major action after the fall) with the story of parents eating their child just after the nuclear holocaust that corresponds to the fall in his new world.

8. Pynchon is not inventing this: both Dornberger and von Braun describe having occupied the target. See Tölölyan's citation of Wernher von Braun and Alan J. Friedman's citation of Walter Dornberger in their respective essays in *Approaches to* Gravity's Rainbow, 47, 99.

9. Tanner, 82. In its symbolic centrality and complexity, the rocket has been likened to Henry Adams's dynamo by Speer Morgan, in *"Gravity's Rainbow:* What's the Big Idea?" in *Critical Essays on Thomas Pynchon*, 84–85.

10. For discussion of the natural cycle and Western technology's violation of this cycle, see Marjorie Kaufman, "Brünnhilde and the Chemists: Women in *Gravity's Rainbow*," in *Mindful Pleasures*, 197–227; Raymond M. Olderman, "Thomas Pynchon," *Contem-*

porary Literature 20 (1979): 500–507; Joseph W. Slade, "Escaping Rationalization: Options for the Self in *Gravity's Rainbow*," *Critique* 18 (1976–77): 27–38; and le Vot.

11. Pynchon's concern with control has been likened to the arguments of Michel Foucault and Norman Mailer by Khachig Tölölyan in "Prodigious Pynchon and His Progeny," *Studies in the Novel* 11 (1979): 224–34, and in "Criticism as Symptom: Thomas Pynchon and the Crisis of the Humanities," *New Orleans Review* 5 (1979): 314–18.

12. See, for instance, Scott Sanders, "Pynchon's Paranoid History," in *Mindful Pleasures*, 139–59, and Louis Mackey, "Paranoia, Pynchon, and Preterition," *Sub-Stance*, no. 30 (1981): 16–30.

13. Many of the often noted oppositions prove to be specific embodiments of the more basic general oppositions. Thus north and south and Apollo and Dionysus reduce to closure and openness or control and freedom, which are variations of each other; European culture and primitive cultures can be translated into breaking the cycle, on the one hand, and living within it, on the other; white skin versus black goes back both to closure/openness and to elect/preterite; white as a color relates to north and death, while black as a color ties into south and to organic life (compost). These are typical examples of such reductions. There are many others.

14. See Carolyn S. Pyuen, "The Transmarginal Leap: Meaning and Process in *Gravity's Rainbow*," *Mosaic* 15 (1982): 33–46; Richard Alan Schwartz, "Thomas Pynchon and the Evolution of Fiction," *Science-Fiction Studies* 8 (1981): 165–72; Schwarzbach; Westervelt; and volume 14 of *Pynchon Notes*.

15. Paranoia in the information age is also explored by such writers as William Burroughs (*Naked Lunch, Ah Pook is Here*) and John Brunner (*The Shockwave Rider*).

16. Dwight Eddins unites the mystical and the ecological in his analysis of Orphism. The unities it prizes include the living genetic molecules, the magic of compost, and the earth as living mind-body. Opposing this is the gnostic attitude, which views the earth as defective and values control and transcendence.

17. The main critics to explore this nexus of values are Wolfley and Cocks.

18. Peter Brier, 43–44.

19. Various kinds of implications of living in the present are discussed by Olderman in "The New Consciousness." Another writer who argues for living in the present and not trying so

desperately to control the future is Russell Hoban, in *Riddley Walker.*

20. William M. Plater, *The Grim Phoenix: Reconstructing Thomas Pynchon* (Bloomington: Indiana University Press, 1978), 154–55.

21. James I. McClintock, "United State Revisited: Pynchon and Zamiatin," *Contemporary Literature* 18 (1977): 480.

22. Mackey, "Paranoia, Pynchon, and Preterition," 20.

23. John M. Krafft, "Anarcho-Romanticism and the Metaphysics of Counterforce: Alex Comfort and Thomas Pynchon," *Paunch* 40–41 (1975): 81.

24. For critical focus on this problem of cusps and choice, see Smith and Tölölyan; Steven Weisenburger, "The End of History? Thomas Pynchon and the Uses of the Past," *Twentieth Century Literature* 25 (1979): 54–72; Ozier; James W. Earl, "Freedom and Knowledge in the Zone," in *Approaches to* Gravity's Rainbow, 229–50; Antonio Márquez, "The Nightmare of History and Thomas Pynchon's *Gravity's Rainbow,*" *Essays in Literature* 8 (1981): 53–62; Schaub, 68–69; and Cooper, esp. chapter 3.

25. For discussions of such intermediate spaces, see Schaub, chapter 5; Joseph W. Slade, *Thomas Pynchon* (New York: Warner, 1974), chapter 5; and Schwarzbach.

4. Mythology and the Individual

1. Joseph Campbell, *The Hero with a Thousand Faces,* 2d ed., Bollingen Series 17 (Princeton: Princeton University Press, 1968).

2. For more elaborate discussion of the pattern with numerous examples of all the stages of the monomyth, see my "Romance: A Perdurable Pattern," *College English* 36 (1974): 129–46. For female variations on the monomyth, see Carol Pearson and Katherine Pope, *The Female Hero in American and British Literature* (New York: R. R. Bowker, 1981); for specifically American variations, see Robert Jewett and John Shelton Lawrence, *The American Monomyth* (Garden City, N.Y.: Anchor, 1977).

3. Erich Neumann, *The Origins and History of Consciousness,* trans. R. F. C. Hull, Bollingen Series 42 (Princeton: Princeton University Press, 1970). Eliade describes initiation rites that parallel this sequence of images in *Rites and Symbols of Initiation.*

4. Bruno Bettelheim, *The Uses of Enchantment: The Meaning and Importance of Fairy Tales* (New York: Alfred A. Knopf, 1976).

5. A.-J. Greimas, *Sémantique structurale; recherche de métode* (Paris: Librairie Larousse, 1966), 172–91; Roland Barthes, "Par où

commencer?" *Poetique* 1 (1970): esp. 4; and Fredric Jameson, "Magical Narratives: Romance as Genre," *New Literary History* 7 (1975): 135–63, quotation 148–49.

6. That Pynchon's characters are not realistic has been explained and aesthetically defended by Thomas Moore, "A Decade of *Gravity's Rainbow,* The Incredible Moving Film," *Michigan Quarterly Review* 22 (1983): 78–94; and Carol F. Richer, "The Prismatic Character in *Gravity's Rainbow,*" *Pynchon Notes* 12 (June 1983): 26–38.

7. Quotations from Goethe come from *Faust,* vol. 3 of *Goethes Werke,* 4th ed. (Hamburg: Christian Wegner Verlag, 1959).

8.   Behind me only be the shining sun!

....

But O how glorious through the storm there gleams
The changeless, ever changeful rainbow bent,
Sometimes distinct, sometimes with shattered beams,
Dispensing showers of cool and fragrant scent.
Man's effort is there mirrored in that strife.
Reflect and by reflection comprehend:
There in that rainbow's radiance *is* our life.

Goethe, *Faust,* trans. Charles E. Passage (Indianapolis: Bobbs-Merrill, 1965), 170.

9. Lawrence Kappel, "Psychic Geography in *Gravity's Rainbow,*" *Contemporary Literature* 21 (1980): 246.

10.   And this is wisdom's final say:
Freedom and life belong to that man solely
Who must reconquer them each day.

....

Such in their multitudes I hope to see
On free soil standing with a people free.
Then to that moment I could say:
Linger on, you are so fair!

Goethe, *Faust,* trans. Passage, 393.

11. The problems of will and decisiveness in *Gravity's Rainbow* are discussed by Smith and Tölölyan and by Earl.

12. For a discussion of these wagnerian parallels, see Kaufman.

13. For useful descriptions of Wagner's themes, see L. J. Rather, *The Dream of Self-Destruction: Wagner's* Ring *and the Modern World* (Baton Rouge: Louisiana State University Press, 1979).

14. See Kaufman; Olderman, "The New Consciousness"; Slade, "Escaping Rationalization"; Craig Hansen Werner, *Paradoxical*

Resolutions: American Fiction since James Joyce (Urbana: University of Illinois Press, 1982), 181–94; and Smith and Tölölyan.

15. David Cowart mentions some of Pynchon's allusions to Wagner in his discussion of Pynchon's use of opera in general; see his *Thomas Pynchon*, 12, 130–31. He equates the rocket limericks with the minnesinger contest in "Pynchon's Use of the Tannhauser-Legend in *Gravity's Rainbow*," *Notes on Contemporary Literature* 9 (1979): 2–3. Joseph W. Slade also discusses the Tannhäuser allusions in his *Thomas Pynchon*, 207–8, as does J. O. Tate in "*Gravity's Rainbow*: The Original Soundtrack," *Pynchon Notes* 13 (October 1983): 3–24. Both Cowart and Slade discuss Orpheus as well.

16. Pynchon uses the medieval wasteland legends but also of course T. S. Eliot's "The Wasteland." For discussions of various kinds of wasteland imagery throughout Pynchon's canon, see Tanner; for its role in *Gravity's Rainbow*, see Slade, "Escaping Rationalization"; for links to Eliot's poem through use of the tarot see David Seed, "Further Notes and Sources for *Gravity's Rainbow*," *Pynchon Notes* 16 (Spring 1985): 25–36.

17. See Norman N. Holland, *The Dynamics of Literary Response* (New York: W. W. Norton, 1975), 42–44, for discussion of the array of fantasies associated with the phallic stage.

18. See Kappel for interconnections between the the Zone and Oz.

19. This point is made by Frank D. McConnell in *Four Postwar American Novelists: Bellow, Mailer, Barth, and Pynchon* (Chicago: University of Chicago Press, 1977), 197.

20. See John Toland, *The Dillinger Days* (New York: Random House, 1963).

21. Dionysus presides over the "phancy phalli" of Roger and Pig Bodine (708, 710), over their explosively repellent menu suggestions (715–17), and over the preterite kazoo and harmonica players on the Los Angeles freeways (756).

22. See Hume and Knight, "Orchestration" and "Orpheus," for much more detailed analysis of Pynchon's use of music and the Orpheus myth. For Pynchon's orphic mysticism, see Eddins; also Thomas A. Bass, "*Gravity's Rainbow* as Orphic Text," *Pynchon Notes* 13 (October 1983): 25–46.

23. Elizabeth Sewell, *The Orphic Voice: Poetry and Natural History* (New Haven: Yale University Press, 1960), 3–4.

24. See Walter A. Strauss, *Descent and Return: The Orphic Theme in Modern Literature* (Cambridge: Harvard University Press, 1971);

Gerald L. Bruns, "Poetry as Reality: The Orpheus Myth and Its Modern Counterparts," *ELH* 37 (1970): 263–86; Gerald L. Bruns, *Modern Poetry and the Idea of Language: A Critical and Historical Study* (New Haven: Yale University Press, 1974); and Sewell.

25. See Strauss, 171, 181.

26. Ihab Hassan, "The Dismemberment of Orpheus: Notes on Form and Antiform in Contemporary Literature," in *Learners and Discerners: A Newer Criticism,* ed. Robert Scholes (Charlottesville: University of Virginia Press, 1964), 135–65.

27. Rainer Maria Rilke, *Sonnets to Orpheus,* German text with translation by C. F. MacIntyre (Berkeley and Los Angeles: University of California Press, 1960); and *Duino Elegies,* 4th ed., German text with translation by J. B. Leishman and Stephen Spender (London: Chatto and Windus, 1975). The lines from part 1, sonnet 22 in the MacIntyre translation read "Boys, on speed waste no courage or power, or on trials of flight."

28. Geoffrey Cocks puts it well when he says, "The answer is not heroism, for that is a return to precisely that anxious ideal which elevates the few at the expense of the many. [Ernst] Becker, in reading from Otto Rank and Erich Fromm, sees the whole problem of heroes, villains, leaders, and the led in the context of the human need for control" (Cocks, 373). The same is true of saviors. They are not part of Pynchon's picture. The savior hero is especially strongly established in American popular culture, as Jewett and Lawrence argue in *The American Monomyth.*

29. Fowler, in "Pynchon's Magic World," notes that Pynchon's favorites frequently resemble children (58).

30. Schwarzbach expresses this aspect of Pynchon's ethos as follows: "Accepting life in all its degradation, remaining fallible, mortal, and above all humane, is the 'answer' to that original question— 'To expect any more, or less,' we are warned, 'is to disagree with the terms of Creation.'" He goes on to argue that degradation, "when it is done, as Ludwig demonstrates, out of love, selfless surrender on behalf of another, then life itself may be the result" (Schwarzbach, 43).

5. Chaos and Cosmos Integrated

1. Betty Edwards, *Drawing on the Artist Within* (New York: Simon and Schuster, 1986), 175. The L-mode of perception corre-

sponds roughly but not exactly to left-hemisphere brain functions, R-mode to right. Saturation refers to the stage in which
one has gathered data on a problem; if the creative process
works, something will trigger insight.

2. See John Protevi, "Multiple Metaphysics: Nietzschean Language
of Power in *Gravity's Rainbow*," (Master's thesis, The Pennsylvania
State University, 1984).

3. Wolfgang Iser, *The Act of Reading: A Theory of Aesthetic Response*
(Baltimore: Johns Hopkins University Press, 1978), 84. Jeremy
Gilbert-Rolfe and John Johnston discuss the importance of gaps
and note, "According to Mallarmé, it is through gaps in the
surface that organization and therefore the most crucial levels
of signification emerge; the work's transitions are the work"
("*Gravity's Rainbow* and the Spiral Jetty," *October* 1 [Spring 1976]:
83). See also Laurence Daw, "The Ellipsis as Architechtonic in
Gravity's Rainbow," *Pynchon Notes* 11 (February 1983): 54–56.

4. Friedman and Puetz recognize that science is being put to literary
use in "Science as Metaphor." Ozier discusses the fact that uncertainty is newly accepted as a principle in the discipline of
history; it has hardly stopped the order- seeking activities of that
field. I may be drawing too definite a line between the subatomic
and the macroscopic levels; according to *Science News*, 8 February
1986, a number of ongoing experiments are uncovering quantum mechanical effects on the macroscopic level, but macroscopic there means at the level of a few atoms, not at the level
of everyday human activity.

5. Warner Berthoff, "Fiction, History, Myth: Notes toward the Discrimination of Narrative Forms," in *The Interpretation of Narrative:
Theory and Practice,* ed. Morton W. Bloomfield (Cambridge: Harvard University Press, 1970), 278. See also Hayden White, *Tropics
of Discourse: Essays in Cultural Criticism,* especially "Interpretation
in History" and "The Historical Text as Literary Artifact" (1978;
reprint, Baltimore: Johns Hopkins University Press, 1985).

6. As a frivolous parallel, I cite David Lodge's novel about contemporary critical theory and theorists, in which the chief decon-
structor, Morris Zapp, after being released by Italian kidnappers,
confesses, "I've rather lost faith in deconstruction. . . . Death is
the one concept you can't deconstruct. Work back from there
and you end up with the old idea of an autonomous self. I can
die, therefore I am. I realized that when those wop radicals
threatened to deconstruct *me*" (*Small World: An Academic Romance*
[1984; reprint, Harmondsworth: Penguin, 1985], 328).

7. A somewhat different sequence of reader responses is discussed by David Leverenz in "On Trying to Read *Gravity's Rainbow*," in *Mindful Pleasures*, 229–49.
8. Jorge Luis Borges, *Labyrinths: Selected Stories and Other Writings*, ed. Donald A. Yates and James E. Irby, augmented ed. (New York: New Directions, 1964), 201.
9. Richard Poirier, "The Importance of Thomas Pynchon," *Twentieth Century Literature* 21 (1975): 154.
10. Victor Shklovsky coined the term "ostraneniye" or "defamiliarization" for that function of art which makes us focus on the stoniness of the stone. See "Art as Technique," in *Russian Formalist Criticism: Four Essays*, ed. and trans. Lee T. Lemon and Marion J. Reis (Lincoln: University of Nebraska Press, 1965), esp. 12. He is, however, talking about representational art, not about art that pulverizes the stone.
11. Although his definition of postmodernism is at odds with most literary uses of the term, Jean-François Lyotard makes an interesting argument when he says, "A work can become modern only if it is first postmodern. Postmodernism thus understood is not modernism at its end but in the nascent state, and this state is constant" (Lyotard, 79). In this context, the first reading of *Gravity's Rainbow* is an experience of this postmodernism, the breaking of all the rules; subsequent readings however let us sense the new rules which the text establishes, both for our reading of it and for subsequent fiction to follow or react against. For the related problems of multiple exposures to a work of music, see Leonard B. Meyer, *Music, the Arts, and Ideas: Patterns and Predictions in Twentieth-Century Culture* (Chicago: University of Chicago Press, 1967), esp. chapter 3, "On Rehearing Music."
12. The need to insist on one or the other reading seems misguided. Richard Rorty makes a useful point, less frivolous than it sounds, when he says, "No constructors, no deconstructors. No norms, no perversions. Derrida (like Heidegger) would have no writing to do unless there were a 'metaphysics of presence' to overcome. Without the fun of stamping out parasites, on the other hand, no Kantian would bother to continue building" (*Consequences of Pragmatism: Essays 1972–80* [Minneapolis: University of Minnesota Press, 1982], 108). The two approaches comment on and correct each other.
13. Surprisingly little has been done on the relationship between Pynchon's works and those of other writers. Scott Simmon links *Gravity's Rainbow* to the American tradition, via Leslie Fiedler's

formula for the American novel, in "*Gravity's Rainbow* Described," *Critique* 16 (1974–75): 54–67; Cooper, in his chapter 1, places Pynchon in the context of contemporary fiction; Petillon notes parallels to *Moby-Dick;* and Bo Green Jensen links Pynchon to writers of the beat and postbeat generation in "A Screaming comes across the sky . . . ," *Vinduet* 1 (1986): 10–17.

14. For a more detailed discussion of Calvino's mythology in structuralist terms, see Kathryn Hume, "Italo Calvino's Cosmic Comedy: Mythography for the Scientific Age," *Papers on Language and Literature* 20 (1984): 80–95.

15. I have not discussed Doris Lessing's Canopus in Argos series (five volumes to date) because she is not centrally concerned with flexibility and interactivity, but as a mythographic writer, she is similar to Grass in her series' millenially long span of time, various quasi-divine narrators, and, in *Shikasta*, a concern to fill in the gap between origins and what we are now, to try to explain how we became what we are. Her various zones let her explore some of the issues concerning Pynchon in his Other Side.

16. See Jules Siegel, 122. Joseph W. Slade argues that Pynchon is religious and that he sees the problem of our culture as the atrophy of religious sensibility. See Slade, "Religion, Psychology, Sex, and Love in *Gravity's Rainbow*," in *Approaches to* Gravity's Rainbow, 153–98. Eddins insists that the book is essentially and primarily religious.

17. I owe information on mystic experience in *Gravity's Rainbow* to Peter Malekin (University of Durham, England) who describes thus a Zen account of satori: "for an unenlightened man a mountain is just a mountain, for one moving towards enlightenment it is something else, not just a mountain, for the enlightened again a mountain is just a mountain—the same but different" (letter to the author, 19 May 1985).

18. See Olderman, "Thomas Pynchon," and George Levine, "Risking the Moment: Anarchy and Possibility in Pynchon's Fiction," in *Mindful Pleasures,* 113–36.

19. After describing how a mandala ultimately teaches the user that the mandala itself does not exist, that it is just an arbitrary means of ordering chaos, Malekin makes the following point: "One consequence is a very interesting treatment of time. Here Pynchon goes beyond the Theosophists and Spiritualists and most eastern sages, using and developing the ideas in modern western science. Time comes out as a Gestalt, part of the Gestalt being status of consciousness . . . hence Mondaugen on time-band and

ego and Rathenau's premature pronouncement of the 'cosmic bomb', and hence the vagueness 'in time' of so much of the material" (letter to the author, 19 May 1985). Another critic to recognize some of the parallels between *Gravity's Rainbow* and mandalas is John M. Muste, who focuses on the surface elements and visual images of what would be drawn were this the traditional pictorial mandala.

Bibliography

Ames, Sanford S. "Pynchon and Visible Language: Ecriture." *International Fiction Review* 4 (1977): 170–73.

Barthes, Roland. *Mythologies.* Translated by Annette Lavers. London: Granada, 1973. Original French, 1957.
————. "Par où commencer?" *Poetique* 1 (1970): 3–9.

Bass, Thomas A. "*Gravity's Rainbow* as Orphic Text." *Pynchon Notes* 13 (October 1983): 25–46.

Berthoff, Warner. "Fiction, History, Myth: Notes toward the Discrimination of Narrative Forms." In *The Interpretation of Narrative: Theory and Practice,* edited by Morton W. Bloomfield, 263–87. Cambridge: Harvard University Press, 1970.

Bettelheim, Bruno. *The Uses of Enchantment: The Meaning and Importance of Fairy Tales.* New York: Alfred A. Knopf, 1976.

Black, Joel D. "Pynchon's Eve of De-Struction." *Pynchon Notes* 14 (February 1984): 23–38.

Borges, Jorge Luis. *Labyrinths: Selected Stories and Other Writings.* Augmented ed. Edited by Donald A. Yates and James E. Irby. New York: New Directions, 1964.

Brier, Peter A. "Caliban Reigns: Romantic Theory and Some Contemporary Fantasists." *Denver Quarterly* 13 (1978): 38–51.

Brunner, John. "Coming Events: An Assessment of Thomas Pynchon's *Gravity's Rainbow.*" *Foundation* 10 (1976): 20–27.

Bruns, Gerald L. "Poetry as Reality: The Orpheus Myth and Its Modern Counterparts." *ELH* 37 (1970): 263–86.

―――. *Modern Poetry and the Idea of Language. A Critical and Historical Study.* New Haven: Yale University Press, 1974.

Caesar, Terry. "'Trapped inside Their frame with your wastes piling up': Mindless Pleasures in *Gravity's Rainbow.*" *Pynchon Notes* 14 (February 1984): 39–48.

Calhoun, John C. "The Concept of Revolution and Its Influence on the Genesis of Art in the Work of Thomas Pynchon." *Perspectives on Contemporary Literature* 2 (1976): 40–52.

Calvino, Italo. "Myth in the Narrative." In *Surfiction: Fiction Now . . . and Tomorrow,* edited by Raymond Federman, 75–81. Chicago: Swallow Press, 1975.

Campbell, Joseph. *The Hero with a Thousand Faces.* 2d ed. Bollingen Series 17. Princeton: Princeton University Press, 1968.

Clerc, Charles. Introduction to *Approaches to* Gravity's Rainbow, edited by Charles Clerc, 3–30. Columbus: Ohio State University Press, 1983.

Cocks, Geoffrey. "War, Man, and Gravity: Thomas Pynchon and Science Fiction." *Extrapolation* 20 (1979): 368–77.

Cooper, Peter L. *Signs and Symptoms: Thomas Pynchon and the Contemporary World.* Berkeley and Los Angeles: University of California Press, 1983.

Cowart, David. "'Sacrificial Ape': King Kong and His Antitypes in *Gravity's Rainbow.*" *Literature and Psychology* 28 (1978): 112–18.

―――. "Pynchon's Use of the Tannhauser-Legend in *Gravity's Rainbow.*" *Notes on Contemporary Literature* 9 (1979): 2–3.

―――. *Thomas Pynchon: The Art of Allusion.* Carbondale: Southern Illinois University Press, 1980.

Daw, Laurence. "The Ellipsis as Architectonic in *Gravity's Rainbow.*" *Pynchon Notes* 11 (February 1983): 54–56.

Duyfhuizen, Bernard. "Starry-Eyed Semiotics: Learning to Read Slothrop's Map and *Gravity's Rainbow.*" *Pynchon Notes* 6 (June 1981): 5–33.

————. Introduction to *Pynchon Notes* 14 (February 1984): 3–6.

Earl, James W. "Freedom and Knowledge in the Zone." In *Approaches to* Gravity's Rainbow, edited by Charles Clerc, 229–50. Columbus: Ohio State University Press, 1983.

Eddins, Dwight. "Orphic contra Gnostic: Religious Conflict in *Gravity's Rainbow*." *Modern Language Quarterly* 45 (1984): 163–90.

Edwards, Betty. *Drawing on the Artist Within*. New York: Simon and Schuster, 1986.

Eliade, Mircea. *Rites and Symbols of Initiation: The Mysteries of Birth and Rebirth*. Translated by Willard R. Trask. New York: Harper and Row, 1965.

————. *The Myth of the Eternal Return; or, Cosmos and History*. Translated by Willard R. Trask. Bollingen Series 46. Princeton: Princeton University Press, 1971. Original French, 1949.

Eliot, T. S. "Ulysses, Order, and Myth." *The Dial* 75 (November 1923): 480–83.

Fowler, Douglas. *A Reader's Guide to* Gravity's Rainbow. Ann Arbor, Mich.: Ardis, 1980.

————. "Pynchon's Magic World." *South Atlantic Quarterly* 79 (1980): 51–60.

Friedman, Alan J. "Science and Technology." In *Approaches to* Gravity's Rainbow, edited by Charles Clerc, 69–102. Columbus: Ohio State University Press, l983.

————, and Manfred Puetz. "Science as Metaphor: Thomas Pynchon and *Gravity's Rainbow*." *Contemporary Literature* 15 (1974): 345–59.

Frye, Northrop. *Anatomy of Criticism: Four Essays*. Princeton: Princeton University Press, 1957.

————. *The Secular Scripture: A Study of the Structure of Romance*. Cambridge: Harvard University Press, 1976.

Gardner, John. *Grendel*. 1971. Reprint. New York: Ballantine, 1972.

Gilbert-Rolfe, Jeremy, and John Johnston. "*Gravity's Rainbow* and the Spiral Jetty." *October* 1 (Spring 1976): 65–85; 2 (Summer 1976): 71–90; and 3 (Spring 1977): 90–102.

Goethe, Johann Wolfgang von. *Faust*. Vol. 3 of *Goethes Werke*. 4th ed. Hamburg: Christian Wegner Verlag, 1959.

———. *Faust*. Translated by Charles E. Passage. Indianapolis: Bobbs-Merrill, 1965.

Gombrich, E. H. *Art and Illusion: A Study in the Psychology of Pictorial Representation*. 2d ed. Bollingen Series 35, no. 5. Princeton: Princeton University Press, 1969.

Gould, Eric. *Mythical Intentions in Modern Literature*. Princeton: Princeton University Press, 1981.

Greimas, A.-J. *Sémantique structurale: recherche de méthode*. Paris: Librairie Larousse, 1966.

Hassan, Ihab. "The Dismemberment of Orpheus: Notes on Form and Antiform in Contemporary Literature." In *Learners and Discerners: A Newer Criticism*, edited by Robert Scholes, 135–65. Charlottesville: University Press of Virginia, 1964.

Hayles, N. Katherine. "Cosmology and the Point of (No) Return in *Gravity's Rainbow*." *Markham Review* 12 (1983): 73–77.

———. *The Cosmic Web: Scientific Field Models and Literary Strategies in the Twentieth Century*. Ithaca: Cornell University Press, 1984.

Hite, Molly. "'Holy-Center-Approaching' in the Novels of Thomas Pynchon." *Journal of Narrative Technique* 12 (1982): 121–29.

———. *Ideas of Order in the Novels of Thomas Pynchon*. Columbus: Ohio State University Press, 1983.

Holland, Norman N. *The Dynamics of Literary Response*. New York: W. W. Norton, 1975.

Hume, Kathryn. "Romance: A Perdurable Pattern." *College English* 36 (1974): 129–46.

————. "Visionary Allegory in David Lindsay's *A Voyage to Arcturus.*" *Journal of English and Germanic Philology* 77 (1978): 72–91.

————. "Italo Calvino's Cosmic Comedy: Mythography for the Scientific Age." *Papers on Language and Literature* 20 (1984): 80–95.

————, and Thomas J. Knight. "Orpheus and the Orphic Voice in *Gravity's Rainbow.*" *Philological Quarterly* 64 (1985): 299–315.

————, and Thomas J. Knight. "Pynchon's Orchestration of *Gravity's Rainbow.*" *Journal of English and Germanic Philology* 85 (1986): 366–85.

Iser, Wolfgang. *The Act of Reading: A Theory of Aesthetic Response.* Baltimore: Johns Hopkins University Press, 1980. Original German, 1976.

Jackson, Rosemary. *Fantasy: The Literature of Subversion.* London: Methuen, 1981.

Jameson, Fredric. "Magical Narratives: Romance as Genre." *New Literary History* 7 (1975): 135–63.

Jensen, Bo Green. "A screaming comes across the sky. . . ." *Vinduet* 1 (1986): 10–17.

Jewett, Robert, and John Shelton Lawrence. *The American Monomyth.* Garden City, N.Y.: Anchor, 1977.

Kappel, Lawrence. "Psychic Geography in *Gravity's Rainbow.*" *Contemporary Literature* 21 (1980): 225–51.

Kaufman, Marjorie. "Brünnhilde and the Chemists: Women in *Gravity's Rainbow.*" In *Mindful Pleasures: Essays on Thomas Pynchon,* edited by George Levine and David Leverenz, 197–227. Boston: Little, Brown, 1976.

Krafft, John M. "Anarcho-Romanticism and the Metaphysics of Counterforce: Alex Comfort and Thomas Pynchon." *Paunch* 40–41 (1975): 78–107.

Leach, Edmund R. "Genesis as Myth." In *European Literary Theory and Practice: From Existential Phenomenology to Struc-*

turalism, edited by Vernon W. Gras. 317–30. New York: Delta, 1973.

Leverenz, David. "On Trying to Read *Gravity's Rainbow.*" In *Mindful Pleasures: Essays on Thomas Pynchon,* edited by George Levine and David Leverenz, 229–49. Boston: Little, Brown, 1976.

Levine, George. "Risking the Moment: Anarchy and Possibility in Pynchon's Fiction." In *Mindful Pleasures: Essays on Thomas Pynchon,* edited by George Levine and David Leverenz, 113–36. Boston: Little, Brown, 1976.

Lévi-Strauss, Claude. *Tristes Tropiques.* Translated by John Weightman and Doreen Weightman. Harmondsworth: Penguin, 1976. Original French, 1955.

———. "The Structural Study of Myth." In *Myth: A Symposium,* edited by Thomas A. Sebeok, 81–106. 1955. Reprint. Bloomington: Indiana University Press, 1965.

———. *The Raw and the Cooked.* Translated by John Weightman and Doreen Weightman. New York: Harper and Row, 1970. Original French, 1964.

le Vot, André. "The Rocket and the Pig: Thomas Pynchon and Science-Fiction." *Caliban XII,* n.s. 11 (1975): 111–18.

Lippman, Bertram. "The Reader of Movies: Thomas Pynchon's *Gravity's Rainbow.*" *Denver Quarterly* 12 (1977): 1–46.

Lodge, David. *Small World: An Academic Romance.* 1984. Reprint. Harmondsworth: Penguin, 1985.

Lyotard, Jean-François. *The Postmodern Condition: A Report on Knowledge.* Translated by Geoff Bennington and Brian Massumi. (Appendix on "Answering the Question: What is Postmodernism?" translated by Régis Durand.) Minneapolis: University of Minnesota Press, 1984. Original French, 1979 (appendix 1982).

MacAdam, Alfred. "Pynchon as Satirist: To Write, To Mean." *Yale Review* 67 (1978): 555–66.

McClintock, James I. "United State Revisited: Pynchon and Zamiatin." *Contemporary Literature* 18 (1977): 475–90.

McConnell, Frank D. *Four Postwar American Novelists: Bellow, Mailer, Barth, and Pynchon.* Chicago: University of Chicago Press, 1977.

McHale, Brian. "Modernist Reading, Post-Modern Text: The Case of *Gravity's Rainbow.*" *Poetics Today* 1 (1979): 85–110.

————. "'You used to know what these words mean': Misreading *Gravity's Rainbow.*" *Language and Style* 18 (1985): 93–118.

Mackey, Louis. "Paranoia, Pynchon, and Preterition." *SubStance* no. 30 (1981): 16–30.

————. "Thomas Pynchon and the American Dream." *Pynchon Notes* 14 (February 1984): 7–22.

Malekin, Peter. Letter to author, 19 May 1985.

Márquez, Antonio. "The Nightmare of History and Thomas Pynchon's *Gravity's Rainbow.*" *Essays in Literature* 8 (1981): 53–62.

Mendelson, Edward. "Gravity's Encyclopedia." In *Mindful Pleasures: Essays on Thomas Pynchon,* edited by George Levine and David Leverenz, 161–95. Boston: Little, Brown, 1976.

Meyer, Leonard B. *Music, The Arts, and Ideas: Patterns and Predictions in Twentieth-Century Culture.* Chicago: University of Chicago Press, 1967.

Morgan, Speer. "*Gravity's Rainbow:* What's The Big Idea?" In *Critical Essays on Thomas Pynchon,* edited by Richard Pearce, 82–98. Boston: G. K. Hall, 1981.

Moore, Thomas. "A Decade of *Gravity's Rainbow,* The Incredible Moving Film." *Michigan Quarterly Review* 22 (1983): 78–94.

Muste, John M. "The Mandala in *Gravity's Rainbow.*" *Boundary 2* 9 (1981): 163–79.

Nadeau, Robert L. "Readings from the New Book of Nature: Physics and Pynchon's *Gravity's Rainbow.*" *Studies in the Novel* 11 (1979): 454–71.

Neumann, Erich. *The Origins and History of Consciousness.* Translated by R. F. C. Hull. Bollingen Series 42. Princeton: Princeton University Press, 1970. Original German, 1949.

Olderman, Raymond M. "Thomas Pynchon." *Contemporary Literature* 20 (1979): 500–507.

———. "The New Consciousness and the Old System." In *Approaches to* Gravity's Rainbow, edited by Charles Clerc, 199–228. Columbus: Ohio State University Press, 1983.

Ozier, Lance W. "The Calculus of Transformation: More Mathematical Imagery in *Gravity's Rainbow*." *Twentieth Century Literature* 21 (1975): 193–210.

Pearson, Carol, and Katherine Pope. *The Female Hero in American and British Literature.* New York: R. R. Bowker, 1981.

Petillon, Pierre-Yves. "Thomas Pynchon et l'espace aléatoire." *Critique* (France) 34 (1978): 1107–42. (A translation appears in *Pynchon Notes* 15 [Fall 1984]: 3–46 as "Thomas Pynchon and Aleatory Space," translated by Margaret S. Langford with Clifford Mead.)

Plater, William M. *The Grim Phoenix: Reconstructing Thomas Pynchon.* Bloomington: Indiana University Press, 1978.

Poirier, Richard. "The Importance of Thomas Pynchon." *Twentieth Century Literature* 21 (1975): 151–62.

Protevi, John. "Multiple Metaphysics: Nietzschean Language of Power in *Gravity's Rainbow*." Master's thesis, The Pennsylvania State University, 1984.

Pynchon, Thomas. *V.* 1963. Reprint. New York: Bantam, 1964.

———. *The Crying of Lot 49.* 1966. Reprint. New York: Bantam, 1967.

———. *Gravity's Rainbow.* New York: Viking, 1973.

———. "Is It O.K. To Be a Luddite?" *New York Times Book Review,* 28 October 1984.

Pyuen, Carolyn S. "The Transmarginal Leap: Meaning and Process in *Gravity's Rainbow*." *Mosaic* 15 (1982): 33–46.

Rather, L. J. *The Dream of Self-Destruction: Wagner's* Ring *and the Modern World.* Baton Rouge: Louisiana State University Press, 1979.

Richer, Carol F. "The Prismatic Character in *Gravity's Rainbow*." *Pynchon Notes* 12 (June 1983): 26–38.

Ricoeur, Paul. *Interpretation Theory: Discourse and the Surplus of Meaning.* Fort Worth: Texas Christian University Press, 1976.

Righter, William. *Myth and Literature.* London: Routledge and Kegan Paul, 1975.

Rilke, Rainer Maria. *Sonnets to Orpheus.* German text with translation by C. F. MacIntyre. Berkeley and Los Angeles: University of California Press, 1960.

————. *Duino Elegies.* 4th ed. German text with translation by J. B. Leishman and Stephen Spender. London: Chatto and Windus, 1975.

Rorty, Richard. *Consequences of Pragmatism: Essays, 1972–1980.* Minneapolis: University of Minnesota Press, 1982.

Russell, Charles. "Pynchon's Language: Signs, Systems, and Subversion." In *Approaches to* Gravity's Rainbow, edited by Charles Clerc, 251–72. Columbus: Ohio State University Press, 1983.

Sanders, Scott. "Pynchon's Paranoid History." In *Mindful Pleasures: Essays on Thomas Pynchon,* edited by George Levine and David Leverenz, 139–59. Boston: Little, Brown, 1976.

Schaub, Thomas H. *Pynchon: The Voice of Ambiguity.* Urbana: University of Illinois Press, 1981.

Schuber, Stephen P. "Textual Orbits/Orbiting Criticism: Deconstructing *Gravity's Rainbow.*" *Pynchon Notes* 14 (February 1984): 65–74.

Schwartz, Richard Alan. "Thomas Pynchon and the Evolution of Fiction." *Science-Fiction Studies* 8 (1981): 165–72.

Schwarzbach, F. S. "Pynchon's Gravity." *New Review* 3 (June 1976): 39–43.

Seed, David. "Further Notes and Sources for *Gravity's Rainbow.*" *Pynchon Notes* 16 (Spring 1985): 25–36.

Sewell, Elizabeth. *The Orphic Voice: Poetry and Natural History.* New Haven: Yale University Press, 1960.

Shklovsky, Victor. "Art as Technique." In *Russian Formalist Criticism: Four Essays,* edited and translated by Lee T. Lemon and Marion J. Reis, 3–24. Lincoln: University of Nebraska Press, 1965.

Siegel, Jules. "Who Is Thomas Pynchon . . . and Why Did He Take Off with My Wife?" *Playboy,* March 1977.

Siegel, Mark R. "Creative Paranoia: Understanding the System of *Gravity's Rainbow.*" *Critique* 18 (1976–77): 39–54.

———. *Pynchon: Creative Paranoia in* Gravity's Rainbow. Port Washington, N.Y.: Kennikat Press, 1978.

Simmon, Scott. "*Gravity's Rainbow* Described." *Critique* 16 (1974–75): 54–67.

Slade, Joseph W. *Thomas Pynchon.* New York: Warner, 1974.

———. "Escaping Rationalization: Options for the Self in *Gravity's Rainbow.*" *Critique* 18 (1976–77): 27–38.

———. "Religion, Psychology, Sex, and Love in *Gravity's Rainbow.*" In *Approaches to* Gravity's Rainbow, edited by Charles Clerc, 153–98. Columbus: Ohio State University Press, 1983.

Smith, Marcus, and Khachig Tölölyan. "The New Jeremiad: *Gravity's Rainbow.*" In *Critical Essays on Thomas Pynchon,* edited by Richard Pearce, 169–86. Boston: G. K. Hall, 1981.

Stark, John O. *Pynchon's Fictions: Thomas Pynchon and the Literature of Information.* Athens: Ohio University Press, 1980.

Strauss, Walter A. *Descent and Return: The Orphic Theme in Modern Literature.* Cambridge: Harvard University Press, 1971.

Tanner, Tony. *Thomas Pynchon.* London: Methuen, 1982.

Tate, J. O. "*Gravity's Rainbow:* The Original Soundtrack." *Pynchon Notes* 13 (October 1983): 3–24.

Toland, John. *The Dillinger Days.* New York: Random House, 1963.

Tölölyan, Khachig. "Criticism as Symptom: Thomas Pynchon and the Crisis of the Humanities." *New Orleans Review* 5 (1979): 314–18.

———. "Prodigious Pynchon and His Progeny." *Studies in the Novel* 11 (1979): 224–34.

————. "War as Background in *Gravity's Rainbow.*" In *Approaches to* Gravity's Rainbow, edited by Charles Clerc, 31–68. Columbus: Ohio State University Press, 1983.

Weisenburger, Steven. "The End of History? Thomas Pynchon and the Uses of the Past." *Twentieth Century Literature* 25 (1979): 54–72.

————. "The Chronology of Episodes in *Gravity's Rainbow.*" *Pynchon Notes* 14 (February 1984): 50–64.

Werner, Craig Hansen. *Paradoxical Resolutions: American Fiction since James Joyce.* Urbana: University of Illinois Press, 1982.

Westervelt, Linda A. "'A Place Dependent on Ourselves': The Reader as System-Builder in *Gravity's Rainbow.*" *Texas Studies in Literature and Language* 22 (1980): 69–90.

White, Hayden. *Tropics of Discourse: Essays in Cultural Criticism.* 1978. Reprint. Baltimore: Johns Hopkins University Press, 1985.

Wolfley, Lawrence C. "Repression's Rainbow: The Presence of Norman O. Brown in Pynchon's Big Novel." *PMLA* 92 (1977): 873–89.

Index

Marvy, Major Duane, 44, 146, 150
Melville, Herman: *Moby–Dick*, 201
Mexico, Roger, 40, 53–54, 123, 127, 152, 163; and counterforce, 60, 81, 130; and intermapping, 113, 115–16, 117; and Jessica, 6, 62, 123, 159; and other realities, 95, 179–80; and probability, 120, 181
Meyer, Leonard B., 239n.11
Midgets, 62, 115–16, 154
Mittelwerke, 44, 102, 146, 154–55, 177
Mondaugen, Kurt, 42, 44, 99–100, 107, 122
Moore, Thomas, 235n.6
Morgan, Speer, 232n.9
Mossmoon, Scorpia, 62, 115
Mucker-Maffick, Tantivy, 48, 128
Munchkins, 62
Music, 53, 76, 172, 198, 206, 214
Muste, John M., 226n.6, 241n.19
Myth, definition, 13–18, 23–24, 87–88
Mythological action or cycle, 12, 89–108; for the rocket, 100–104; for science and technology, 104–7; for Tyrone Slothrop, 96–100; for Western culture, 89–96
Mythological cosmos: definition, 35–37; physical characteristics, 38–45
Mythological literature, definition, 18–23
Mythology: definitions, 18–20, 136; *Gravity's Rainbow* as

mythological literature, 21–23, 87, 89, 185; Pynchon's mythology, 195–99, 206–7

Nadeau, Robert L., 230n.11
Närrisch, 92, 124, 165
Neumann, Erich, 138
Nibelungs, 62, 154
Nietzsche, Friedrich, 170, 188–89, 197

Offenbach, Jacques: *Orphée aux Enfers*, 53, 173
Olderman, Raymond M., 229n.7, 232–33n.10
Omnipon, André, 54
Orpheus: as cultural figure, 67, 117, 142, 177–79, 183, 198, 214, 219; as model for Slothrop, 6, 53, 168–75; as pinball, 53, 63, 66
Orpheus Theatre, 7, 174
Orwell, George: *1984*, 95, 107
Other Side, 83–84, 110, 139–40, 152, 194, 198; as alternative reality, 181, 218; as binary opposition to This Side, 119, 132–33, 135; and its inhabitants, 71, 80, 99; as part of mythological cosmos, 11–12, 43, 45–63
Ozier, Lance W., 78–79, 193, 230n.9, 234n.24, 238n.4

Pan, 169, 215, 220; as lover of Geli and Katje, 48–49, 115; and Titans, 55, 67
Paranoia, 97–98, 107, 110; as a principle of organization, 10, 30, 60, 80–81
Parker, "Yardbird," 53, 68, 174

Rocket-City. *See* Raketen-Stadt
Rocket limericks, 44, 93–94
Rocketman, 99, 142, 155, 161, 165
Rockets, 8, 70, 73, 110–11, 119; and atomic weaponry, 10, 45, 108; and Gottfried, 112, 117, 207; mythological action concerning, 100–104; and Slothrop, 6, 112–13; and *Tannhäuser*, 154–56
Rorty, Richard, 239n.12
Rossini, Gioacchino, 98
Russell, Charles, 3–4

Sachsa, Peter, 46, 109, 129
Schaub, Thomas H., 79, 225n.5, 229n.3, 234n.24
Schlabone, Gustav, 54
Schwartz, Richard Alan, 187–88
Schwarzbach, F. S., 231n.14, 234n.25, 237n.30
Science, 187–90, 195
Seed, David, 236n.16
Sewell, Elizabeth, 169–70
Shakespeare, William: *Measure for Measure*, 16; *The Tempest*, 15–16
Shklovsky, Victor, 239n.10
Siegel, Jules, 227n.18
Siegel, Mark R., 227n.12, 230n.9, 232n.6
Silence, 53–55, 172
Simmon, Scott, 239–40n.13
Slade, Joseph W., 216, 233n.10, 234n.25, 240n.16
Slothrop, Broderick, 93, 98
Slothrop, Constant, 97
Slothrop, Nalline, 67, 98, 168
Slothrop, Tyrone: and Faust, 143–53; and Floundering

Four fantasies, 98, 159, 163–64; as infant, 7, 59, 106; and intermapping, 109–14, 142–43; and juvenile heroes, 158–67; and Orpheus, 168–74; and *sparagmos*, 17, 22, 63, 67, 76, 168; status at end of novel, 215–18; and wagnerian heroes, 153–58
Slothrop, William, 97, 104, 113; and hymn, 74, 218; and pigs, 63, 89–90, 127, 128
Smith, Marcus, 79, 229n.6, 234n.24, 235n.11
Springer, Der. *See* Göll, Gerhardt von
Stapledon, Olaf: *The Last and First Men*, 21
Stark, John O., 229–30n.9
Strauss, Walter, 171–72
Structuralism, 23, 25–29, 30, 88
Structuralist approach to *Gravity's Rainbow*:
—binary oppositions, 88, 96, 118–35; control and freedom, 39–40, 77, 118, 124–26, 135, 151, 158; death and life, 119, 128–30; elect and preterite, 63, 118, 135; eros and thanatos, 119, 122–23, 135; openness and closure, 39–40, 77–78, 118, 124–26; paranoia and antiparanoia, 119–22, 134; zero and one, 118–21, 126
—mediations, 88, 96, 118–35
—redundancies and repetitions, 88, 108–18
Swanlake, Jessica, 6, 62, 95, 115–16, 123, 159

Kathryn Hume, who received degrees from Radcliffe and the University of Pennsylvania, has served on the faculties of Cornell and The Pennsylvania State University, where she is now Professor of English. Professor Hume has published widely in areas as diverse as medieval studies (particularly studies in medieval romance and the Old Norse Sagas) and narrative theory, recent evidence of which is her *Fantasy and Mimesis: Responses to Reality in Western Literature.*